AN AUSTRALIAN ODYSSEY: FROM GIZA TO GALLIPOLI

AN AUSTRALIAN ODYSSEY: FROM GIZA TO GALLIPOLI

GARRIE HUTCHINSON

S

SCEPTRE

A Sceptre Book

∫

SCEPTRE

Published in Australia and New Zealand in 1997
by Hodder Headline Australia Pty Limited,
(A member of the Hodder Headline Group)
10–16 South Street, Rydalmere NSW 2116

National Library of Australia Cataloguing-in-Publication data

Hutchinson, Garrie, 1949– .
An Australian odyssey: from Giza to Gallipoli.

Bibliography.

ISBN 0 7336 0387 4.

1. Hutchinson, Garrie, 1949– – Journeys – Middle East.
2. Middle East – Description and travel. I. Title.

915.60453

Typeset by Bookhouse Digital Publishing Services, Sydney
Printed in Australia by McPherson's Printing Group, Victoria

For Alexander the Great II, and the girls I left behind:
Esther, Isobel and Karen

CONTENTS

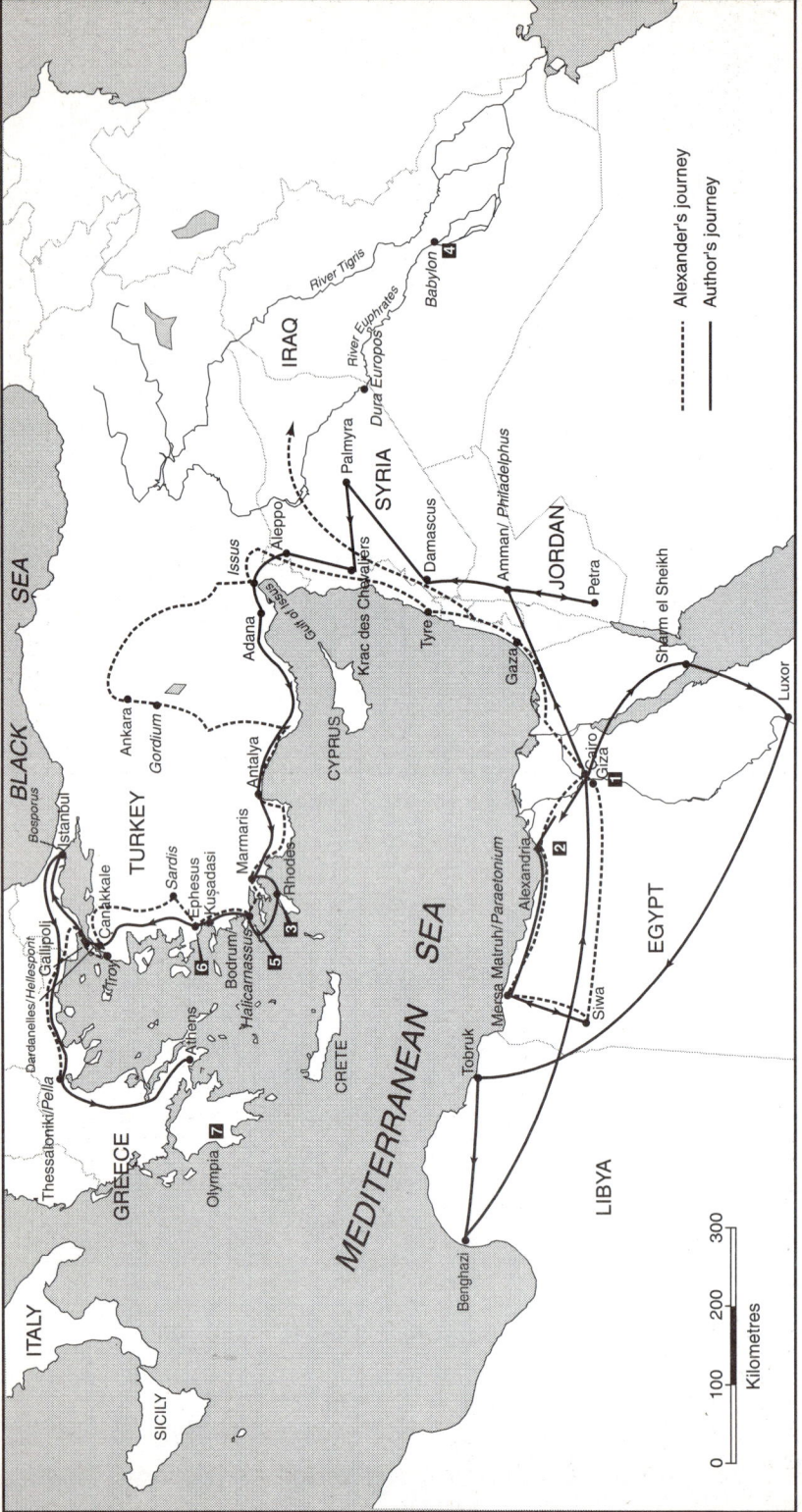

The author's travels in the eastern Mediterranean

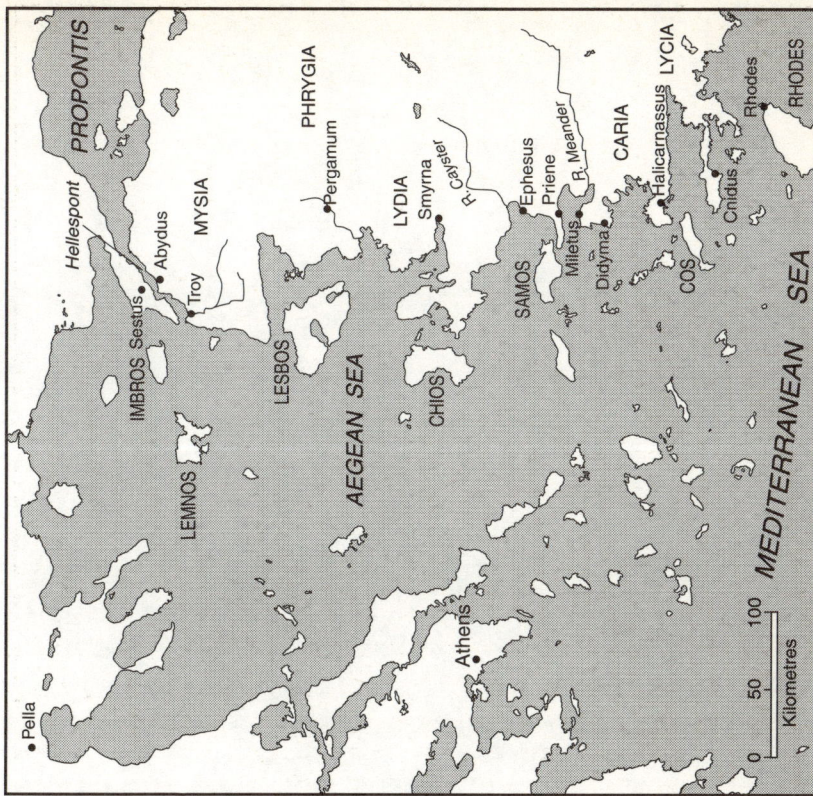

The ancient Aegean coastline

The Seven Wonders of the Ancient World
1 Pyramids of Giza
2 Pharos of Alexandria
3 Colossus of Rhodes
4 Hanging Gardens of Babylon
5 Mausoleum at Halicarnassus
6 Temple of Artemis at Ephesus
7 Statue of Zeus at Olympia

Alexander the Great

356 BC	Born Pella, Macedonia
336 BC	Acclaimed king on assassination of father, Phillip II
334 BC (May)	Crosses Hellespont (Dardanelles)
334 BC (May	Visits Troy; defeats Darius and Persians at River Granicus
334 BC (July/August)	Visits Ephesus, stays at Priene, captures Halicarnassus and Miletus, visits Didyma – all in Caria
334 BC (September)	Cuts Gordian knot at Gordium in Phrygia
333 BC	Defeats Darius again at Issus
332 BC (July)	Siege of Tyre is finally successful
332 BC (September)	Wounded at Gaza
332 BC (November)	Crosses into Egypt
332 BC (December)	Founds Alexandria
331 BC (January–February)	Visits oracle at Siwa, via Paraetonium
331 BC (August)	Final defeat of Darius at Gaugamela, near Ninerva; occupies Babylon
330 BC	Successful invasion of lands to the east: Bactria through modern Afghanistan as far as India
323 BC	Dies at Babylon

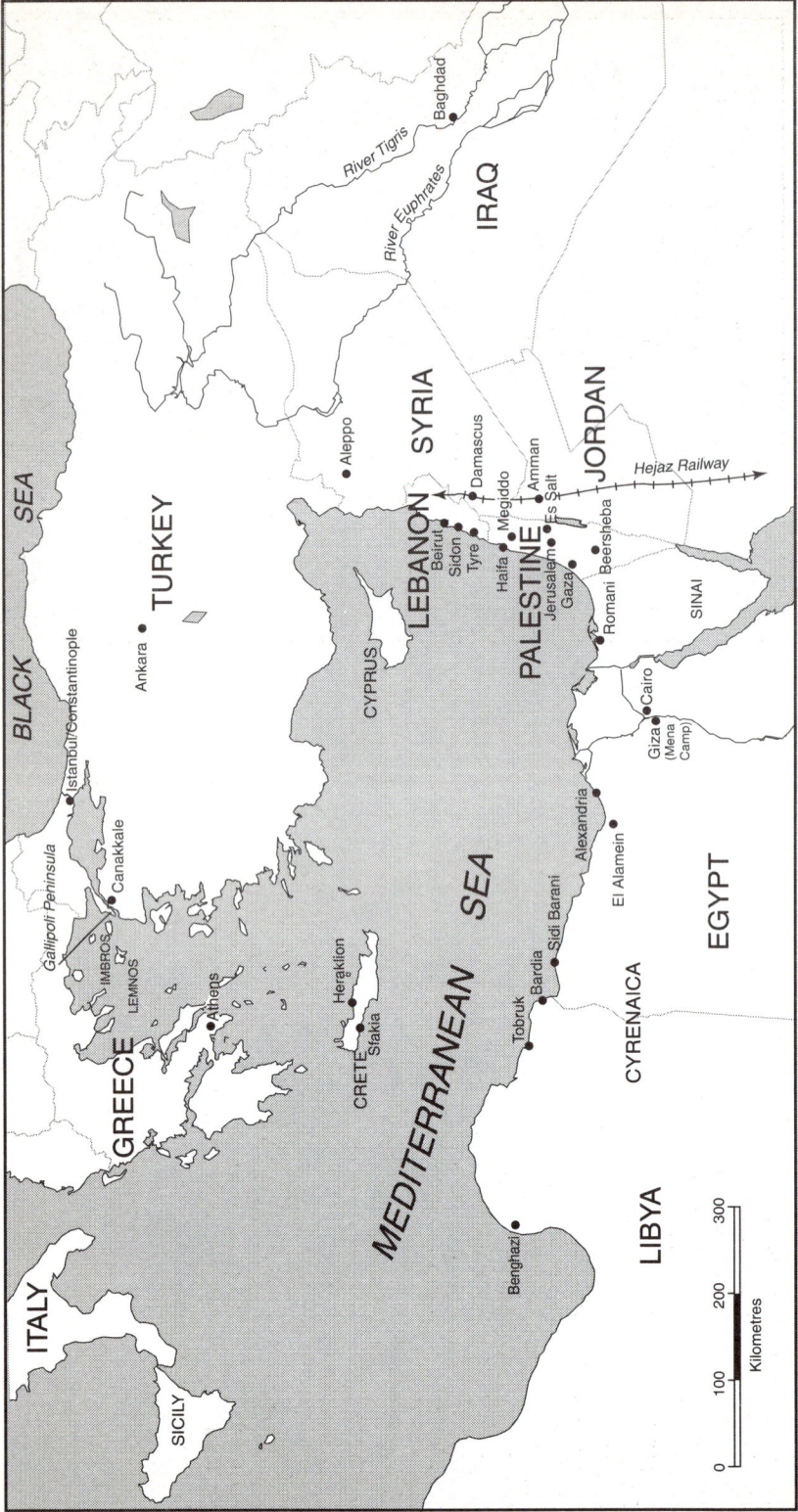

Australian military actions in World Wars I and II

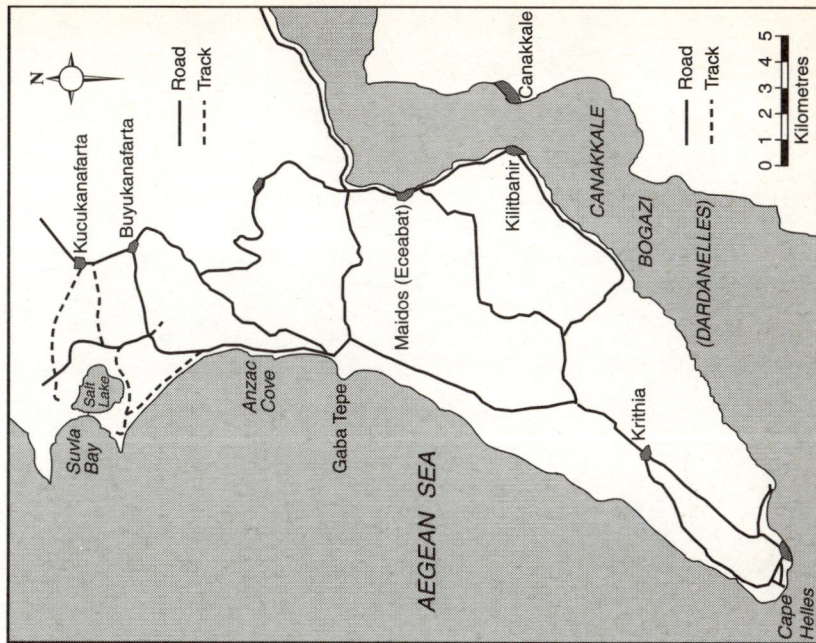

The Gallipoli Peninsula

The Light Horse in World War I

December 1914	First arrivals in Cairo
25 April 1915	Landing at Gallipoli
20 December 1915	Evacuation of Anzac area at Gallipoli
4 August 1916	Battle of Romani
26 March 1917	First Battle of Gaza
19 April 1917	Second Battle of Gaza
31 October 1917	The Charge at Beersheba
7 November 1917	Third Battle of Gaza
9 December 1917	Capture of Jerusalem
30 March 1918	The raid on Amman
1 May 1918	Battle of Es Salt
19 September 1918	Battle of Megiddo (Armageddon)
30 September 1918	Capture of Damascus
30 October 1918	Armistice with Turkey

World War II in the Middle East

January 1941	Tobruk taken by 6th Division
March 1941	9th Division besieged at Tobruk
April 1941	German invasion and Allied withdrawal from Greece
May 1941	German invasion and Allied withdrawal from Crete
June–July 1941	7th Division in Syria and Lebanon
October 1941	9th Division relieved at Tobruk
February 1942	PM John Curtin recalls 6th and 7th Divisions from Middle East
July–October 1942	9th Division involved in battles at El Alamein

ACKNOWLEDGMENTS

I would like to thank the following people, who made the trip and the book possible.

To EgyptAir in Sydney, *shukrun* – especially Mr Khalek, Hayam, and Karen Halaby for providing travel from Australia to Egypt and back, as well as the unexpected diversion to Libya. The book would not have been possible without this assistance.

Mena House Oberoi, especially Mrs Nehad al Saady at Giza and Genevieve Prieto in Sydney, for sanctuary at Giza.

Mike and Angela Smith, for hospitality and diplomatic skills of the highest order in Cairo.

In Syria, Mohammad Muslli for yarns and safe driving, Jim Dolymore for hospitality, Colonel Dick Clarke for clues.

In Athens, Irene Morfinos and family for Sunday lunch.

In Australia, John Ross for my absence when I should have been dealing with leg-breaks not nearly breaking legs.

Ian Cartwright, Deputy Director, Office of Australian War Graves, for arranging permission stay at the Anzac Rest House.

Paul Molloy at the Department of Foreign Affairs and Trade, for points of contact.

Ross McMullin, for valued advice.

Gary Hearst, Tim Hakins and Diane Muttatall at Ya'lla Tours, for effective connections in Jordan and Syria.

The Friday seminar on work and travel at the inaptly named Provincial Hotel, Fitzroy.

Lisa Highton for believing there was a book in the idea and waiting for it, editors Pauline McGuire and Susie Rourke for saving me from most errors though not from pigheadedly sticking to others.

PREFACE

This is a book of stories about the people and places I encountered on a journey from Giza in Egypt to Gallipoli in Turkey, with one or two diversions, in March and April 1996. The stories have evolved from the places and people I encountered on the journey, mixed with what I realise now is a lifetime of accidental reading. Some of the stories will be familiar, but not all, I hope. They have three tracks, or purposes: the journey itself, and the two 'organising' ideas. I wanted first to see what remained of as many of the Seven Wonders of the Ancient World as I could get to, and second, to track as many of the Australian connections as I could along the way, principally those to do with the Light Horse and the first Anzacs in Egypt, Turkey, Palestine and Syria.

I also carry around, physically and mentally, the baggage of a number of writer and painter heroes who have worked in the Eastern Mediterranean over the past 5000 years. The mostly anonymous creators of the images to be found in the great museums of Cairo, Damascus, Istanbul and Athens are part this encumbrance, as are the writers of the Bible stories, the stories of the Thousand and One Nights, and the writers Homer and Herodotus.

But equally powerful in my imagination are the Australian writers and painters of the period around World War I: Charles Bean and Harry Gullett, C. J. Dennis, George Lambert, H. Septimus Power and Arthur Streeton. Their paintings are to be found in the Australian National Gallery, the National Gallery of Victoria, the Art Gallery of New South Wales, but the greatest war paintings are in the Australian War Memorial: they are not lesser works of art for being across the lake from the official art establishment.

My indebtedness to these writers and artists, as well as to a legion of specialists in the fields of archeology and military history is obvious. I trust that anyone whose special interest has had its toes stepped on by this blundering autodidact will forgive me. I have plundered every idea and work I could find in making my own way around the monuments and meanings of this vast swag of territory and time. Anyone who, like me, wants more about the detailed archeology and history of the Seven Wonders should immediately search for John and Elizabeth Romer's *The Seven Wonders of the World*.

In a year when the great achievement of Australian democracy – that of creating a diverse, absorbent and tolerant society which seemed at last to be coming to terms with its recent history and its ancient geography – was abused by a few ignorant loud-mouths, it seemed appropriate to be travelling around some of the African, Asian and European territories from which all our ancestors migrated. Though, with a few exceptions, everyone I met was hospitable, it made me daily more grateful for the society we have constructed so laconically in Australia.

I have also come to believe, naively perhaps, that a great force for peace and reconciliation is the tide of what might be called archeological tourism that is sweeping through the countries of the eastern Mediterranean. If only more people could afford to visit: more Turks in Greece and Greeks in Jordan, more Egyptians in Syria and Syrians in Israel and Israelis in Italy, and more Palestinians in Palestine, too, I suppose. And more Australians everywhere. The more people come to see and touch their complex and intertwined histories, the more understanding they might come to have of the present. We're all in this together! So let's have more tourism in the region. Let's open (and of course, conserve) the tombs and temples everywhere. And let *all* the stories be told.

Note on languages
The transcription of words and placenames from Arabic, Greek, ancient Egyptian and other old languages is notoriously fraught. In this book I have made the choices that I am comfortable with,

and my editors have tried to make me consistent in using them. Failings in choice are my own. I prefer Cairo to Al-Qahirah, Giza to Gizah, Gallipoli to Gelibolu, Aleppo to Halab, Cheops to Khufu, Tutankhamun to Tutankhamen, Nefertiti to Nefertari and so on.

Note on currencies
When I travelled, the following exchange rates applied in the more official exchange bureaux: A$1 = 75 cents US, 2.2 Egyptian pounds (E£), half a Jordanian dinar (JD), about 50 Syrian pounds (S£), about 75 000 Turkish lire (TL), about 187 Greek drachmae (dr).

CHAPTER ONE

A DREAM
OF WONDERS

THROUGH THE MURKY WINDOW of an EgyptAirbus named *Cleo Express*, after a long night's journey into day, I felt before I actually noticed the tantalising hint of a shape just by the gleaming bronze stripe of the Nile: the shadow of the pyramids.

All my dreaming life had had this moment and this place lurking beneath its surface. Cairo: the beginning of stories, the starting-point of my journey, the focus of memories.

My dreaming had been of ancient Egyptians, the Arabian Nights, Gallipoli, Alexander the Great, the Trojan War, the Australians' crusade in World War I through Palestine to Damascus, the legacy of the Australians in Cairo – an Australian odyssey.

Egypt, and the journey, and the prospect of seven or even more wonders was mixed up in a doze as the plane circled and slowly descended, almost as if it was gliding on an eddy of the ancient hazy air dancing up from Cairo below.

I had not been to Egypt before, but thousands of Australians had, as soldiers in two world wars, as tourists, travellers, writers and painters. Even for an Australian, this is one of the roads most travelled. Egypt is the original tourist destination, one of the places the very first travel writer, Herodotus, wrote about 2500 years ago in his book *The Histories* when he came to see one of the Seven Wonders of the Ancient World. Not much hope of original insights here, you might think. Yet in coming to see the sites of Australian experience in this part of the world, in the context of a journey from Cairo to Gallipoli and on to Athens, I hoped there would be.

Thousands of Australians lie buried in the countries of the eastern Mediterranean, from Tobruk in Libya around the coast to Egypt and modern Israel, through Jordan, Lebanon and Syria to Turkey and Greece, including Crete.

These are the lands which for thousands of years have made a culture of graveyards, tombs and monuments to the dead. These mausoleums chronicle the progress of civilisation, and the memorials to the Australian dead tell of our part in this story. And

overleaf: Medusa head, Apollo Temple, Didyma, Turkey

not just the dead. The birthplace of modern Australia is perhaps also to be found around here; the Mediterranean lands are the birthplace of millions of living Australians.

I wanted to visit the sites of Australian battlefields and cemeteries and six of the wonders mostly by bus, train and ferry. I had about six weeks to get from Cairo to Athens.

Sights and sites. In Greek, the word used originally to describe or distinguish the wonders was *theamata*, which means 'things to be seen'; that is, sights. This came in the centuries after one Philo of Byzantium wrote the earliest and fullest description of the ancient wonders in Alexandria, Egypt around 225 BC. The Greek word which came to be used to describe these things was *thaumata* which means 'wonders'. Today, both sights and wonders have become, for the most part, simply sites.

While a journey involves missed connections and choices at forks in the road, it also needs a mental map, a reason to go from one place to the next. Without a jotted map in mind, there is no journey, there is aimless wandering.

The Seven Wonders of the Ancient World offered some directions and stopping points. To begin in Egypt, there are the pyramids at Giza, which is now a suburb of Cairo, and the Pharos or Lighthouse at Alexandria. In Greece there is, or was, the Colossus at Rhodes, the island off the coast of Turkey. In Turkey itself are the ruins of the Temple of Artemis at Ephesus and the Mausoleum at Halicarnassus, now the town of Bodrum. At Olympia, on mainland Greece, is the site of the statue of Zeus, which I might not have time to see, and in Iraq is the place where the Hanging Gardens of Babylon once flourished.

I hoped to see six of the seven sites. Babylon would have to remain in the imagination because I had no real desire to go to Saddam Hussein's Baghdad, which is only a few miles from the site of Babylon.

Philo of Byzantium, who first described the Seven Ancient Wonders, was a scholar–scientist at the ancient research institute

in the Mouseion–Library complex at Alexandria, the city founded
by Alexander the Great around 331 BC. Philo did not invent the
list; it came into existence, or into the consciousness of the people
of the ancient world, in the century after Alexander's death in
Babylon in 323 BC. Many of the wonders were built around
Alexander's time: the Pharos, the Colossus, the Temple of Artemis
and the Mausoleum. For me, travelling in the reverse direction to
Alexander, back past his birthplace at Pella near Thessaloniki in
Macedonia, some of Alexander's own sites were another focus.
He had been all over the area, defeating the Persians at Granicus
near Troy, calling in at Priene and Halicarnassus, consulting the
oracle at Siwa, and buried, probably, in Alexandria.

Philo wrote: 'Everyone has heard of the Seven Wonders of the
World, but very few have seen all of them for themselves ... Only
if you travel the world and get worn out by the effort of the journey will the desire to see all the wonders of the world be satisfied, and by the time you have done that you will be old and
practically dead ...' He said that he would 'remove the necessity
to travel' and describe the wonders, because reading about them
provided an 'education' which 'allows one to see those things
with one's mind if not with one's eyes.' It 'displays the beautiful
and amazing things in one's very own home.'

Over 2000 years ago, the wonders were described so that the
armchair traveller could see them with his mind's eye, avoiding
the perils of the trip. This part of the world is no less perilous now
than it was in Philo's day, but having read Philo's and others'
descriptions, I still wanted to see them for myself. I wanted to see
them with an Australian eye.

I knew that aside from the pyramids ('mountains built upon
mountains' wrote Philo) there was not much to see at the modern-
day sites of these wonders, so I decided that I would find seven
extant wonders from the ancient world as well: wonders that
would be as evident and wondrous as the pyramids. My prelimi-
nary list of extant places to visit included the Temple of Karnak

at Luxor in Upper Egypt, the Oracle Temple at Siwa in Egypt which Alexander the Great visited, Petra in Jordan, Palmyra in Syria, the great Crusader castle Krac des Chevaliers in Syria, the Roman town of Ephesus, and Troy in Turkey.

The tombs at Luxor in the Valley of the Kings and the Valley of the Queens, Priene, Jerash, Aleppo, Miletus, Athens, Rhodes, other citadels, castles and cities – well, I would see them too.

But I had an idea that there were, as well as those ancient wonders, seven Australian sites in the area that might make another list of wonders: our wonders. I made a jotted list of the places I wanted to try to visit, to see whether there was anything there, in addition to cemeteries, which would qualify them as Australian wonders of the Middle East. Gallipoli in Turkey, Tobruk in Libya and El Alamein in Egypt were obvious candidates. Beersheba, now in Israel, site of the great charge of the Light Horse in 1916, was another one. Damascus in Syria, liberated in both world wars, was a place of romance and possibility. Cairo itself, and the site of the Mena Camp at Giza, where Australian soldiers camped in both world wars was another. There was Amman in Jordan, which the Light Horse raided and eventually took in 1917, and Greece and Crete, scenes of bitter fighting and strategic withdrawals in 1941.

I would not be able to get to all of these places this time, but there were plenty of places to mix on the itinerary with the older wonders.

But first I had to begin at the beginning: in Cairo.

As a boy, reading that delicious but shocking book of stories, *The Arabian* (or *Thousand and One*) *Nights*, I came across my first impression of what Cairo was supposed to be like in the lubricious 'Tale of the Jewish Doctor'. I had wanted to visit ever since.

This salutary tale is about what happens if you tarry in Damascus on the way to Cairo. You might, for example, be seduced by two of the most beautiful sisters imaginable, but also learn that there is a price that must be paid by waking up beside one of them after she's had her head cut off. All that before being paid to marry the third sister and live happily ever after.

The story begins with the doctor of the title hearing about the wonders of Cairo from his uncles, and wanting to go there.

> He who hath not seen Cairo hath not seen the world: her soil is gold, her Nile is a marvel; her women are like the black eyed houris of Paradise; her houses are palaces; and her air is soft, more odorous than aloes wood, rejoicing the heart. And how can Cairo be other-wise when she is the Mother of the World.

What worked on the doctor had a similar effect on me. Black-eyed houris! Where would I find some of them?

A more recent literary spur was reading the Egyptian novelist Naguib Mahfouz's surprising, evocative and sad Cairo Trilogy, the major work for which he won the 1988 Nobel Prize for Literature.

The three novels, *Palace Walk*, *Sugar Street* and *Palace of Desire*, tell the story of the family of Al-Sayyid Ahmad, his wife Amina, and their children – notably Kamal, who was born in 1911, making him around the same age as Mahfouz was at the end of World War I – during the 1919 attempted nationalist revolution in Cairo. The Cairo Trilogy is the story of the city, and of Egypt, in the years of transformation of family life and a renewed, modern kind of nationalism. It is told indirectly, delicately, even nostalgically.

In *Palace Walk*, Al-Sayyid Ahmad would often come home late at night, after drinking and listening to the black-eyed houris sing, and discuss the matters of the day with his wife:

> He proceeded to discuss household matters with her. He told her he had directed a merchant he knew to buy up a reserve of clarified

butter, wheat, and cheese for the house. He attacked the rise in prices and the scarcity of necessary commodities caused by this war, which had been giving the world a pounding for the past three years. As always when he mentioned the war, he began cursing the Australian troops who had spread through the city like locusts, destroying the land.

The truth was that he had a special reason for resenting the Australians. Their tyranny separated him from the Ezbekiya Garden entertainment district, which he had abandoned in defeat, except for the few rare opportunities he could snatch. He could not stand to expose himself to soldiers who openly plundered people of their possessions and took pleasure in abusing and insulting them without restraint.

Could that have been us? Locusts? Destroying the land? Plundering people, abusing and insulting them? Australians had participated in some high jinks and even a kind of race riot in Cairo in 1915 – C. J. Dennis wrote a poem about it called 'The Battle of the Wazzir' – before the Anzacs headed off to Gallipoli, but surely that couldn't have created the sort of anger felt by Naguib Mahfouz as a boy.

Palace Walk was first published in Arabic in 1956 – that other great year of Egyptian national awakening when the Suez Canal was nationalised by Gamal Abdul Nasser. This action provoked the cockeyed military intervention of the fading imperial powers Britain and France, launched after the delegation led by Australian Prime Minister Robert Menzies failed to convince Nasser of the error of his ways. Menzies had been instructed to tell Nasser to let the British and French run the Suez Canal just like they always had. Nasser called Menzies 'that Australian mule', a reference to the World War I Egyptian joke that Australian soldiers were like Australian mules, which ate twice as much as Egyptian mules but did half the work. Nasser sent Menzies packing and, after much Egyptian blood was shed, the Suez Canal remained nationalised, despite invasion and the 1956 war. A minor side effect of this episode was that Egypt broke off diplomatic relations with Australia and did not come to the 'Friendly' Olympic Games in Melbourne a few months later.

Mahfouz assuredly would have had a quiet chuckle at the Australian political misfortunes and Menzian misjudgments in 1956. His memory of Australians went back to his boyhood, particularly to the events of 1919, where Australians did seem to have caused the sort of hurt and resentment that Naguib Mahfouz would remember as a defining childhood moment. In putting down the Saad Zaghloul nationalist uprising of 1919, the Light Horse killed Egyptians and burned villages, such as Surafend. This Australian service in Britain's imperial interest was something of a puzzle for nationalist Egyptians. Could it be that, from the Egyptian point of view, we Australians in 1919 were just as brutal as the enemy we had defeated in 1918?

The First AIF had begun their association with Egypt well before this, in December 1914, when they had stopped off for training in warm and sunny Egypt before joining the fighting in France, as was originally intended.

One soldier's first impressions of Cairo were of a 'panorama of strange realities'. On Boxing Day 1914, Major Coe of the 12th Field Artillery wrote:

The shops never close. The natives won't work on Friday. They say their prayers in the open. Women are beasts of burden, child marriage, harems, high palaces and indescribably filthy stinking houses in which the donkeys, bison, fowl, sheep and goats all sleep together with the natives. Camels, overloaded donkeys. Arab horses, motor cars, phaetons, pyramids, Sphinx, tents, desert, cultivation, electric trams, plough drawn by camel and donkey harnessed together, scorpions, huge beetles, mosquitoes, morning temperature forty-five, midday temperature ninety-eight, no rain, bell *tents, marquees, the smell of the east, home memories – mix the lot and that is Egypt for you, as I know it …*

Their first impressions perhaps tainted their later relationship with Egyptians. They came by boat, some of them on a troopship called *Ulysses* and others on the *Euripides* on which 500 men received ptomaine poisoning, allegedly from food bought from boats that had accosted them before and during the trip up the Suez Canal. A poisoned welcome …

'Mr Garrie, please fasten your seatbelt.'

'Breakfast? Another breakfast?'

'No, we are landing soon. *Inshallah.*'

The Airbus landed; the warm dusty air perfumed with kerosene smells hit like a mugger. This was Cairo, at last.

CHAPTER TWO
ALONE IN GIZA

THE EGYPTAIR TERMINAL HAD been modern in the 1960s but was now, like the pyramids, in an advanced state of preservation in the desert air. The air of Cairo had yet to shake off the effects of a huge dust storm that had blown through a few days before. The desert is always near, the combination of dust and car exhaust lying like a doona over the city. Inside the terminal it was not much better, as people lit up Cleopatra cigarettes with the enthusiasm of desiccated travellers arriving at an oasis.

My in-flight companion, George, a Scottish Australian in Cairo for a big expo – he was travelling in sanitary ceramics – was met by a party of greeters. It was off to a hotel and a diary of meetings for him in the solicitous hands of those chaps from the government. In Egypt they love groups travelling with guides, whether on the business of business or the business of seeing the sights. Individuals are a bit of a bother.

I passed through to the Immigration Desk. A cheerful 'g'day' met with no response from the official, a pencil-thin man with a big cap and a crayon smear of moustache who disdainfully picked up my passport with the tips of two fingers.

'Mr Garrie? What is this?'

I admit it was not a mint condition item. My passport had come back from a trip to Turkey in 1993 in the pocket of a shirt that went straight from sweaty back to washing machine after walking stiffly through the door at home. It was ragged around the edges, with smudged stamps and leaky signature, but still valid – at least I thought so. My photo made me look like a fugitive with a prison haircut.

The immigration man studied my visa, which had cost all of A$42 from the Egyptian consulate in Melbourne, and waved me out of the way. He retained the passport: uh-oh.

A few minutes later he called me back and wordlessly handed it to me. I took a surreptitious look while waiting for the luggage: a stamp, no notes. Looking at the immigration official's booth, I saw that he waved everyone through while he consulted the

overleaf: the Mena House, Giza

details on the computer. But he didn't want you to watch him – just in case something came up.

'Hello. Where are you from? England America Germany?'

'No mate. Australia.'

'Synneymelbun?'

'Melbourne.'

'I have many frens in Melbourne. You know Knox?'

'Nice talking to you, but I'm just getting my luggage, and …'

'You with group?'

'No, I am travelling by myself.'

'Travelling alone? Ah! Maybe I can help you.'

'No thanks, I've got things to do.'

'My name means Morning Sun.'

'Glad to hear it.'

'I wait. You see me, my badge.'

My interrogator was another thin person – where are the fat Egyptians? – a boy in scuffed black pants and dark blazer. He was hesitant, even offhanded. He walked away while I stood waiting.

Finally my blue backpack, another souvenir of the visit to Turkey, emerged onto the luggage carousel. I had purchased this backpack for US$20 from a member of the Russian whitewater canoeing team on the River Çoruh, up near the border with Georgia, in 1993. We were all in that part of the somewhat cultivated Anatolian wilderness (apricots, tomatoes, poplars, rice in the river valleys) for the World Whitewater Championships. The Russian team had brought a lot of gear to sell for hard currency, including this excellent pack. They were trade-goods rich but dollar poor – like Egypt.

My other gear included the famous sandy coloured Thomas Cook (the Australian Thomas Cook) photographer's vest, a magical combination of pockets for all the bits and pieces you cart around: camera lenses; spare batteries; newspapers; Swiss Army knife; notebooks; passport; various wallets with cash in five currencies; traveller's cheques; cards; souvenir pebbles; a guidebook or two; locally purchased maps and museum catalogues; a plastic bottle of water; cap (when not on head); and paper bags of nuts, dried figs and apricots. It weighed about fifteen kilos fully loaded. A pocket for everything and everything in its pocket.

I was struggling to put it on while holding my camera bag, when my new friend Morning Sun turned up again.

'Come. I will take you to my boss friend. No obligation.'

'No thanks. Please, I need to think ...'

'No, come, I am official guide, not one of these – ptah! – tourist touts. Look, I have badge!'

He did, too, and I found myself walking none too steadily with him. Morning Sun was steering me, by pushing one side or the other of my pack, towards the door and into a Cairo morning.

The solicitous behaviour of Morning Sun seemed to mean that business was a bit slow at seven in the morning, and anyway, I did need to ask someone where the buses and taxis left from. I knew Giza, where I was staying for first few nights at the Mena House, was some distance from the airport, on the other side of the Nile.

Once out of the door, he propelled me to the left and around a corner where a number of offices – more like small cement cells – huddled under a staircase. I could barely fit through the doorway.

Here 'the Boss' touted his wares in a desultory sort of way. At last, a fat Egyptian. Perhaps he could see that I was not interested in the *One Day Tour of Cairo*, *Pyramids with Aircon*, *One Day to Saqqara*, or *Nile River Cruise Including Dinner and Belly Dance*.

Travellers in the old days always picked up a dragoman (translator, guide, fixer) to accompany them around Egypt, but I was feeling rather put upon. And besides, I wanted to make my own mistakes.

'When you go?'

'I don't need anything, thank you.'

'Where you stay?'

'I'm already booked at the Mena House.'

'Very far away.'

'Very close to the pyramids.'

'Very expensive.'

'Very nice.'

'Of course.'

With that I tried to stand up, but my pack caught on the doorhandle and I plopped down again. This seemed to break the ice in these high-level negotiations, because the Boss laughed, pulled me to my feet, and pointed the way to the taxis. 'Pay him just £20,' he said.

Well, I tried. Cairo taxis are black and white and held together with bits of string, wire and probably hommos. Some are larger, indestructible Peugeot 504s, known in Egyptian English as 'Poo-joes'. Others are smaller Renaults and Fiats of *une certain vintage*, and there are also, from Eastern Europe, mock-cars called Ladas. I found a Lada that looked like it had gone five rounds with a camel and tried my first bit of negotiation.

I pondered the possible impact my name would have in Arabic; that is, a 'gharry' is a wheeled conveyance. It was a bit like being called Truck or Wagon or perhaps Taxi in English. But then a *gamal* is a camel is a four-legged conveyance, and there are plenty of *gamals* about in Egypt.

'Mena House in Giza – how much?' asked the experienced bargainer.

'Sixty.'

'Thirty,' I said. Experienced bargainers halve the first offer and meet somewhere in the middle. The driver shook his head. Why should I starve for you? his body language said. I have wives, children, and possibly camels – *gamals* and *gamals* …

'Fifty,' he said.

'All right, forty.'

'Okay.'

Bargaining honour satisfied, or so I thought, we set off into the traffic.

Connoisseurs of traffic in large cities love Cairo. Cairo, they say, has twelve or fourteen or sixteen million people at night – and twenty million in the day. Cairo has no traffic lights that anyone obeys and no lanes that anyone stays in. Nevertheless, despite the lack of a system, despite camels and donkey carts, and hundreds of officious traffic policemen, there is rarely a traffic jam that sees cars sitting in one place for hours, drivers dying from the fumes.

Being amidst it all can be quite disturbing, as Egyptian drivers are addicted to the horn, as well as to loud Arabic popular music with which they frequently sing along.

'You like Arab music?'

'Of course.'

'Umm Kalthoum, okay?'

'If you say so.'

You can't avoid the music, and after awhile you can't avoid liking it. It's everywhere, and to the untrained Western ear, it essentially sounds like the same song.

The sound of traffic is like a weird Western symphony, *Turangalila* perhaps, by Olivier Messiaen, a suite for the intruments of chaos: one million car horns, the clashing rhythm of life and a choir of screams. Add to it the street theatre – large billowing and bellowing buses, donkeys solo, donkeys with carts, the occasional camel, women in head-to-toe black sacking seemingly blind to their surroundings, and flocks of generally reckless and suicidal pedestrians – and that's an off-peak drive in Cairo.

I didn't see a serious accident, but I saw sweepers with a more frustrating job than painting the Sydney Harbour Bridge. Their job involved waving long brooms at the sand, dust and debris by the side of the road. They made the labours of Hercules seem small jobs. And I saw daily, hourly, scrapes and traffic bumps. Every Egyptian car has some body damage – the only pristine ones seemed to bear diplomatic plates or chauffeur-driven businessmen on their way from the duty free showroom for the first time.

Cairo is not as ancient a city as Damascus (which city is?), though ancient sites nearby, such as Babylon (not to be confused with the one in Iraq), Memphis and the pyramids at Giza, are testimony to the age of settlement and civilisation on the banks of the Nile. The Persians established the fortress named Babylon in 500 BC, and people lived around the site, which became known as Fustat, for a thousand years after that. The Jews and, later, groups of Christians, notably the Copts, built synagogues and churches in the area that is now known as Old Cairo. The Muslims took over in 640 AD, after winning a battle at Heliopolis, and then a complicated sequence of caliphs ruled for hundreds of years.

Today's Cairo – or Al-Qahirah in Arabic – dates back to a day in June, 969 AD. Al-Qahirah might be translated as 'City of Mars', and this is how it came about.

A new set of rulers had appeared. The Fatimid caliphate was in charge of the Islamic world, and a general named Gawhar wanted a new city built, down the Nile from Fustat. He had the area pegged out with strings with small bells on them. Before starting to dig, he waited for a sign from his astrologers. Days passed. Eventually, a crow landed on one of the strings, sounding the bells, just at the time the planet Mars was in the ascendant. Work began, and the city was to be called Al-Qahirah, City of Mars the Conqueror. Or so they say.

The airport is close to the planned suburb of Heliopolis on the site of the Pharaonic centre which flourished at the same time as Memphis. We passed the baroque 'castle' or 'Hindu Villa' and next to it another building which had been used by the Australians as a hospital in World War I and was remembered vividly by the many Anzac nurses who had worked there. There had been an Australian camp near here, as well as the Mena Camp at Giza, in both world wars.

Heliopolis was built by and developed by the Belgian tramways concessionaire Baron Empain in 1905, and mostly designed by another Belgian, Alexander Marcel, as a sort of self-contained enclave. It was stratified by buildings, into social classes: large palace-type buildings for the top Europeans, villas for middle-class Europeans, and apartment blocks for 'les indigenes', as Egyptians were known to the Baron.

Baron Empain brought the tram to many cities in the region, between Cairo and Constantinople. As a tram lover, he was an honorary Melburnian, a fact not lost on the first AIF diggers who used to catch his trams from the Mena Camp at Giza back to Cairo.

The tree of Cairo is not the palm tree – though there are plenty of those – it is the Australian eucalyptus. Where did they come from? Who brought them here? Some – those beside the zoo and the Nile – look just like river red gums. Others are scruffier, maybe a local genetic adaptation: eucalyptus nondescriptus, perhaps. Are gum trees Australia's revenge for the rabbit, or our greatest contribution to the look of Cairo, and many other countries of the eastern Mediterranean?

We crossed the Nile, then the island of Gezira, the Nile again, and soon drove down Al Ahram: Pyramids Road. From the taxi, the city looked dusty, busy, self-contained. I spotted the Cairo Tower, not as impressive as the Nile itself, and thought that Cairo really had no need of additional landmarks, because – those pyramids, there they are! Looming on the horizon like a dream come true.

I once stood on a track in a park in Zimbabwe and asked a friend in the car where the giraffes were. He said, 'Right next to you.' I was looking beneath one. That's what the pyramids are like – they are so big you can't see them, so old they've always been there.

Half an hour from the airport I arrived at the Mena House Oberoi, the historic hotel where there are plenty of Rooms with a View. The pyramids are just across the road. The Australians had camped out the back.

We swung in the gate of Mena House, past a security check-point. The driver wheedled under the awning. 'Baksheesh, baksheesh.' I gave him the E£10 I thought I'd saved by bargaining. Welcome to Egypt.

I felt at home straightaway, mainly because of the great gum trees that thrived near the entrance. These particular trees are the offspring, and may well be the originals, of the avenue of eucalypts which lined Pyramids Road from the hotel to the Nile, as noted and photographed by men in the First AIF when they waited for a tram to take them to the fleshpots of Cairo.

'Please, what your name first please?' asked the flashing eyes behind the desk at the Mena House.

'Garrie.'

'Welcome in Egypt, Mr Garrie. You are with group?'

'No, I am alone.'

'Alone! And you are only in Cairo?'

'No I am going to … I don't know … Siwa, Petra, Damascus, Palmyra, Halicarnassus, Rhodes, Ephesus, Gallipoli …'

'Oh! Mr Garrie you must be having a wonderful odyssey.'

As I turned from the desk, the sound of an Arab song floated into the foyer from somewhere inside the hotel, which called to mind the first impressions of another Australian traveller.

Ninety-nine years ago, in February 1897, the Australian painter Arthur Streeton had arrived in Cairo. His first impression was to remark how wonderful it was '… at night to pass through strange crowded thoroughfares and perfumed gardens on [our] way to hotel, to our bed to [be] awoken by music at one o'clock the next morning; throwing ajar the window shutters to hear a tramp of revellers passing below and singing in concert the finest music.'

Later he wrote to the *Bulletin*:

I've been so excited endeavouring to get some of the Cairo lightness in my work that I let everything else slide. 'Tis a wonderful land, this

Egypt: I've been time after time through the slipper, brass and bronze, jewellery, perfume, silks, ring, curio bazaars ... I did a quick sketch of a spice bazaar ... I write with a stick of incense under my nose, the mosquitos are very bad. These bazaars are the sight of Cairo, with the grand design of some of the mosques and the fine arches and fastnesses of the city.

Streeton made some nice sketches of other subjects, such as water sellers and the striped mosque, taking photographs and being photographed, like everyone since their invention, on a beast in front of the Sphinx and the pyramids.

Streeton, one of the first Australian tourists, was also quite professional in his attitude to painting. He stayed for three months, intending to 'cash in' on the taste for 'oriental' subjects. I'd seen two of these paintings, reworked from his sketches, in a grand retrospective of Streeton's work. They were minor works, I suppose, in the Streeton legacy, but brightly, freshly painted: a water seller, and the striped mosque near the Khan el Khalili bazaar.

At the beginning of 1918, having served as a medical orderly in London, Streeton was appointed an Official War Artist. He was too late for Gallipoli, Egypt and Palestine, and so he painted in France, producing a number of battle-as-landscape pictures around Villers-Bretonneux. Somehow in these paintings France looks like Australia, whereas the palette in Egypt was brighter, pinker, and did not. Streeton wrote, 'True pictures of battlefields are very quiet looking things, there's nothing much to be seen – everybody and everything is hidden and camouflaged.'

The Mena House was operated in the early part of the century by an extraordinary individual named George Nungovich, who had also gained the concession to provide food for the AIF. His culinary style and the provision – or lack of it – of the rations were the source of much controversy. Nungovich had begun business as a porter at the Cairo Railway Station – said to be as good an entree to business there as starting as a paperboy would be in Australia.

The gum trees are not the only Australian associations with this splendid hotel. Unlike Shepheard's, the other historic hotel in downtown Cairo, the Mena House is still at its original location, where it was built in its first incarnation by the Khedive Ismail in the 1860s as a resthouse and hunting lodge. The Khedive was the Governor of Egypt under the Ottoman Empire.

The building was expanded for the celebrations marking the opening of the Suez Canal in 1869, and was used infrequently by other royal acquaintances of Ismail in the 1870s before being 'privatised' along with the rest of Egypt when the British asserted their influence on the ailing Ottomans in the 1880s.

In 1881 it was bought by a wealthy Englishman named Frederick Head. Frederick's wife Mary was the Australian daughter of the squatter and Queensland Treasurer of 1866, John Donald McLean. The Heads gave the building the name Mena House.

The next owners of the hotel, Hugh Locke-King and his wife Ethel, took over in the late 1880s. Ethel was the daughter of the Tasmanian Governor of the 1860s, Sir Thomas Gore Browne.

It was Ethel who created the beautiful public rooms and restaurants at Mena House, ordering the brass candelabra, wonderful *mashrabia* (wooden fretwork) screens and ornate Arab-inspired plasterwork ceilings.

During World War I, Mena House became a hospital staffed by Anzac nurses. After the war, some Australians who had been associated with the Light Horse in Egypt and their successful crusade through Palestine and Syria came back to Cairo. Perhaps they were among the men who could not bear to leave their horses in Egypt, because one of them, Frank Cullen, ran the Mena House Riding School from the stables.

The owners of these beasts today are among the most sticky individuals in the world of tourism, and are the single unpleasant feature of the environs of Mena House and the pyramids. You may want to be alone, as I did, to just walk around and hope to be struck by some awe. The touts make this impossible, and getting rid of them will not only cost you baksheesh, but also a certain amount of distress (I saw several travellers in tears having made the mistake of stopping to take a picture), and a diminution in the experience itself.

I know the guides and jockeys and touts have to earn a living and so on – which in a city the size of Cairo is not easy – and that they have traditionally held the pyramid concession, but all the same, distressing individual tourists is a bit counterproductive. The Egyptian tourist business needs all the help it can get, and travellers, even those not in groups following a guide with a flag on a stick, need to feel welcome in Egypt, having taken the decision to visit in the first place.

The men of the First AIF camped behind the pyramids. They trained for Gallipoli by running up and down the Great Pyramid, riding camels, making a nuisance of themselves in Cairo, as well as doing a bit of more-formal soldiering and sandy-square bashing. There were also quite a few games of cricket and football.

Mena Camp was one of three or four camps and hospitals created by the Australians in and around Cairo at the end of 1914. The Light Horse were stationed at Mahdi; Colonel John Monash and the 4th Brigade were at Heliopolis; the First Australian Division camped here at Mena, as did official war correspondent Charles Bean.

Every nation needs its own epic, its own national story or set of stories – it's one of the major qualifications for nationhood. And one of our Australian stories was written by Charles Bean in *The Official History of Australia in the War of 1914–1918*, published in fifteen volumes between 1921 and 1943. Bean wrote *The Story of Anzac* in two volumes, and Harry Gullett wrote the volume concerned with the campaign through Palestine and Syria.

To me, Bean is, above Lawson, Paterson or Dennis, Australia's Homer or Herodotus, and his story of Anzac and Gallipoli is the primary Australian story, as it is largely told through accounts of what individuals did. Never mind that it was in the imperial service, that is part of the Australian nationalist paradox. The fact that Gallipoli, Egypt, Turkey, ancient Greece and Troy are all in the same part of the world is more than a coincidence for me. It is why I am here, and why Australians are at home here. Our story is part of the great collection of stories told in this area from back beyond the Bible.

Before Charles Bean was elected Official War Correspondent by his peers in 1914, he was a *Sydney Morning Herald* journalist. He went to Cairo in December 1914, then to Gallipoli and later to France. He returned to Gallipoli in 1919 as head of the Australian Historical Mission to collect relics, supervise burials and answer questions about the campaign. He travelled back overland to Cairo by rail from Istanbul in 1919. My own journey would be very much in Bean's actual footsteps, as well as in his emotional debt.

Bean, known to his mates as Captain Carrot, and the Australian soldiers in late 1914 and 1915 were quite impressed by the pyramids rising next to them in the hazy, dusty light.

What was the camp at Mena like? Bean left no description in his diary, but the *Egyptian Gazette* of 18 December 1914 described the Light Horse camp at Mahdi, across the Nile:

Although the camp is not yet quite fixed, the men seem cheerful and at home. Large wood fires burn beneath and around oval iron pots of tea; toast, too, seems a great favourite, baked and sadly burned in the wood ashes. The many lines of beautiful and much-loved horses strike the onlooker immediately; they have practically constant attention night and day. Being packed on the boats as they were the whole time from Australia, standing for seven or eight weeks, has for the time being weakened and stiffened their legs and joints and at present not one of them is being ridden. They are exercised daily, at first gently, increasing to ten-mile exercises and training they are now undergoing. There are wild and almost-wild horses amongst them, many of which were presented to the regiments before they left.

The lines of tents are like most lines of tents but for a few of the officers', which showed an almost oriental brightness with their linings of brilliant orange, and the huge canteen tents built of native tenting. Mascots of the regiments are, of course, a chief and interesting sight, and a motley crew they are. One regiment is the proud possessor of two great birds of the kind called laughing jackasses whose shrieked mirth can be heard by the inhabitants of Mahdi, half a mile away. There was also a rock kangaroo or wallaby.

Mena Camp was like this too: lines of tents, the pyramids looming nearby. Pictures of it in World War II, twenty-five years later, look just the same. There were also horses and mules here.

The stables at Mena House are still at their long-established location on the other side of the road from the main entrance to the hotel. They are sunk below road level, the road climbing up onto the plateau on which the pyramids were built. It is like a mine site, alive with hundreds of animals and their handlers readying themselves to prey upon tourist and traveller alike.

The soldiers of the First AIF, especially the Light-horsemen, knew all about horses, and a bit about camels but they did not know much – anything – about Egyptians.

Cairo was a big shock to their systems: their systems of belief, hygiene, and human relationships. I had encountered something like this culture shock, and I had some appreciation of what had caused the trouble between the Australians and the people in and around Cairo in 1915 and 1919 – events which colour the background to relationships eighty years later.

'People who say there are slums in Melbourne don't know what they are talking about. They have no idea what slums are.

The lowest lanes in Carlton are clean and the houses palaces compared to the places in Cairo.' This is what Lieutenant J. D. Campbell wrote home in 1916, when C. J. Dennis was creating a rosy version of those slums, and the sentiments of the first diggers in *The Moods of Ginger Mick*. (*Songs of a Sentimental Bloke* was published in 1915, and Dennis sent Ginger Mick to war in the *Moods*, published in October 1916. Both books were published in huge editions for the Anzacs, who treasured them.)

Mick was on his way to war having heard 'stern jooty's call' to fight for king, empire and to preserve the values of 'old' Australia that Dennis celebrated with a small fraction of the racism of compatriot Henry Lawson and the local knowledge of 'Banjo' Paterson.

Paterson was another storytelling Australian who passed through Cairo in World War I. After serving in an ambulance in France, Captain Paterson, who was also an honorary vet, brought horses from Australia to Egypt and was commissioned in the 2nd Remount Unit, AIF in October 1915. Wounded and later promoted to major, 'the Banjo' served in Egypt, Palestine and Syria until 1919. He would have had a look at the stables at Mena.

For older Cairenes, the memory of the boys and men of the Light Horse and other regiments of the First AIF is not of the heroes of Gallipoli or the dashing crusaders who beat Lawrence of Arabia into Damascus. They have a different view. But just as there are only a handful of the First AIF left alive in Australia, so there are very few people in Cairo today who can report on the Australian presence eighty years ago.

Naguib Mahfouz begins his Cairo Trilogy during World War I, when traditional Egyptian family life was on the cusp of change. One of the younger members of the family he writes about was caught up in nationalist demonstrations and the Saad Zaghloul uprising of 1919.

The idea that there was anything wrong in Australia (newly a nation, if still within the thrall of imperial Britain) undertaking any of these dirty tasks of empire did not occur to anyone, least of all Bean or Paterson, although Bean was uncomfortable with the idea that his Anzac heroes might have tarnished their reputation.

What the Egyptians thought of the matter was of even less concern to anyone at the time. The British government proclaimed Egypt a British protectorate from 20 December 1914, just after the first Australians arrived. Any thought by Egyptian nationalists that Australian colonials would join their brothers in Egypt to throw off the British yoke was soon seen to be risible.

The First AIF were 'loyal' to a man – a sentiment the Sultan of Egypt thought was a good example of wartime patriotism. The Sultan's view was that becoming an active part of the British Empire was better for Egyptians than being a forgotten backwater of the faded Ottoman Empire, which Egypt had officially been, even though Britain had effectively occupied the country since 1882.

But from today's perspective, the idea that five years later some of those soldiers who helped to create our national identity of Gallipoli and Palestine would be used to put down an Egyptian nationalist event is paradoxical, to say the least.

Egyptians did distinguish between the bigger, healthier, more insolent Australians with their great horses, and the weedier and more obedient English, but that was not necessarily a favourable comparison in a society where civility in language was at the heart of its culture.

Tewfik al-Hakim wrote in *The Prison of Life*, 1964: 'We in the cities did not experience the war to any great extent, except in so far as we had to put up with the insolence of the Australian soldiers and the drunken English, or their grabbing what passers-by had in their pockets at night and what street vendors had in their hand during the day.'

This upsetting of street sellers' trays and stalls by Australians was much remarked upon, and universally thought of by Egyptians as boorish behaviour.

In 1996 I was on the lookout for, but did not encounter any, 'special' treatment. In 1914–15 Australian soldiers, who were paid more than the British (or so the Egyptians thought – it may have been the buildup of unspendable pay from the weeks on the ship), became the 'chosen prey of the exploiter'. 'Special prices for Australians' was a sign often used; it was soon found to mean 'twice as much as what others have to pay'. This understandable but unpleasant commercial behaviour is at the heart of the expression 'being gypped'.

CHAPTER THREE

ON EATING
A CAMEL

I WALKED OUT THE front door of the Mena House, past the swimming pool, through the car park and beyond the security gate manned by lazily observant guards. Their eyes flicked over the dusty pedestrian parade: European, okay; Japanese, okay; American, okay; Egyptian, whaddya want? The obstacles supposedly preventing unauthorised invasion of the enclave by cars might stop a camel, but not the determined taxi I dodged as it weaved through the barriers like a slalom skier.

Across the road and up the hill past the crater where the stables exude flavoursome odours of camel and pony, drawn by the looming pyramids. Accosted by a kid: blue *galabyia*, white scarf, small, his hand beseeching.

'Whereyoufrom?'

Struck thoughtless by the view of the pyramids growing larger and more unbelievable with each step: 'Australia.'

'Synnymelbun?'

'Melbourne.'

'Ahh, Melbun best place Aussie,' he said, as if he had been there last week. 'Wanna see pyramids horsee camel donkey?'

'No thanks. I'm just walking.'

'No ticket?!'

'I am buying a ticket up there.'

The ticket office was up the incline beyond the stables. The boy was insistent, tugging at my sleeve and scurrying beside me like a demented fox terrier. Despite myself, I found I was walking down into the stables.

'I am walking. I don't want a camel.'

'But why, why, why not? Is too far. See everything.'

We kicked dust and dung through the yard, watched by amused cameleers, ponyjocks and donkeymen. They watched as they would a puppy attack a large and stupid dog.

'Alone! *Imshee!*'

The kid stopped on the edge of the stable yard. I stopped too.

overleaf: Joma and Camel 107, Giza

I was faced with a hill of sand leading up to the road and the ticket office. The kid said, 'Camel is better than walking.'

I was so annoyed that I just started to climb up the sandhill, kicking camel turds like footballs. Two steps forward and one step back. So this is Egypt! I was tired, upset, jetlagged, excited. I wanted to look at the pyramids. Couldn't they understand?

The kid chased me up the hill. He just wouldn't let go. 'Meester! Meester!'

I turned towards him. He was holding something, which I recognised just as I was about to launch into a blast of '*Imshee!*' It was my camera case. It must have fallen out of my pocket.

'Camel?' he said, with a cute smile.

'Nick off. But thanks.'

At the top of the sandhill there was a road in the desert which was not deserted. It was peopled with camels, ponies galloping erratically up and down, bands of tourists keeping close together like phalanxes of Roman soldiers, and a few stragglers – backpackers gazing, easy meat.

I bought a ticket. Ten Egyptian pounds seemed a fair price, even if it was just to walk around. It cost an extra E£10 for pictures inside, and the same again to see the 'solar boat'. For now, I just wanted to walk around and find a place to take a picture.

The pyramids are a bit like Uluru: both hypnotise photographers, both rise like a rocket straight from the ground, and both have the certainty, the majesty of huge objects that have been around for as good as forever. They are so big you cannot take them all in at once. You have to walk around them, stand back from them, watch the patterns of light and look for the shadows.

Uluru is awe-inspiring because it is a natural weather-beaten red rock, as old as the earth itself, squatting in the centre of our ancient Australian continent. The pyramids are awe-inspiring because people actually built them, and their perfect shapes sit in silent criticism of every building built after them.

The locals of the Uluru-Kata Tjuta country, the Anangu, call tourists 'ants', for that is what we look like climbing the great rock. At the pyramids, tourists are more like sheep, hounded by wolves. I climbed Uluru once, despite the Anangu not actually liking us ants doing it. But here the locals would have just loved to lift a hundred pounds or so to guide Mr Garrie up to the top – perhaps that is why I didn't.

I walked around the base of the Great Pyramid, named for Khufu but more familiarly known as Cheops. It's not at all smooth; more like an enormous heap of large stones which at the bottom are more than two metres high, sandy and dusty.

I was no New Age pyramidologist, and I had an open mind on the astronomical and even astrological significance of the place. Whether or not the pattern of the pyramids on the ground at Giza replicated a pattern in the stars, whether it levitated at midnight, whether the angle of some of the interior tunnels pointed to stars didn't bother me in the slightest. I'd made it – I was standing at the beginning, not of time but of modern time. Building these first 'state' buildings was the beginning, for better or worse, of making our mark on the world.

I knew that the Great Pyramid of Cheops was orientated on the points of the compass, that it was the biggest and most accurate stone building ever constructed – angles are right and true – and that it comprised more than 2 300 000 stones. It was originally 440 cubits square, which in metric terms is 227 metres wide and 137 metres high. It is so well made that it has stood, alone of all the wonders, these 4500 years, a complete and integral snub to time. 'Man fears time, but time fears the pyramids', as the Arab saying goes. As Napoleon said before the Battle of the Pyramids on 21 July 1798, 'Soldiers! From the top of these pyramids forty centuries look down on you ...' Napoleon's adventure in Egypt was a military farce made art because it began the modern discovery of Egypt, archeology, art, the Rosetta Stone – a considerable and greater achievement than mere military domination would have been.

The pyramids seem almost to float in the air – which is why they are irresistible to photographers. They cast no shadow that I could see, because the top is narrower than the base.

Herodotus, the great historian from the town of Halicarnassus (now Bodrum, in Turkey) visited 2000 years after the pyramids were built and heard saucy tales about the method used by the Pharaoh Cheops ('no crime was too great for Cheops') to build one of the smaller pyramids – the middle one of the three. Cheops is supposed to have installed his daughter in a brothel and had her charge a certain amount of money for her services. She did so, but, wanting to leave a monument, asked the visitors to bring a stone as well; hence, perhaps, the small pyramids of the Queens. Or one of them, that is. Two were actually used for the wives of Menkaure, the builder of the third of the big pyramids. As Herodotus wrote, 'so the story goes'.

Herodotus wrote about the number of workmen it would have taken to build the Great Pyramid, and of the smooth limestone casing (long since stolen), and noted that an 'inscription is cut upon it in Egyptian characters recording the amount spent on radishes, onions and leeks for the labourers, and I remember distinctly that the interpreter who read me the inscription said the sum was 1600 talents of silver.' A lot of money, but Herodotus asked the practical question: 'If this is true, how much must have been spent in addition on bread and clothing for the labourers during all those years the building was going on, not to mention the time it took (not a little I should think) to quarry and haul the stone …'

Herodotus was born about 480 BC. His book *The Histories*, while largely the story of the Greek struggle against the invading Persians, is also a colourful account of his travels. Herodotus went around and looked at things from Scythia on the north coast of the Black Sea, to this spot in Egypt. He wrote from his own observations. He came to the Great Pyramid and 'measured it myself'. Even then the pyramids were thousands of years old. It's hard to get the correct emotional perspective on that.

Herodotus, Napoleon, 'Banjo' Paterson, Arthur Streeton and me, and millions of other men and women, we've all stood right *here* and wondered the same thing: boy, these pyramids are bloody big and bloody old. And just how did they build them?

Overwhelmed by the scale of things, I walked away, and was accosted by boys with free turquoise-coloured scarabs.

'Free? Bullshit. You just want to sell me something.'

'No, I don't.'

'My name is Greta Garbo. I want to be alone.'

'You German?'

'No. Australian. *Imshee! Imshee!*'

Having circumnavigated the base, located the solar boat museum, the entrance and the surroundings – sand and cemeteries – I climbed inside the Great Pyramid of Cheops.

The entrance is about five metres above the level of the roadway. There are steps up but no signs. Inside, a guard rips your ticket, and you walk about twenty metres down until a second passage joins.

Bend your back up the new passage, as it is only a metre and a half high and about forty metres long. It then widens into the higher, steeper, and – yes – amazing Grand Gallery, which is nearly nine metres high and nearly fifty metres long. This is constructed of finely jointed stone, with holes for the beams which once held back the huge stone blocking 'plugs'. Excavated, it now has a wooden floor with slats on it to stop you slipping.

At the top is a passage leading to the king's chamber with an empty red granite sarcophagus inside, looted in very ancient times. The whole feeling is warm, dim, close and spooky, though the ventilation, from the original shafts, is excellent.

Because I was alone, I was approached by the guard at the bottom, who asked if I wanted to climb down to another tomb chamber.

'Is cloze. But shhh, shhh, come, come.'

This chamber is a hundred metres down in the bedrock beneath the pyramid. Down here there is absolutely nothing, just a rough-cut floor.

I paid the guard his E£10 and then another ten for his mate. They allowed me time outside to sit on a stone and dry off, because I was swimming in sweat; it had been very hot work inside. My leg muscles stiffened up in the breeze. The books don't tell you that Egyptology requires a level of fitness for real enjoyment.

It was an experience you had to have – even if there was almost nothing to see inside except extraordinary masonry skills. And why did't it just fall down, collapse under its own weight? How could the architect–engineers have known that it would not?

It was late afternoon by this time. Business around the pyramids must have been pretty slow, because as I was dreaming on the stone, I became aware of a camel standing quietly by me, and of being gazed upon by a small Bedouin man. He was weathered by the sand, and was aged somewhere between thirty and fifty.

'Hello where are you from?'

'Australia.'

'Oh. Synnymelbun?'

'Melbourne.'

'You are welcome. Welcome in Egypt.'

Something about the way he said welcome made me take notice. Perhaps he meant it. Perhaps I had found a true cameleer. Perhaps I was just feeling vulnerable.

'Come,' he said. 'I show you the pyramids. Better than walking. Good price.'

Nothing ventured, I thought. My legs felt like they had just run a marathon and, really wanting to ride on a camel anyway, I succumbed. 'How much?'

'One hour thirty pounds. See everything. You unnerstan'?'

'Okay.'

'My name is Joma and this is Camel 107, the Cadillac of the desert. His name is Michael Jackson.'

An uneasy thought popped into my head just then – didn't Michael Palin ride a camel called Michael Jackson in his television series 'Around the World in Eighty Days'? Perhaps all camels are named after the moonwalker. Perhaps this is the very one.

Having overcome my rapidly stiffening quads and staggered aboard, I waited as Joma sprang lithely onto the front of the beast, and we swayed off.

Joma had a repertoire of squeezes, flicks with a fly whisk, and vocalisations to keep Michael Jackson plodding in the right direction and maintaining an agreed height above the ground. A sound like 'ahhrrr ahhrrr' softly in the back of the throat told Michael to keep going. 'Chhhu chhhu' through the teeth meant kneel on the ground. The camel responded with little growls and grumbles, but eventually did what Joma wanted.

We circumnavigated the Great Pyramid again, then padded over to Khafre and Menkaure, and then on to a high sand dune for pictures of me in Bedouin outfit, Joma and Camel 107, the pyramids, careworn desert, the view.

Every Australian who comes to see the pyramids ends up on a camel. Bean, Streeton and Paterson were no exceptions; neither were the men of the First AIF.

Sergeant Roy Whitelaw was in the Army Motor Transport Service when he came to the pyramids and rode his camel in April 1916. He wrote home:

Last Wednesday two pals and myself went to Mena where we climbed the Pyramids, talk about a crawl, Alpine climbing wasn't in it, we carved our names on the top stone 486 ft high & over 5,000 years old, slid down again & told each other with sweaty faces how we enjoyed it, but never again for mine.

Sergeant Whitelaw took a picture of an Egyptian doing the carving, wearing a white *galabyia* and white skull cap, and captured a rare shadow of the pyramids falling on Mena village and its irrigation allotments. They are now all part of the dusty, dirty city.

There's another picture of Sergeant Whitelaw and two mates, Stan Laver and Syd Leigh, sitting proud in the saddles of three camels, with front legs jauntily resting on the beasts' necks. The Sphinx stares enigmatically into the distance, the fuzzy outline of the Great Pyramid behind it. Resting against the foot of Whitelaw's camel is the number 97. Could this have been Camel 97? Or is it photo 97? Alongside the camel, a boy: white skull cap, dark coloured *galabyia*, a little smile, proud eyes, bare feet. Could this boy be one of the 'niggers' or 'nigs' Whitelaw referred to in his letters? One of the 'natives' who started the riot in 1919 and were shot, or one of the 'bedowins' who got 'a bad doing' at a place called Wardan?

While I was taking a picture of the sand-blasted Sphinx, Joma was approached by another man on a camel. They had a muttered conversation and Joma presented the man with a bundle of money.

'Licence,' he said when the man had gone. 'Tourist police.' It seemed that he was only approached because he had a 'fare', and that the man was just taking some baksheesh not to dob Joma in to his superiors for not having a 'licence'.

An Egyptian evening's violet shades were falling. We ambled off to the routine stops. I told Joma that I was not interested in buying, and that his cut wouldn't amount to anything. He didn't seem to mind. 'Money come, money go, what care I?' he said. 'You unnerstan'?'

We stopped at a dark chamber of an entrance hall, then entered a sunken pit lined with couches, and walls glowing like Aladdin's cave from bottles of yellow, turquoise, dark blue and a variety of greens. A personable young man with glistening hair and some practised patter welcomed me. Joma slipped outside into the shadow of the building – he'd heard all this before.

The patter: 'All pure ingredients, natural oils, smell same same as others. What you like – Chanel Five? We have. This oil of lotus. Smell beautiful, yes? Pure oil no alcohol. Look set match to oil no burn okay? You buy big bottle, big big bottle, little bottle, not much. In box. You smell nice now, not camel.'

'I buy a bottle of Nefertiti "original recipe" okay? Thirty pounds.'

When the Australians arrived in World War I, smell was one of the things they noticed: the odours of the city and the perfumed men they came across in the markets. Lemon-scented and other colognes were evidently as popular then in Egypt as they are now – and as unpopular with Australian men.

Next came an even less satisfactory visit to a 'papyrus institute', which sold not very good paintings on papyrus (really, banana leaves). 'All done by hand of professor not stamped!' said the pretty young girl delegated to follow me round. 'I am student. Just help my cousin, no commission. I speak you English. Just write on this paper what you like – easy to forget! We do you very good discount. All prices in dollars or pounds whatever you like. Credit cars. Anyway you like it.'

Smacking his lips, Joma said, 'Very pretty, you unnerstan'?' and asked whether I would like to come to his house for some *chai*.

Camel 107 took us through the back streets of Nazlat al Samman, which appeared, like a lot of Cairo, to be both falling down and being built at the same time. Streetlights and shadows were widely spaced, kids played football, fluorescent lights glowed over small businesses: sillhouettes fixing bicycles and motor bikes, dilapidated taxis and small electrical appliances, people making brooms.

Joma's house was a three-storey affair in a three-camel wide sand-street. The front door was a gate in the wall, allowing entrance to the livestock quarters. A kid appeared to take the camel and we dismounted outside the front door.

Camel 107's quarters were not his alone. There was also another camel – Camel 108? – and a donkey living in three straw-filled, cement-lined stables that comprised one of the ground-floor rooms. Opposite was another room with a couple of days' supply of bright green lucerne, and next to it a storeroom and stairs up to the first floor.

I was ushered into a large living room with hard cushioned benches covered in red-patterned Bedouin carpets on three sides, and a shelf with tin cooking bowls and tin plates to eat from. I was bid sit on a cushion, Joma did the same, and the boy brought the *chai*.

I paid Joma E£50 for the afternoon. He told me he worked every day, every day, sometimes for no money. 'It comes, it goes, you unnerstan'?' There was a lot of competition. 'Many of Bedouin out there. All looking for few tourists.' Things had been bad for many years. Not enough tourists. That is why they chase you. 'They hungry, you unnerstan'?'

Joma didn't want his kids to drive camels near the pyramids, though it was tradition in his family. His father ... his father gave him the house. But now ... other Bedouin come in from other places. They have not licence, like Joma. That is why today: 'Man ask, I pay. But I say to him: what about these boys? Make them pay also.'

Joma said again, 'Money come, money go. I am Bedouin – you eat, you drink, you have children, you are happy.' His daughter was fourteen and she would marry the following year. His sons, they must stay at school. 'No more camel drivers. You unnerstan'?'

Joma's wife brought in a tin pot of a stew and a plate of a tomato and vegetable dish. Of the stew Joma said, 'Is camel. Is good. You eat.'

Having jolted around on a camel, my stomach was disinclined

towards eating the same, but I managed to down a plate of it. It tasted like goat. Joma's wife and children waited. They would eat what was left over. I left some of mine on the plate – back into the pot it went.

Joma then introduced his wife, a brighteyed and smiling woman, his daughter Saba and sons Shaben, Ahmed and Rajab. They giggled and wanted to have their photograph taken. I was urged to eat more. 'Have more *chai*. Please, I insist, you unnerstan'?'

I was invited to stay the night, but pleaded another engagement. Joma told me I was welcome in his house any time. 'Bring your wife. Stay two weeks. Plenty food. Very good water, hot cold, all the time. Clean. Come, I show you.' We leaped off the cushions and went upstairs, where there were three more rooms with rolls of blankets, cupboards and, yes, a kind of bathroom with taps that worked. Joma demonstrated. 'Plenty water. When you come?'

Soon, I promised. But now I had to go back to the hotel. Joma said he would take me.

'Don't wake up Michael Jackson. I'll walk.'

'No, you cannot walk from here. Is not safe. My cousin has taxi.'

We went outside, Joma banged on a door down the street, the cousin appeared, and we drove through the sand-street to the roundabout outside the Mena House.

On the way I arranged to meet Joma again at eight the following morning for a ride to Saqqara on my own camel, to Memphis, and to the place of the Step Pyramid, the first big stone building ever made.

My engagement that night was with Mrs Nehad of the Oberoi, who had promised me dinner aboard the *Cleopatra*, the hotel's floating–sailing restaurant on the Nile.

The pre-dinner dinner might have been fun, but it had also

consumed some time. I'd quite forgotten that Australia were playing Sri Lanka in the World Cup final just a couple of time zones away in Pakistan.

The cricket was another reason I was glad to be at the Mena House: it had a satellite TV sports channel. By the time I tuned in, Sri Lanka were in the last triumphant over, Aravinda da Silva and Arjuna Ranatunga grinning from ear to ear. There was then the chaos of the presentation, the vision of Ian Chappell being jostled on the podium. 'Hey Chappelli! That woman you are standing next to is the Prime Minister of Pakistan. *Inshallah*,' I said to the TV screen. I knew that in Cairo, even at the pukka Gezirah Sporting Club on the island in the Nile, they hardly cared.

Cricket never really took off in Egypt despite a hundred years of the British, although some famous matches were played at Gezirah and in Alexandria by Lindsay Hassett and an AIF team against the British in 1941. (We won, of course.)

I saluted the TV, marched out through the grand halls of the hotel, dropped my key. There was absolutely no-one to commiserate with. I had half an hour to negotiate Pyramids Road to get to the landing stage on the Nile. It had been a long day. I took the first taxi and we set off into the night. The traffic was slower than a Shane Warne leggie. It took fifty minutes to do a trip that would take fifteen on a slow afternoon.

At the landing place there was no sign of anyone, let alone the good ship *Cleopatra* or Mrs Nehad. The driver looked at me as if I were stupid, which I suppose I was. But hell, we had just lost the World Cup. I thought for a moment, then looked down by the black, glistening immensity of the Nile: a ticket office, a glow, a woman.

'Sorry, Mrs Nehad … the traffic … the World Cup.'

'Don't please be worry, Mr Garrie. I have boat.'

'Yes, but … the boat has sailed.'

'I have another boat.'

There was a little cabin cruiser down the steps in the gloom. Obviously people had been late before.

We climbed aboard. Mrs Nehad was wearing a number of black professional woman's items; I was in my pyramid-dusted travelling gear. I thought that she probably had better things to do than squire visiting writers around. She had a family. But Mrs Nehad also had a job, and in the hotel business that was twenty-four hours a day.

We chugged off, slowly it seemed to me, into the Nile and the night. It was cool. The stars glowed through the dusty sky; the night lights of the buildings on the riverbank were reflected in the dark water. Up ahead was a strange sight: a golden glowing two-storey barge sedately ploughing through the water. A fifteen-minute sail and we'd caught up. We pulled alongside, a waiter offered a hand, and it was an easy step into a large two-tiered dining room. Our table was by a window on the lower deck. We were just in time for the entree platter of dips and delicacies, a cold beer and a hot belly dancer.

I asked Mrs Nehad whether this dancer was a good example of the art. She said she thought she was good, but not the best. For the best dancers and singers I should go to a nightclub, but they only started at midnight and I would be too tired, okay?

Belly dancing is not my favourite form of dancing to watch, but I was intrigued by the pleasantly dazed expression this girl maintained throughout the proceedings, a sign of enthusiasm and concentration. She perspired daintily and gyrated like a waterbed. It seemed she was – at least she gave the impression of being – under the thrall of the music, directed from the electronic organ by a seemingly sadistic young man who would slow down, speed up, or add special trills that had the dancer going even faster. This performance, with added whoops and encouragements from the drummer, was met with complete lack of interest from the throng of paying customers.

There was also a plaintive singer of Arabic love songs, and a single dervish who whirled for about ten minutes. They were fish out of water, as I was, and *I* was fading fast. I realised that I had been more or less awake for forty-eight hours since leaving Australia, battered by Egypt in ways that I didn't quite understand.

CHAPTER FOUR

THE BATTLE OF THE WAZZIR

A PERFECT, WARM SUNLIT morning. It was 8.20 a.m. and Joma hadn't waited twenty minutes for me. I looked for him at the stables. I walked around the pyramids again, and I visited the extraordinary so-called 'solar boat', or funeral barge, found undisturbed by Kamal el-Mallakh in 1954 in a stone-roofed pit south of the pyramid of Cheops. 'Solar' because the body of the Pharaoh was taken from the Nile west towards the setting sun. It had lain there for 4500 years or so, a dismantled flat-bottomed boat that may have actually been used during the funeral rites of Cheops himself on the Nile, powered and steered by the six sets of oars found with it. It had taken fourteen years to reconstruct and was a wonder of a boat. The airconditioned building it was housed in was mercifully free of touts.

But Joma was nowhere to be found. I had thought I knew Joma a little after riding the afternoon before, eating with his family – enough to think he would consider me worth waiting for. Even if I had been just another tourist, I was also a job, a day's pay. As he had said, two days work a week and he could live like a bey. Perhaps something had gone wrong: he'd eaten a bad bit of camel, or fallen off, or Michael Jackson was not well, or his saddle had broken – anything might have happened. But I was a traveller with a schedule to keep, and I wanted to see the Step Pyramid at Saqqara; if not by camel, then by car. This was easily arranged back at the Mena House.

I was soon riding south to Saqqara with Mr Zen in an oldish Mercedes. Mr Zen was an oleaginous middle-aged man who drove with one hand and set about teaching me Arabic numbers from the number plates of cars with the other. First lesson, the numbers go left to right in Arabic just as they do in Australia and unlike the script, which goes the other way. Simple, but no-one had pointed that out to me before. ٥٦٧٨٥٢ is 567852. And ١٠٠١ is 1001.

Mr Zen once studied photography in Athens. 'No work photo man Cairo. You photo man?'

overleaf: Commonwealth Cemetery, Old Cairo

'No, writing.'

'Ah, not video? Video expense in Egypt.'

I knew what he meant. Taking photographs where allowed ('One camera! No flash!') inside most monuments is relatively expensive – the same price as an admission ticket – and a video camera ticket might be five or ten times the price of admission; that is, E£100 or 200: a discouragement to tourists, but not to anyone who wanted to make a pirate video of Egyptian tombs.

Mr Zen told me that he lived in Heliopolis, had seven children – one a doctor, one an engineer 'and five daughters' – caught the bus to the hotel every morning and every night and was available twelve hours a day seven to seven.

Windows open, the air fragrant with palm groves, *fellaheen* working by the canal beside the Nile not raising their heads as we swept by. Saqqara is about half an hour's drive south of Giza – a few hours by camel. Mr Zen steered the car with a finger through what little remains of Memphis, first capital of Egypt and the place where Alexander came to be made Pharaoh in 331 BC.

The ruins of Saqqara are spread over a very wide area, but the major sight – the world's first large stone building, the Step Pyramid – is ten minutes' walk from the main ticket office and fleetingly visible though the palms and gum trees well before you get there.

The pyramid was built for Zozer in the 2600s BC. Imhotep was a physician, and the Pharaoh's right hand in administration of the ancient kingdom. Imhotep was also the world's first structural engineer and first architect, the person to whom credit has been given for inventing a method of erecting large stone buildings and in devising the divine shape of the pyramid.

Imhotep was not working with huge stones, and solved the engineering problems as he went along in an experimental fashion. First he had a *mastaba*, or platform, built, about eight metres high. After some thought he decided to make it square. He added a few metres to one side so that it was about one hundred metres square, and then put four more *mastaba*s on top, each slightly smaller than the one beneath it, up to a height of eighty metres. Underneath, cut into the bedrock, was a seven-metre square shaft, twenty-eight metres deep, with a burial chamber sealed by a huge granite plug – the burial place of his Pharaoh, Zozer.

This was the first time a tomb had been built that rose so impressively above the ground. Previously, a single *mastaba* and a shaft was as much as a Pharaoh had been allowed. All this was eventually enclosed within a fenced court 500 metres long – which is clearly where the Egyptian notion of building a fence to keep the sand out began.

To get to the pyramid I entered this court through an entrance that follows the ancient causeway up from the ticket office. At the entrance is a colonnaded hall with a tomb containing a very deep shaft where Zozer's entrails were buried. I walked down the hall and looked right across the vast, sandy sun-bleached court to the pyramid, walked towards it, a series of other ritual buildings on my right, and around Imhotep's great work.

I was looking for the exit when a cameleer showed up. Just when you think you are alone in deserted contemplation, a camel is breathing down your neck: a nice looking camel, a tawny colour with a white neck and red Bedouin blanket for a saddle. And the driver is saying:

'Where you from?'

'Australia,' wearily.

'Melbunsynny?'

'Melbourne.'

'You are welcome, Sir.'

Followed by the camel, I walked towards the exit at the far end of the complex from where I had entered, intending to head towards the Serapeum, the underground burial ground of the Apis bulls, which was somewhere Over There.

The cameleer said, 'Come. I take you on my camel to Serapeum.'

'No thanks, I think I will walk.'

'Is far. Very hot.'

'Well I'll go back to the car and drive over.'

'Cannot go by car, must go by camel.'

'What's that over there, a mirage?'

'No is a bus – but no car.'

'I'll walk.'

'This very good camel.'

'That's what they all say.'

'You are from Australia? This camel, he carry Phillip Adam.'

'Phillip Adams?'

'You know him?'

'As a matter of fact, I do.'

'He like this camel.'

'I have had a bad time with camels in Egypt. At Giza …'

'They are robbers!'

I decided I'd give him a go, for the right price.

'Okay, how much?'

'Very good price. How much you want to pay?'

'Twenty.'

'Ohh, wife, children, work, poor camel …'

'All right, thirty. But that's it.'

'Very good idea.'

All aboard the camel Phillip Adams once rode. Nice camel, easily able to take two. After twenty minutes I was glad I was riding. The walk back would have been a killer.

At the Serapeum it is mysterious, cool and dark, with surprisingly wide corridors lit by dim regular lamps. The tomb niches for the Serapis bulls loom out of the darkness, cut from the excellent stone that seems to underlie most of Egypt. This happy geological circumstance, the availability of good stone with which to build and in which to tunnel, was the resource enabling ancient Egypt to function.

Stone and water. The stone paralleled and reinforced the other great unifying natural feature (the superhighway) of Egypt: the Nile, the flood. All the big infrastructure projects over thousands of years were dependent on the working of stone. It was stone that was the basis of technological breakthroughs in building, and it was building that expressed the character and beliefs of Egypt from the most ancient times to the building and destruction of the Pharos and Library at Alexandria. Even today, if one were to choose an industry to be 'in' in Egypt it would be something to do with quarrying, cement making or building.

There are a couple of kilometres of corridors in the Serapeum. Twenty-four of the bull burials are accessible to the casual visitor in the main 200-metre long corridor. Alone, except for the 'guardian' at the other end talking to a phalanx of visitors, I examined the huge sarcophagi. I needed a more powerful torch, but these huge stone enclosures – over three metres high and five metres long, carved from single blocks of granite or basalt or limestone – are mightily impressive.

When the French archeologist Auguste Mariette found the place in 1851, only a few bull bones were left. The rest, apparently, had been eaten under the influence of a high priest from the Temple of Ptah at nearby Memphis.

The cult of Serapis was introduced by Alexander the Great's successor in Egypt, Ptolemy I, as an attempt to give the Egyptians and the colonising Greeks a joint set of beliefs and rituals and official god. It was a kind of ancient policy of multiculturalism.

There are other places devoted to the cult of Serapis. The area beneath Pompey's Pillar in Alexandria is one, where there are some sandy tunnels, and a menacing life-size statue of an Apis bull in the Graeco-Roman Museum. But in terms of tunnels and burials, the Saqqara site is the most intact.

The Apis bulls themselves were an Egyptian contribution predating Ptolemy, having been worshipped since ancient times. The bull that died in the reign of each Pharaoh was buried with ceremony in the Serapeum at Saqqara. Some of the sarcophagi are carved, indicating in which reign they met their end. One is (probably) the bull to which Cambyses, the invading Persian (Pharaoh briefly, 525–522 BC), showed disrespect, enraging Egyptians at the time. The result for Cambyses and his army of 50 000 was to be swallowed up in the sand sea while attempting to invade and destroy the oracle at Siwa in the desert a few hundred kilometres to the west.

The attendant in the Serapeum scurried down the gloomy corridor looking for his contribution. I'd paid already, but, short of cash, he insisted I pay another five pounds for my camera. No flash! It was almost pitch black down there. I defiantly took a flash photograph of a big black sarcophagus, inside and out. It was the only one of the sarcophagi that was accessible in its niche, down a set of steps. It was covered in hieroglyphs on the outside; there was nothing on the inside. No-one said *boo!* (or *moo!*).

On the way back to the pyramid, we stopped at the tombs of Ptah-hotep and Akhjet-hotep. The cameleer told me that everything was okay, just go in, it was part of the fee.

I spoke to the guardian inside the pleasant tomb with its scenes of bulls pulling ploughs and an agricultural figure with a staff and pyramid-shaped apron – perhaps a picture representing Ptah-hotep. Some professional photographers were at work in one room of the chamber, and I borrowed some of their light. Ptah-hotep glowed.

The attendant, dressed in a blue *galabyia*, wanted some baksheesh. I said – abruptly, I suppose – that I had already paid. A hissed and whispered dervish song and dance ensued: I had taken pictures, I had to pay. In the end I handed over £10, annoyed again. Outside I told the cameleer. He was angry – after all, he was the one who was in charge of my 'tour', not the bloke inside. Somehow this affair had interfered with the ethics of the baksheesh system.

'Is not to pay!'

'Don't worry. He has wife, children …'

'How much?'

'Ten.'

'Ptah! I get. Wait with camel.'

A few minutes later he came back brandishing a handful of worn notes. 'Here, your pounds. He is old: no wife, no children. We go. They all want money for nothing! You get good service you come back. Good for me, good for Egypt.'

'We agree on a price,' I said, 'that should be it.'

'A fair price. That is it. Then is happiness.'

Back to the pyramid, clop, plop, pshhh pshhh aboard the Phillip Adams, relaxed in a wavering view of the desert.

At the edge of the great enclosure we stopped for a picture. I was again encased in a scarf for a picture in front of another pyramid. I briefly thought of Imhotep, one of two ancient Egyptian commoners but surely the only engineer ever to be made a fully fledged god, but another ship of the desert approached, with another cameleer aboard. This, it transpired, was my cameleer's boss, chief of the Saqqara Licensed Camel Corps.

I pay Phillip Adams' driver his E£30, which was the price we'd agreed on. He looked at the notes with disappointment. He clearly wanted more.

'But we agreed,' I said.

'Yes, this for him,' indicating the boss, silent and motionless a few metres away. 'What about baksheesh for me?'

I gave him the E£10 he had retrieved from the guardian over at Ptah-hotep's tomb. I didn't like this. It was obvious that a different set of values was involved in camel driving or camel touting than the bargaining values I had been used to in Asia. Here a deal was not necessarily a deal.

I walked in search of more tombs to the south of the Step Pyramid. There are a dozen or more here; some open, some not. One extraordinary place is 124 steps down a beautiful cast-iron staircase, the tomb of the vizier Aper-El and his wife and son, in three chambers cut into the bedrock. It must be nearly seventy metres down – and the same back up again. One of the rooms is painted with a dark blue sky containing hundreds of golden stars. It is an extraordinary place.

Heading back to Pyramids Road, Mr Zen asked if I would care to eat 'Egyptian' with him. Yes, I would. On the way we stopped at a carpet weaving and sales establishment where friendly Mahmoud would have been happy to relieve me of several thousand dollars for a big silk carpet, very nice made on the spot. I made my excuses. Then a silver place. I succumbed and had them make a silver key ring with a made-up cartouche of Alexander, to be delivered to the hotel that night.

We arrived at a cafe with a nondescript exterior, an empty downstairs and my host – a worried, anxious man made worse by the sight of Mr Zen with a guest. He made us go upstairs, where it was busy, wiping down a laminex table for two. The restaurant specialised in pigeon – that was all there was. Mr Zen ordered the special, which was lentil soup (*shubat'ads*), followed by roast pigeon (*hammam*) stuffed with wheat (*freek*), which was eaten with the fingers, bones sucked clean, accompanied by water and pigeon juice in a mug. And bread, of course. It was delicious.

A popular joke at the non-Arabic speaker's expense is to confuse *hammam*, meaning pigeon, with *hamam*, a traditional bathhouse enjoyed all over the Arabic world. Try it. Try both!

We finished dinner and went to his after-work hangout nearby to watch a bit of the Egypt–Morocco football game. It was a kind of meeting house – a front room of a house lit by garish fluorescent light, grubby but clean, with telephone, a few couches, bubbling water pipes, TV, and a tiny man to fetch tea and coffee and stoke up the coals on top of the tobacco in the pipes. There were six or seven interested Upper Egyptian friends of Mr Zen. They all talked at once and were all in the tourism or hospitality business. They regretted that I'd already been to perfume, silver, carpet, papyrus shops. Next time, Mr Garrie, come and get a really good deal.

It was once a tradition in Egypt that a gentleman traveller should hire a dragoman. In these tourist days, if you are not 'with group' it is a matter of doing it yourself by taxi or bus and fighting off the camel drivers. Or, you can hire a car and driver from the hotel such as Mr Zen or his friend Mr Kair (which translates as Mr Beautiful) to get around and do some of the chores of travel, such as getting an Egyptian price for a train ticket to Alexandria, finding the Australian Embassy in order to vote in the Victorian elections, and having a chat with the Ambassador, Michael Smith, about the origin of Egyptian gum trees and the impossibility of visiting Tobruk and Libya.

Next day it was Mr Beautiful's turn to drive. We called in on the Nilometer, a circular well with a column in it used since ancient times to measure the flood and calculate taxes. This version was built in 861 AD, on the southern tip of Roda Island in the Nile. The elegant kiosk covering the well has a conical roof, and the interior is covered in tiles. Since the Aswan High Dam was built after Suez 1956, the Nilometer was not worked. I walked down part of the way to look at the measuring pillar, while Mr Beautiful went to pray. There must always be time allowed for that, whatever the name of one's dragoman.

We stopped below Saladin's citadel at one of the huge cemeteries known to non-Cairenes as the 'City of the Dead'. Mr Beautiful said no one lived there anymore. 'Once, yes, people lived here. But not now.' As a proud Egyptian he was embarrassed at the idea that people would be forced to live in a cemetery. 'For tourists. Not you.'

He drove me to the fabled Egyptian Museum, itself surely a wonder of the world.

This is the Aladdin's Cave of Egyptology. The Egyptians have so much history and so much material, that however much has been looted over the millennia there is still more than can be displayed at any one time in any one place. There are more than 100 000 objects in this cramped old building, and it said that some have sunk into the mud underneath it, requiring them to be re-excavated. Australian visitors feel right at home, because the place is reminiscent of Australian museums built at about the same time – this was begun in 1858 – and untouched by modern whizzbang practices.

Conservation matters aside, the Egyptian Museum is so enjoyable precisely because it doesn't spoon-feed you with audiovisual aids, computer trickery, post-modern display design (where less is supposed to be more) and mood lighting, as modern museums do. It just has an incredible collection of ancient stuff.

I spent an afternoon with the materials from Tutankhamun's tomb, excavated from the Valley of the Kings by Howard Carter in 1922–23. Nothing I have seen, even having seen some of the pieces before on their world tour, quite prepared me for the range and beauty of what this minor Pharaoh had had buried with him.

The gold mask of Tutankhamun lies in a glass case in a darkened room, light coming from an open window. His jewellery is in a room next door, and in a dozen rooms around are the 1700 or so items that were buried with him, including thrones, chairs, coffins, statues, shrines, games, chariots, head rests, Anubis dogs, caskets, amulets, canes, chests and – yes! – boomerangs.

In a corridor outside the mask room is, for me, the most beautiful and evocative piece of all: Tutankhamun's canopic shrine. After embalming, the Pharaoh's viscera (liver, lungs, intestines, stomach) were preserved in four special containers called canopic jars, with lids like stoppers carved from a glowing white alabaster, about twenty-four centimetres high.

The lids are decorated with incredibly and disturbingly beautiful carved heads, with rosy pink lips and kohl-darkened oriental eyes. They are a vision of a kind of androgynous beauty that's neither Asian nor Greek. They don't resemble Tutankhamun, and may have been made originally for someone else. They appeal to me as women. I'd like to think that this is what Helen of Troy, or Cleopatra looked like.

The lids are fitted into the alabaster canopic chest cavities. All this was originally on a sled, and enclosed by a gilded shrine about two metres high and with sides 1.5 metres and 1.2 metres long. On each wall of the third, or outermost, shrine are four gilded goddesses, arms outstretched, their heads slightly turned. They are about ninety centimetres tall, with golden pleated shawls carved in a figure-hugging form, special *khat* head-dresses, big black eyes and insouciant expressions. They are almost alive, the turn of the head a masterstroke of informality – not seen before in art and, of course, hidden from the history of art for thousands of years.

Tutankhamun's body had been returned to its tomb in the Valley of the Kings, where I was going in a few days, but other royal mummies were on display in the museum's Room 52. This had recently reopened after having been closed by President Sadat in 1981 because the display was thought to be disrespectful to the dead.

The mummies were queued in airconditioned repose, skins like puckered leather, protuberant teeth: Ramses II and III, Tuthmosis I, II and III, Amenophis III and Nefertiti herself. Her tomb had also been reopened at Luxor, in the Valley of the Queens. I was going to pay my respects there too.

I don't know that I was able to respond to these bodies, this ancient death, in the proper way. They have a non-human aspect to them that is distancing; they don't have the eyes. That's what it is about those statues in Tutankhamun's tomb: they have eyes. Classical Greek statues, even the greatest, are eyeless, sightless. They don't seem to look at you in quite the same way. Perhaps that is why in the Roman period in Egypt they often painted a portrait in the mummy case of the person inside: so that their original image would live on.

Some of these 'Fayoum portraits' (Fayoum is an oasis south of Cairo where many of them have been found) are on display in the Egyptian Museum. They are hauntingly beautiful, especially one called Portrait of a Young Lady, discovered by Flinders Petrie in 1888. This is a second century woman, dressed in pink and dark red drapery, in three quarters with her head turned to face us. She is stunning, modern, sad, with big dark brown eyes, black hair falling, red lipstick on what the museum catalogue calls an 'undeceived mouth'. Her eyes accuse us of life two thousand years after she lost hers. It is a painting by an ancient impressionist.

Outside the museum, I waited for Mrs Nehad to take me to the Naguib Mahfouz Coffee House in the great Khan el Khalili bazaar, the biggest market in the world.

I stood outside the fence around the museum. It is dangerous to stand still for more than five minutes anywhere near a tourist site because stillness attracts papyrus salesmen like an oasis attracts the thirsty. I had already bought one; I did not need more. Fending them off was almost impossible. Even a tourist policeman tried his hand, and he was on the other side of the fence.

One man must have had little luck during the day. His rates went from two papyrus for E£10, to E£6, then E£2. When I turned this offer down he hissed, 'You Jew!' as if that really was the worst insult in the world, and walked away. Another seller nearby came up to me and shook his head. He offered me six papyrus for E£5, which I wearily accepted. Street corner racism is hardly unique to Cairo, or Sydney, but it was still disturbing. A few minutes later the first bloke came back, having consulted his friends or his conscience, and said he was sorry, he didn't know what he had said, or why, and so on. I was still angry. I waved my six papyrus at him. 'I bought from someone who did not insult me,' I said. He went home; maybe he wouldn't eat. Which one of us was right?

Mrs Nehad arrived in her car, bringing her languid nineteen-year-old daughter Bassan, known to Mr Zen as 'the white girl'.

She was pale with powder and breathy with a charmingly mangled English, spiced with French, a student of French literature.

'English is hard,' she said.

'My French is worse.'

'Oh, Mr Garrie, *merçi*. What is your first language *en Australie*?'

'We speak a kind of English.'

'It is, how you say, quaint?'

'Quaint is a good word for it. It is our own kind of English.'

'Tell me some words in your English.'

'Umm … date.'

'Date?'

'Yes. Assignation.'

'I am going on a date tonight.'

'After the Khan?'

'*Oui*. Now we visit the *magasin*.'

'Oh, the shop, the Khan?'

'*Oui*, yes, big, big *magasin*.'

'Biggest in the world.'

'I like your *campagne*. So wide, so much, everywhere.'

'Yes, the bush.'

'Boosh?'

'That's what we call the countryside: the bush.'

'What you use in Australian: *tu* or *vous*?'

'In Australian, just "you".'

'We eat, and I buy *pour tu*. Special price, okay?'

The Khan el Khalili has everything you could want in a market oriented to trade goods, which it has been for six or seven hundred years: herbs and spices, gold and silver, clothes and cloches, souvenirs of the places you might one day go. At night, we walked the narrow alleyways, covered counters glowing with gold, boys gliding about with tea, proprietors politely inviting us in. It was not as frenetic as the Grand Bazaar in Istanbul, but also a *souk* with the layers of an onion. The outside was for tourists, even with a pretty Egyptian guide; the inner layers of wheeling and dealing were undiscoverable to outsiders.

Dolls turned from wood like clothes pegs caught my eye, as did patterned pyramids and some silver trinkets. Bassan negotiated on my behalf. It was interesting to watch. She never got into an argument or even a discussion. She asked a price, made an offer which was accepted or rejected, and that was that. Unlike the visitor, both the seller and buyer in this case had an idea of what the price actually was. Whether she bought or they sold was a matter of little consequence – someone else was always coming down the alley.

While we were cruising the shops, Mrs Nehad was waiting for us at the Naguib Mahfouz Coffee House. This isn't the one where he used to sit puffing on the *narghile* with his pals, it is an up-market tourist establishment with black marble, brass and carpets inside, tables outside, and potent coffee. It is close to the mosque Arthur Streeton painted, just down the alley, and also not far from where the Australians did battle on Good Friday 1915 in the Battle of the Wazzir, when Naguib Mahfouz was a little boy.

Sergeant Lawrence of the Australian Engineers arrived in Cairo on 21 May 1915, which was after the riot. Lawrence later served with great distinction at Gallipoli and in France, winning the Military Cross, and he wrote a very informative diary which helps give a picture of what the Wazzir was like.

The day after he arrived, he was camped out near Heliopolis ('It is all sand, not unlike St Kilda only a little coarser'). He came to town on a train ('The carriages are very similar to our Tait trains' – like the old red rattlers). It was Saturday night.

The Australian is very well known and is invariably greeted with the remark *'Australe* very good very clean gib it baksheesh'. All they get is a cut on the behind with a cane, without which no man goes about.

I saw Shepheard's Hotel and the Continental ... fancy me seeing the former. Then we went along to the brothel quarter. This is one of the main streets and has been called by the Australians the 'YSER'. They and the New Zealand troops had a battle with the authorities there. The buildings are nearly all five- or six-storey and have window balconies over which the girls hang, clad in the scantiest of garments – some only wearing a coarse net. They are there in dozens and dozens. We went into one ... Up about three flights of narrow stone stairs, past numerous closed doors and into the 'limelight'. Round the reception rooms were seated the 'girls', about eight altogether. Not one of them had on a garment that would for one moment hide one of her charms to a blind man. As a general run they do not appeal to my taste ... Up dark, narrow alleyways past native shops through little dark passages passing numerous native brothels (the others are all French). At the doors of these places the women sit and try and entice the men in, uttering all the time flattering remarks regarding the Australians and even going to the extent of lifting up their clothes to show themselves, at the same time saying 'velly clean, velly nice'. Anyhow out of this sort of thing, as I have seen enough to last me a long, long time. Another lager or two and away to the station. Gee my head just reels, but the disgusting sights I have seen tonight just cap the lot.

The Australians' visit to Cairo was not quite the first time a large group of Australian men had set foot in another country, another culture. Australian cricket teams had, for example, often called in at Ceylon, passed through the Suez Canal, stopped off in Italy, caught the train to Paris. There is not much record of highjinks by them in those places, though there was quite a bit of it among themselves aboard ship. But whatever a party of fifteen or sixteen cricketers might get up to on stopovers was obviously not enough to generate the end of season football club binge such as still takes place today.

But in Cairo in 1915, thousands of Australian men had camped for several very boring months in a very alien place, with the ignorant attitudes to people of other races that they had grown up with, and a marginal attitude to army discipline (these men were volunteers, doing the country and empire a favour), and the inevitable happened.

Charles Bean gave his first-hand impressions in his diary: 'About Christmas time our men certainly began to play up a bit … The same old wasters would break camp every night, and as they were therefore the men Cairo saw most of, we began to get a bad name in Cairo …'

In his entry for 9–30 January Bean wrote about drunkenness, venereal disease, and that some men were being sent home for disciplinary reasons – as 132 were. But he also wrote:

> Except in a very few cases, neither the Australians nor the New Zealanders have acted offensively towards the natives. They have managed to get, I am told, into lower quarters in Cairo than visited by the British troops and have run the risk of making the Egyptians despise them, which is said never to have occurred to British soldiers before, but on the whole they have been kind to the natives … [with] a few vile exceptions …

On 6 February Bean wrote:

> There is a perceptible insolence in the manner of some inhabitants. In Cairo on one of the picture shows the other day, there were shown films of all the nations at war. The audience sat glumly through the pictures of French and Russian troops; when it came to the Germans they cheered. The Kaiser's portrait was cheered and that of the King of England hissed … There was a bit of a row over it …

By 2 March, things had changed. Bean sent an article back to the Australian newspapers 'about the troops being in danger of losing their good name through a rowdy element which ought never to have been allowed to enlist, or at any rate to sail', and it had boomeranged to Cairo and was 'causing a quite unexpected amount of feeling amongst the troops ... I can't see a word in it that anyone in the force – any decent man at any rate – can object to ... [but] I am clearly in for a rocky time.'

By Easter 1915, most men knew that something was up; that they were headed for the war, and for who knew what or where.

Bean's entry for 2 April: 'There was to have been general leave today; and as the Division is not to embark until tomorrow, leave has been granted to 25 per cent of the men ... about five, matters grew into the stage of a serious riot. It is hard to ascertain the facts.'

Bean, as the Herodotus on the spot, reported: 'Some New Zealanders who had picked up certain diseases in a particular street [Haret el Wasser, The Wazzir, The Wozzer] seem to have made up their minds to go in and pay the house back for what they got there. The men heard that a Maori had been stabbed in one of these houses ... or ... hit with a bottle.' But soon there was a 'bonfire', then many bonfires in the street, an Australian Light Horse patrol involved, damage done, five arrests, a bigger crowd, Greeks selling 'vile doctored liquor', men very drunk. Most of the men were 'onlookers' there to 'see the fun'. Four prisoners were rescued from the patrol, the officer hit 'with a staircase' by a big New Zealander, English military police known as 'red caps' called in. They were mounted and carried pistols.

Bean continued:

> I myself went in about ten p.m. and the space in front of Shepheard's [Hotel] was then kept clear by a square British Territorials ... The town was quiet again but the disturbed street was a wreck. I didn't see it but I was told one public house was burnt out. The men were tremendously bitter against the red caps and a few fools would have tried to lynch some of them after the firing. I heard every side argued by Australians who were in it ... Many men are very sick at it having happened at all as it will get Australia and New Zealand a hopeless name in Cairo. At Oxford and Cambridge people only call it 'light-heartedness'.

A week later, on 10 April, Bean, the dismounted Light Horse and other Anzacs sailed for Gallipoli. Reports of the Battle of the Wazzir reached Australia not long afterwards.

C. J. Dennis was not only laureate of the larrikin but also the poet of the diggers, and wrote the verses of 'The Battle of the Wazzir' as an expression of Australian manly vigour, another kind of sport or war, an honourable endeavour at cleaning up Cairo.

At the time, he could not publish the poem with its mock history, sense of justice being done, and the crusading spirit of the Australians. The censor banned it, and it did not appear (except in a small private edition) until another war had passed and it was published in 1946 by Alec Chisholm. It remains, however, perhaps the best bit of Egypt–Australian folk literature, at least from the antipodean side. Here is an edited version of 'The Battle of the Wazzir' by C. J. Dennis. For someone who wasn't there, Dennis had good information.

If ole Pharaoh, King of Egyp', 'ad been gazin' on the scene
'E'd 'ave give the AIF a narsty name
When they done their little best to scrub 'is dirty Kingdom clean
An' to shift 'is ancient 'eap uv sin an' shame.
An' I'm tippin' they'd 'ave phenyled 'im, an' rubbed it in 'is 'ead.
But old Pharaoh, King uv Egyp', 'e is dead.

It was part their native carelessness, an' part their native skite;
Fer they kids themselves they know the Devil well,
'Avin' met 'im kind uv casu'l, on some wild Australian night –
Wine an' women at a secon'-rate 'otel.
But the Devil uv Australia' 'e's a little woolly sheep
To the devils wot the desert children keep.

So they mooches round the drink-shops, an' the Wazzir took their
    eye,
An' they found old Pharaoh's daughters pleasin' Janes;
An' they wouldn't be Australian 'less they give the game a fly …

An' Egyp' smiled an' totted up 'is gains.
'E doped their drinks, an' breathed on them 'is aged evil breath ...
An' more than one woke up to long fer death.

When they wandered frum the newest an' the cleanest land on
    earth,
An' the filth uv ages met 'em, it was 'ard.
Fer there may be sin an' sorrer in the country uv their birth;
But the dirt uv cenchuries ain't in the yard.
They wus children, playin' wiv an asp, an' never fearin' it,
An' they took it very sore when they wus bit.

If old Pharaoh, King uv Egyp', 'e 'ad lived to see the day
When they tidied up 'is 'eap uv shame an' sin,
Well, 'e mighter took it narsty, fer our fellers 'ave a way
Uv completin' any job that they begin.
An' they might 'ave left 'is Kingship nursin' gravel-rash in bed ...
But old Pharaoh, King uv Egyp', 'e is dead.'

The Battle of the Wazzir wasn't the end of the Australian presence in Cairo. The Light Horse and the others came back after the
Gallipoli campaign, and, from 1916, began the crusade against
the Turks through Palestine and Syria.

At war's end, the Light Horse were enlisted to help the empire
deal with the Egyptian insurrection of 1919. The Light Horse
were employed to put down riots and illegal assemblies, killing a
number of Egyptians in the process. In the 1919 actions, the Australians took part in a kind of rural pacification which saw some
villages burned. One was Surafend. There were thirty-three
British casualties in all and, officially, 800 Egyptians killed.

Asked about this, today's Egyptians profess ignorance. Much
water has flowed down the Nile since then, and the incident
occurred at a time when the British (and others) were involved in
all kinds of post-war military action in Russia and Turkey. But
the Australian part in this action leaves me, at least, with a sour

taste, even at this distance in time. It is part of my distaste for the
way an Australian government, prisoner of its time and attitudes,
allowed Australians to be used in a foreign interest. At least the
Egyptians, both then and now, understood that.

One day Mr Zen dropped me off in Old Cairo, which once was
called Babylon. I wanted to look at the old Coptic churches, the
Coptic museum, and the synagogue.

The churches were tiny and fantastic, with ancient icons,
saintly remains wrapped in red, old wooden screens, the smell of
incense and the sound of creaking floors. The seventh century
(AD) 'hanging' church is the Church of the Virgin, suspended over
the Roman gate. The synagogue used to be the Church of Michael
the Archangel, perhaps begun in the fourth century. It was renovated in the nineteenth century, when a vast number of documents
going back nearly a thousand years were found, and became
known as the Geniza hoard. This material provided the factual
base of the Indian Malabar Coast trading part of Amitav Ghosh's
wonderful book *In an Antique Land*, in which parallel ancient and
modern stories recall the *Thousand and One Nights*.

Other churches include those of St Barbara and St Sergius and
Bacchus. Tradition has it that the church of St Sergius and Bacchus is built on the site of a church visited by the Holy Family on
their flight to Egypt. And then there is the Coptic museum: small,
peaceful and containing some magnificent frescos, fabrics and
carvings.

Across the road from the museum was a cemetery – there are
cemeteries everywhere around here. I was looking for the Commonwealth Cemetery where 481 Australians are buried, the most
permanent reminder that we too were here. This particular cemetery, however, was a confusion of crosses and mausoleums – and
no signs. A caretaker showed no sign of comprehending my questions in English. He sat at the entrance stoically, embarrassed.
Just as I was walking out, a small neat man trotted up.

'G'day. Are you Australian?'

'Yeah, I am.'

'So am I. Name's Ron. Just here in this cemetery visiting the grave of my mother. Lived in Sydney for seven years, back here for awhile. What are you looking for?'

'The Commonwealth Cemetery. There are Australians in it.'

'I'm a Maronite – at least my mother was. This is a Christian cemetery. All kinds – Maronites, Catholic, Orthodox. I'll ask this bloke. I've never heard of an Australian cemetery …'

Some chat in Arabic, the caretaker's face lights up, he gestures out the gate. Left, left, left, it's around the back.

Off I went, chatting with Ron to the corner a hundred metres away, turned left and walked through a thriving fruit and vegetable market built into the cemetery wall. Left again, a deserted road along the other wall, then a hundred metres down was a wrought-iron gate, locked.

After a couple of minutes, a gardener emerged from a building inside the gate. He was dressed in a dark blue shirt, a dark blue cap. He let me in.

'Hello. Welcome to Old Cairo cemetery. Where are you from?'

'Australia.'

'My name is Bagdhadi.'

'Mine is Garrie.'

'Mr Garrie, please I show you the book.'

Bagdhadi took no baksheesh. 'It is an honour to show you. Not many Australians here.'

The book was a British guide to the cemetery published in 1930. There were some British Hutchinsons and an Australian Hutchison: William James, 4th Battalion. Died of typhoid on 20 June 1915, and is now in the cleanest, greenest and quietest bit of Cairo. I dipped my lid to all of them.

CHAPTER FIVE

A BEACON
TO MEMORY

RAMSES STATION IN CAIRO has a quietly elegant facade masking half-a-dozen platforms of frenzy. Fortunately, Mr Zen had taught me well in the matter of Arabic numerals, and helped in the matter of buying a ticket. The E£22 I was charged was better than the somewhat elastic E£30 or even E£40 that anyone unaccompanied by an Egyptian might expect to pay. Needless to say, a chat with the pretty girl behind the ticket windows the day before I travelled had helped. These ticket windows are secreted away to the left as you walk in the main entrance of the station, and are supposed to be for Egyptians, it seems, not for non-Egyptian Europeans.

Carriage ٥ (five), seat ٤٦ (46). I bought the English newspapers, bumped into people with my backpack, got in the wrong end of the carriage, bumped into more people, heaved the pack aloft, sat. Unlike buses, which might break down or go anywhere, trains feel big and safe because they go where the rails take them. This train was Turbo ٩١٧ (917), and once it started, would only stop at the two stations in Alexandria two hours or so later.

This train trip is perhaps the most comfortable to be had in Egypt. I travelled in a streamlined, slightly down at heel carriage done out in that pastel lime-green laminex colour beloved of Australian kitchens in the 1950s, and royal blue seats.

Friendly staff sold Coke or *chai*, and a chicken leg, spicy rice and vegetable sort of thing – quite tasty – while I watched the darker green of the delta country roll by. The trolley squeaked along airline fashion, and orders were marked on a ticket poked into a little pocket in the headrest of the seat in front, to be paid for towards the end of the trip.

Across the aisle an officer in the uniform of an Egyptian parachute regiment did a crossword. How would a crossword work in Arabic? I wondered. Five across: which way would that be?

After the palpable pressure of getting around Cairo – the dust, the car horns, the demands for baksheesh – I was looking forward to Alexandria by the sea.

overleaf: Site of the Pharos, Fort Qaytbey, Alexandria

Older generations of travellers to Egypt and Alexandria often had their first encounter from the sea. The First AIF landed at Alexandria and caught the train to Cairo. Before that, for more than 1500 years from the third century BC to the earthquake of 1307, the Pharos or lighthouse shone from Alexandria, gleaming on the low horizon of the African coast, guiding mariners to the safety of the two ancient harbours.

In his *Travels in Upper and Lower Egypt* in 1803, Vivant Denon wrote:

> When the long low shadows of evening had marked the outlines of the city I distinguished the two ports, the lofty walls, flanked by numerous towers, no longer enclosing anything but heaps of sand, and a few gardens, the pale green of whose palm trees scarcely tempered the ardent whiteness of the soil, the Turkish castle, the mosques, their minarets; the celebrated pillar of Pompey; and my imagination went back to the past; I saw art triumph over nature; the genius of Alexandria employ the active hands of commerce, to lay on a barren coast the foundations of a magnificent city as the depository of the trophies of the conquest of the world ...

Denon's 'Turkish castle' was built on the site of the Pharos, one of the Seven Ancient Wonders and the excuse for my visit.

E. M. Forster, who lived in and wrote about Alexandria during and after World War I, wrote that the Pharos 'beaconed the imagination, not only to ships at sea, and long after its light was extinguished, memories of it glowed in the minds of men'.

But Alexandria stood for more than a great lighthouse, as Forster's 1922 book *Alexandria: A History and a Guide*, still the best guidebook to Alexandria (if you can find a copy), points out in loving detail. It was, with the other ancient and lost institutions of Alexandria, emblematic of Western notions of civilisation on the edge of Africa and Asia. The idea that in twentieth-century Alexandria was a place of cosmopolitan civilisation, a beacon of multiculturalism, occurs in the work of writers such as the poet C. P. Cavafy, his friend E. M. Forster and, a war later, Lawrence Durrell and Naguib Mahfouz. At the same time as celebrating these qualities of Alexandria, they all lamented an Alexandria that had already gone, or was in the process of disappearing.

Mahfouz's novel *Mirimar* about some Alexandrines living in the aftermath of Nasser's 1950s revolution (Nasser was born and went to school in Alexandria) begins with an evocation: 'Alexandria. At last, Alexandria, Lady of the Dew. Bloom of white nimbus. Bosom of radiance, wet with sky-water. Core of nostalgia, steeped in honey and tears.' The novel ends unhappily for all concerned. Alexandria then was not what it once had been.

Lawrence Durrell, in the first of the Alexandria Quartet, *Justine*, writes that World War II Alexandria is 'the fevered city, clinging to the minds of old men like traces of perfume upon a sleeve: Alexandria, the capital of Memory'.

The 'capital of memory'. Surely, I thought, hurtling north on the train, there must also be stones and ruins, even people who remembered an earlier version of Alexandria. If all that remained were memory, I might as well have stayed in Australia reading the books, or talking to my friend George who was born there but whose family, like most Greeks of Alexandria, was harassed out of Mahfouz's city in the 1950s.

Searching for the remains of the Pharos would surely be a less forlorn expedition than it would at the other sites of the ancient wonders. Of course nothing could compare with the hulking existence of the pyramids, but at least in Alexandria there were supposed to be a few stones that had once formed part of the Pharos's foundations, built into the base of the fort at Qaytbey.

Alexandria had always had the tang of a seedy seaside resort, from the days when Helen (she of Troy) was supposed to have first had a fling with Paris on what was (or could have been), in those palmy days before the Trojan War, the island of Pharos.

Alexandria now had no wonder of a lighthouse; no great

library, of which Ptolemy boasted before the beginning of the
first millennium that it had a copy of every book written; no tomb
or celebration of Alexander (he was a non-Egyptian European,
after all); and almost all of the later flowerings of Alexandrian
culture have been forgotten or ignored in the development of
another Mediterranean summer resort.

Alexandria had become, in the past forty years, an Egyptian
city. This was hardly news, but it was nevertheless a literary sadness. On the train up from Cairo, like hundreds before me, I
couldn't help rehearsing what I would not see.

The taxi touts besieged passengers as we struggled off the train at
Masr Station. I tottered down the steps of the carriage with my
pack and marched imperiously down the platform, pretending I
was looking for someone important. Outside, a great line of
Alexandrine yellow and black taxis queued. I looked for the least
interested.

One pulled up, dropping a fare. I got in and asked to be taken
for a ride: put the meter on! I declined the opportunity of staying
at the legendary but pricey Hotel Cecil, and asked for the Metropole – it was supposed to be modest and central.

The driver agreed and off we went. On the map, the hotel
wasn't far away, but Alexandria has a perverse road system governed by the fact that the city has spread in a strip along the coast,
jammed between the sea and Lake Mareotis. For wine lovers
(such as Cleopatra) Lake Mareotis has a special significance,
because on its shores the vines for the world's first commercial
wine are supposed to have been cultivated – and even today it is
where Egypt's famed Omar Khayam brand is made.

From being one of the world's first planned cities, designed
by Alexander, Alexandria has become a hodge-podge of geography and accident, especially in the last forty years.

The story of the design of Alexandria is told by the Roman

historian Plutarch, and involves Alexander the Great's love of the poet Homer.

When Alexander had defeated Darius at Issus a few months before (this episode occurred towards the end of 332 BC), the booty had included a beautiful casket. Alexander asked his friends what he should keep in it, and decided he would keep his copy of Homer's *Iliad*. The next year, having decided to found a port on the Egyptian coast, to be the first of the seventeen cities he named after himself, he had a dream. In it, a greybeard recited lines from Homer's *Odyssey*: 'There is an island called Pharos in the rolling seas off the mouth of the Nile, a day's sailing with a roaring wind astern.'

Next morning Alexander went there and studied the geography. He saw the great natural advantages of the place: a strip of land between sea and lagoon, and a spacious harbour. He said that Homer, as well as having other admirable qualities (among them, in my opinion, being the world's first and still one of the best sportswriters), was 'a very far-seeing architect'.

Alexander then drew a map on the ground. Lacking chalk, he used barley meal to make a flattened semicircle with spokes radiating from the inner arc to the circumference – rather like the design of the military cloaks they wore. While they were admiring the symmetry of the design, Plutarch continues, a flock of birds descended and ate the barley. Initially disturbed by this omen, Alexander was reassured by his astrologers that it meant the place not only would be abundant, but that it would be 'the nurse of men of innumerable nations'.

Leaving aside the possibility of a bit of multicultural hindsight on Plutarch's part (he was writing in the first century AD, 300 years after Alexander's time), that phrase has an Alexandrian ring to it of which everyone from Alexander's time to 1956 would have approved – seeing the city as a nurse to men of innumerable nations.

In modern Alexandria it is easy to drive parallel to the coast, but crossing the city is difficult. Only a few streets, it seems, go the right way; others are jammed to a standstill or go the other way. It isn't as crazy as Cairo, but it is demented by ordinary standards.

Around we went and arrived at the Metropole to find that it was dark and seemingly closed for renovations. As I was about to get out, the driver said, '*Non*, wait, mister. Hotel?'

'Yes. What about the Cecil?'

'*Très* expensive.'

'I know.' But a modern Justine haunts it still, perhaps …

'Special rate, my friend hotel.'

'Okay.'

Off we went again, winding down to the Corniche and zooming along it at a juddering clip in the car, another Lada, that must have fallen off the back of a ship from Poland.

After about ten minutes of zooming, it was apparent that this okay special deal was not to be had in the central part of Alexandria. We were headed for the Nile – possibly the Suez Canal.

'Very far now?'

'Yes. Very close.'

The Corniche is lined with faded splendours – five- or six-storey seaside apartment blocks and mansions made of a grey cement render covered in off-white washes and tan ochre colours. Newer hotels jut out at angles to take advantage of the view of the beach and the lapping Mediterranean. Fifteen minutes drive from the Metropole, we stopped at one of these angled establishments, the Hotel Mekka or Mecca depending on which sign I read. It was eight shabby out-of-season storeys high, and had a small lobby facing a lane off the Corniche.

A sign of the times was a large billboard nearby. An Alexandrian, with a kind of Mark Antonian profile, was captioned with the English words: 'Concrete. The Masculine Look.' The Pharaohs used no cement, but since then the whole of Egypt (the whole of the Middle East) has been built with cement, with its thousand and one uses. There is almost no wood in Egypt (except for the gum trees) so everything is built from stone and cement. No wonder this advertisement for hair care products (for that is what I took it to be) had adapted the name of that most valuable and ubiquitous product.

Inside the Mecca's lobby was a cheap-looking set of mirrors and, past the lift, a motley collection of tables and chairs – presumably the restaurant. It was lit by the garish red light of the setting sun and pink fluorescent tubes.

The taxi driver had followed me in and nodded encouragingly.

'A room? How much? One hundred fifty. Too much? Okay, special rate one hundred twenty.'

That was about A$54, not the E£30 or less I had wanted to pay, but it was getting dark and I'd already wasted money on the taxi. 'Okay, but I want to see it first.'

I was led by a boy in a threadbare red jacket into the lift, which staggered to the seventh floor. We emerged into a narrow corridor to the sound of laughter. The shy but curious young cleaning women had a tea-making establishment by the stairs to the lift. '*Salaam alakum*,' I said in my best accent. They giggled, bold eyes under their scarves.

The room was small, but the window opened onto a small balcony with a tremendous view of the too-orange sun setting behind Fort Qaytbey and the site of the Pharos at the other end of the beach. Who cared about the bed or hot water, I'd take the view. They had known I would.

Morning was crisp and breezy with the door to the balcony still open. Outside, Fort Qaytbey gleamed, a cool light grey bastion at the far end of the sweep of the eastern harbour. The Pharos had been four or five times the height of the fort, and would have been an immense building, as high as this hotel.

I took a taxi down the Corniche, curving around to the right, across the narrow strip of land to a wet dropping-off point near the fort. The narrow connection joins the original coastline to what was the island of Pharos. The road was being remade, very gradually it seemed, and there was much confusion between buses, taxis and private cars, and the demands of the port on the eastern harbour.

It must have been school visit day, because the fort was overrun with groups of singing, chanting and even ululating kids of primary- and secondary-school ages. The boys especially, arm in arm in arm, had some special song-like chants – similar to what you might hear at the soccer but longer and more elaborate.

There's nothing like a fort to wander around in, find a nook or cranny to sit in, and maybe have a conversation with a friend of the Opposite Sex. In urban Egypt, courting cannot be as difficult as it seems to be in some parts of the Islamic world, but it is difficult enough.

The best place to get a feel for what the Pharos was like is on the ground floor, where you can gaze upwards inside the tower of the keep. In the ancient Pharos, a central staircase wound its way around the core of the first level, higher than this, and some 60 rooms or apartments were kept for workers and supervisors.

The main entrance to the fort had re-used some dark grey granite column bases and lintels from the Pharos, which I stopped and gave a rub. Not a kosher conservation technique, but irresistible. Outside the fort the sea beat on old foundations, and my attempt to storm the foundations from a little beach to the west, along a narrow ledge, was defeated by spray.

In the harbour here must lie more remains. Recent archeological diving has sighted and claimed large marble blocks for the Pharos, and other sculptures for the palace of one of the seven Cleopatras. There has been quite a shift in the shoreline here over the last thousand years or so, especially since the fourteenth century earthquake which destroyed the last of the lighthouse, and a good deal else might be under the water. Actually, I believe that the remains of the palace in which Cleopatra VII used the asp are still in town outside the Hotel Cecil, but archeological digging has hardly begun in the city itself – how could it? – and the site of Cleopatra's palace remains mysterious.

The fort, and the lighthouse before it, stood on what was once the island called Pharos. The island became solidly connected to the mainland, first by a mole and later through infill building, silting and subsidence. It is now a narrow promontory dividing the eastern and commercial harbours.

On her first visit, Helen reputedly complained that all she could see in the moments she looked beyond the flap of the love nest with Paris were seals. But the place must have had some other attraction, because Helen was back ten years later with her husband Menelaus. According to Homer, Menelaus gave the place its name, mishearing a local's grumbly local dialect when he asked who owned the island. The local said 'Pharaohs' – they having ruled Egypt for thousands of years. But, with absolutely no evidence at all, I reckon the local mistook Menelaus for Helen's previous companion, Paris, and Menelaus the cuckold heard what he wanted: Pharaohs possibly, or Paris, and Pharos it became. Menelaus' account also transformed the pesky seals into nymphs, giving to the Greeks back home a more romantic view of the rock.

The Pharos of Alexandria, the first and greatest lighthouse, took its name from the island and, like some of the other wonders, gave currency to the words as generic objects: mausoleum, colossus, pharos, pyramid.

An old tradition has it that construction of the Pharos was begun by Alexander's friend and general, founder of the Ptolemaic dynasty, Ptolemy I Soter (Soter means Protector) in 323 BC. Building most probably began, however, a few decades later in 297 BC under Ptolemy II Philadelphus.

The Pharos shone from its 120 metre plus height until 1307 AD, when an earthquake destroyed much of it. By 1326 the Arab traveller Ibn Battuta reported it in ruins, and again in 1349 as being in even worse condition after another earthquake.

Most probably the tower was first built simply as a tall building that could be seen from the sea. Fire used as a signal was mentioned until early Roman times. Although there were stories of lenses being used, there was probably simply an oil-fired flame on the topmost section reflected in polished bronze mirrors – enough to give sailors a warm glow of arrival.

The building had a square base of around fifty-seven metres, an eight-sided centre section of twenty-seven metres, and a round seven or eight metre tower on top, surmounted by a large statue of Zeus. Over the centuries, this topmost tower was damaged by storm and earthquake, and replaced by different structures – in its last years by a mosque-like cupola with Islamic moon. There were no statues of Zeus after the 600s.

Almost from the day Alexander left, in 332 BC, before a shovel of sand had been turned by his architect and town-planner Dinocrates of Rhodes, people have lamented what has been lost. It's like the fisherman – 'You shoulda been here yesterday' – or the Australian travellers to Bali, who say we shoulda been there in the seventies, sixties, fifties, thirties or 1520s before it was ruined by the Javanese, Dutch, Japanese and Australians. But it's not just the usual tourist talk. The lament for Alexandria is different. Even at the various peaks of its fame, Alexandria always seemed to have something greater that was gone. You shoulda been in Alex when Alex was here, when the library was thriving, when the Pharos shone, when the Pharos fell over, when Saladin dropped in, when Napoleon invaded, when Rommel was just down the road.

In the Graeco-Roman Museum at Alexandria are two small terracotta lanterns about twenty centimetres high which are models of the Pharos made, the labels say, in the third century BC. They are the only evidence in all Alexandria of what the lighthouse looked like. Hunt high and low in the *souk*, or in the second-hand bookshops, or in the numberless tourist trivia shops and stalls around the city – these objects are all you'll find. Small, brown, lopsided and charming, I thought that in any one of the old Alexandrias some sharp thinking potter would have turned these out in their thousands for souvenir hunters such as me.

Down the coast a bit, forty kilometres away, E. M. Forster wrote of a mini Pharos, a one-to-five scale model, at Abusir on Lake Mareotis marking the entrance to the ancient port of Taposiris. It had – still has – the same square, octagonal and round design, but was only thirty metres tall.

I didn't see this one. All I saw was a lighthouse at Montazah at the eastern end of the Alexandria beach strip, where there is a strange and wonderful palace built at the turn of the century as a copy of aspects of the Palazzo Vecchio in Florence. It was a hospital in World War I – E. M. Forster worked there for the Red Cross. Later it was used by King Fuad and by King Farouk, who was in residence when the 1952 coup took place. Nasser sent a message: 'Let us spare Farouk and send him into exile. History will sentence him to death.' An Alexandrian point of view.

President Mubarak uses it for visiting guests. The gardens are open to the public, there is a nice beach, international hotels nearby – and a small toy-like lighthouse.

Like Alexander himself, the Pharos is forgotten in its city.

One night, tearing myself away from the silhouette of Fort Qaytbey, I considered the evening ahead. Alexandria! Dinner at Pastroudis's, maybe, where Lawrence Durrell's World War II reprobates were wont to hang out, but first a visit to the Cavafy Museum, located in his old apartment on Rue Lepsius, now Sharia Sharm el Sheikh. Number four. Upstairs.

Down at the lift a taxi driver waited, already laughing with the bloke behind the desk. Got a live one here, I imagined them saying to each other in Egyptian Arabic. I comprehended two things at that moment, seeing one and hearing another. The driver looked like Don King the rascal boxing promoter, right down to the frizzy shock of grey hair. And I heard that my Arabic was nonexistent. I had been able to get my eyes adjusted to numbers in Arabic, thanks to the lessons of Mr Zen in Cairo, but adjusting my voice to even saying something as simple as Cavafy Museum – *Al Mat-haf* … Cavafy … Sharia Sharm el Sheikh – was almost impossible.

El Donking, as he had become to me, said, 'Mr Garrie, okayokayokay,' as if he had visited Cavafy's apartment every Saturday for lunch all his life.

We roared down the Corniche, then into the rabbit warren of streets in the middle of the city, and after fifteen minutes squeaked to a stop outside the closed and deserted terracotta coloured portico of the Graeco-Roman Museum. '*Al Mathaf!* The museum!' said El Donking triumphantly.

'*La'shukrun*. No, thank you,' I said, one of the few other words even vaguely appropriate to the situation that I could remember. '*Fein Cavafy?* Where is Cavafy?' The soldier at the entrance to the museum waved us on. In the taxi I wrote 'Sharia Sharm el Sheik, Cavafy Museum' on a card again.

We stopped. These streets were quiet and must have only operated during business hours. There was light coming from an inside office in a solid stone building. 'Speaking Inglisi,' said El Donking, and rushed inside. A few minutes later he rushed out. 'Speaking Inglisi coming,' he said, and went inside again, the sound of pattering feet echoing out.

I got out of the taxi. The street was tree-lined. All the buildings were large and made from stone. A muezzin sounded from some nearby loudspeaker. El Donking brought a woman, no scarf, who said, 'Excuse me, I speak little English.'

'More than my Egyptian. I am looking for the Cavafy Museum – Sharia Sharm el Sheik.'

'Oh yes,' she said, 'Sharm el Sheik,' and launched into a torrent of Arabic accompanied by a semaphore of gestures, while El Donking nodded and copied a few of the hand signals.

'Okayokayokay,' he said, and we roared off in a new direction.

We then had to find a new guide, as El Donking had discovered that he was in the wrong place.

'Cavafy?' the next woman said. 'Famous poet? I've lived here twenty-five years and I have not heard of him. So sorry.'

Poor Cavafy, dead for a comparatively few sixty-three years, the great singer of the songs of Alexandria, forgotten, now an unsung hero to the locals. This is a prose translation of what he wrote of Alexandria in his poem 'The City':

> You will find no other countries, no other seas. This city will always be with you; you will be walking along these same streets, growing old in these same familiar districts and your hair will turn white beneath these same roofs. You will always find yourself in this city. As for leaving – vain hope – there is no boat, no road that you can take. As you have ruined your life in this corner of the earth, so you have destroyed it everywhere else in the world.

Forty years ago, during the Nasser years after the revolution and the arrival of the republic, was when most of the last Greeks sailed across the Mediterranean, and Alexandria became an Egyptian city for the first time since it had been founded – by a Macedonian, almost a Greek.

Friends of mine, Alexandrines of Greek extraction but of Egyptian nationality, came to Australia under the pressure of not being wanted in their birthplace in 1958, an example of some of the 'ethnic cleansing' that has gone on in this part of the world for thousands of years: Greeks out of Turkey, Khazaks out of the Crimea, Greeks out of the area around the Black Sea, Turks out of Greece.

Of course the Greeks had invaded Turkey in the washup of World War I, until driven out by Mustafa Kemal (Atatürk) who was born in Salonika when it was part of the Ottoman Empire and not part of Greece. Salonika, now Thessaloniki, was part of Macedonia. Alexander's father, Philip II, is buried at Vergina, just down the road.

I read somewhere that there are fewer than 500 Greeks living in Alexandria now, most of them in the restaurant business. I don't know if there are any Macedonians, or Turks.

We stopped again, at a chemist shop. 'Anyone here speak English,' I asked.

A pretty girl in a white lab coat emerged from the dispensary part of the shop. 'I am happy for practice,' she said.

'I am looking for the museum, the apartment of Constantine Cavafy, the poet – lived in Alexandria for fifty years.'

'I know him,' said the vision in white with coal black eyes. 'He is near.'

I realised that this was one of the few Egyptian women I had been close to while in this perfumed country. I got a whiff of something floral as she came around the counter to discuss matters with El Donking. I didn't know what C. P. would have made of this – he being more inclined in the other direction – but I was sure he would understand the scent of nostalgia.

'*Shukrun*,' I said. 'Thank you.'

'*Afwan*,' she replied. 'You are welcome.'

'Okayokayokay,' said El Donking.

Back to the taxi, around two corners, and we stopped outside a darkening apartment building, opposite a shoemaker, who was working under a fluorescent light.

'Cavafy Museum?' I asked, and he nodded, pointing opposite. I walked up two flights of wide stairs. At the top was a solid wooden door. I pushed it open.

Inside, a young man in a white shirt said, in English, 'You are late,' as if he had been waiting all day.

'I have come a long way,' was my tired reply.

Expecting to pay, I must have raised an eyebrow, for the young man said, 'It is five pounds – but only for Greeks.'

'I am Australian.'

The young man said, 'You are welcome.'

Cavafy's apartment, where he had lived from 1907 until his death in 1933, contained many of the things he used or was supposed to have used: bed, desk, chairs, lamps, mirrors, books. It also contained his death mask, a composed and peaceful face that looked in plaster as old as a marble mask of Homer.

It is said that when Cavafy died of cancer of the larynx, his last act was to draw a perfect circle on a blank sheet of paper, and then draw a period, a dot, in the centre. Make of that what you will. In Arabic a dot represents zero, but Cavafy was an Alexandrine Greek – perhaps he meant it as a joke. It seemed to me to be the gesture of a writer on the edge of infinity, curious about what would happen next.

Cavafy was born in 1863 and lived and worked in Alexandria for most of his life in the days when the city, if not the most cosmopolitan city in the world, was the liveliest Greek city in the world. He worked in private and sang the songs of his birthplace and its heroes, puzzling over love and passion, the Greekness of the eastern Mediterranean, the history of the city. He was a Greek citizen; his parents came from Constantinople.

For most of his life, Cavafy worked in the Irrigation Service of the Ministry of Public Works, promoted from clerk in 1892 to Assistant Director at his retirement in 1922. He was also a stockbroker and punter on the Egyptian Stock Exchange, occasionally making a 'killing'.

He lived alone in this apartment lined with books near the ancient centre of Alexandria, and close to where the Mouseion (a kind of scientific research institute) and the great million-scroll library once stood.

In the Mouseion, part of the library, ancient scientists such as Eratosthenes calculated the diameter of the earth (it is round!) at 12 560 kilometres, only eighty kilometres out, and Euclid worked on the principles of geometry. Aristarchus in 239 BC added a leap year to the calendar. It was adopted by Julius Caesar as the world standard after he worked in the library–Mouseion in 48 BC. The surgeon Celsus and the physician Galen also worked there, as did the geographer Strabo and Claudius Ptolemy who in the 130s, devised a map of the world that was used until medieval times.

As for the library, a third century BC Ptolemy ordered its scholars to compile a definitive edition of Homer's *Odyssey* – where the island of Pharos was mentioned. This first text of the second great work of western storytelling (Homer's *Iliad* was number one) was edited by Aristarchus, just a few steps from Cavafy's apartment.

I thought of Cavafy standing here, thinking that he was the heir to all that, to all that was Alexandria, not yet knowing that he would become a museum, a library of his city, himself.

The shoemaker hammered across the street. I heard the low rumble of traffic, a wailing song, perhaps of lost love, in Arabic from a nearby ghettoblaster, the clack of backgammon and dominoes – the sounds of the city.

E. M. Forster, as well as being a friend of Cavafy's, was the chief promoter of his work in his lifetime. Forster lived in Alexandria during World War I, and was smitten with the city – as he was by a number of its inhabitants. Forty years after their meeting, Forster would say that meeting Cavafy was the greatest thing in his life.

Forster also wrote for the *Egyptian Mail* (still the English language newspaper of Egypt) under the pen name Pharos. He imagined the ancient intersection of the Canopic Way (Sharia Horreya) and the Street of the Soma (present-day Sharia Nebi Danyal) in his collection of pieces from the paper, published in 1923 under the title *Pharos and Pharillon*, the story called 'Between Sun and Moon'.

Beginning at the Gate of the Sun (by the Public Gardens) it traversed the city uninterruptedly until it reached the waters of Harbour (near

Minet el Bassal), and here stood the Gate of the Moon, to close what the sun had begun. The street was lined with marble colonnades from end to end, as was the Rue Nebi Daniel, and the point of their intersection (where one now stands in hopeless expectation of a tram) was one of the most glorious crossways of the ancient world.

Clitophon [a character in 'post-classical' Bishop Achilles Tatius's 'improper novel' which Forster was using to recall the place] paused there in his walk, and looked down the four vistas, over whose ranks rose temples and palaces and tombs, and he tells us that the crossways bore the name of Alexander, and that the Mausoleum close to them was Alexander's tomb.

He does not tell us more, being in search of a female companion named Leucippe, whom he deems of more permanent interest, but there is no reason to doubt his statements, for Achilles Tatius himself lived here and dare not cause his characters to lie. The passage gleams like a jewel among the amorous rubbish that surrounds it.

The vanished glory leaps up again, not in architectural detail but as a city of the soul. There (beneath the Mosque of Nebi Daniel) is the body of Alexander the Great. There he lies, lapped in gold and laid in a coffin of glass. When Clitophon made his visit he had already lain there for eight hundred years, and according to legend he lies there still, walled into a forgotten cellar ...

And, Forster concluded in 'Between Sun and Moon', despite paganism being dead, the twin luminaries of paganism preside over the street still: 'In the evening the western vista can blaze with orange and scarlet, and the eastern, having darkened, can shimmer with a mysterious radiance, out of which, incredibly large, rises the globe of the moon.'

No moon tonight. Dark clouds scud above. I wanted to go to the great intersection and eat at Pastroudis's Cafe, which is close to the spot. I made my farewell to Cavafy. I bought a copy of the Third Kavafiz International Symposium 1993 and a poster of C. P. I kissed my fingers and placed them on the cold plaster of his mask. I signed the visitors' book, and I went down the stairs, to search for the taste of Durrell, Justine, Balthazar, Clea and the others. El Donking lurked at the bottom.

Pastroudis's Cafe has been an Alexandrian institution for generations, reaching the height of its fame in the 1930s and 1940s when its dark-panelled walls throbbed with cosmopolitan life.

Lawrence Durrell sat here from time to time during that period, watching world and war go by and storing the character of Alexandria for the now neglected but extraordinary novel sequence The Alexandria Quartet.

> All indeed whom war or time threw up
> On this littoral
> And tides could not move
> Were objects of my study and my love.
>> (Alexandria)

Pastroudis's is on a wedge of corner along Sharia Horreya. Durrell knew this street as the Rue Fuad, and Cavafy as Rue Rosette, but in ancient times it was the Canopic Way, because it was the road to Canopus, a town on the end of the Canopic branch of the Nile, now dried up.

According to Plutarch, it was along this road, at about midnight on 31 July 30 BC, that Mark Antony heard the sound of the departing god before his final battle with Octavian. He had lost the Battle of Actium; now it was clear that the world and the gods were on the side of Octavian (as emperor, Augustus) not on his and Cleopatra's. The end of the 300-year-old Macedonian dynasty of the Ptolemies and the independence of Egypt were about to end.

Cleopatra was back at the palace, and Mark Antony ordered his servant to fill his cup with wine more generously than usual. He thought that it would be the last time, and that the next day he would be 'lying dead, a mummy, or nothing'. The departing god was Dionysus, and it was 'a marvellous sound of music was heard, which seemed to come from a consort of instruments of every kind, and voices chanting in harmony, and at the same time the shouting of a crowd in which the cry of Bacchanals and the ecstatic leaping of satyrs were mingled, as if a troop of revellers was leaving the city, shouting and singing as they went'.

I like the idea of Cavafy sitting in Pastroudis's Cafe, Plutarch's words in his head.

> At midnight, when suddenly you hear
> an invisible procession going by
> with exquisite music, voices,
> don't mourn your luck that's failing now …
>
> Go firmly to the window
> and listen with deep emotion,
> but not with the whining, the pleas of the coward;
> listen – your final pleasure – to the voices,
> to the exquisite music of the strange procession,
> and say goodbye to her, to the Alexandria you are losing.
>
> (C. P. Cavafy, 'The God Abandons Antony')

Next day Mark Antony suffered a humiliating loss as his troops and fleet deserted him, just as they had done at Actium. He thought that the Egyptian troops had been ordered to do so by Cleopatra, in an act of betrayal and in hope of dynastic survival. He was furious, and she fled to her palace – up the road, near where the Hotel Cecil now stands – locking the doors and sending word that she had killed herself because Antony had grievously doubted her. (If this sounds a bit romantic, so be it. Shakespeare liked the yarn.)

Antony, naturally, thought that she had shown more courage than he had, and asked a faithful servant named Eros (!) to kill him. Eros instead turned the sword on himself. Antony, according to Plutarch, said: 'That was well done, Eros. You have shown me what I must do, even if you had not the heart to strike the blow yourself.' Then, as they say, he fell on his sword.

But he did not die. Soon, Cleopatra's secretary arrived with a message to come to the queen. She was not dead! He was not dead! He was carried to the palace nearby. Cleopatra would not open the doors, so Mark Antony was, instead, dragged by ropes up to the high first-floor window by Cleopatra and two servant women.

'Those who were present say that there was never a more pitiable sight than the spectacle of Antony, covered with blood, struggling in his death agonies and stretching out his hands towards Cleopatra as he swung helplessly in the air,' wrote Plutarch.

Antony's cynicism about his great lover was perhaps understandable. Despite great wailing and the disfigurement of her body, Cleopatra did not die for some days, and perhaps even then it was an accident. She wanted assurances from Octavian for her children, for her dynasty. She had previously experimented with poisons and poisonous snakes on slaves, but none of these deaths were to her taste. Octavian put to death her son by Julius Caesar, and made some other threats, but did not kill her as he might have done. He locked her away from suicidal temptation.

A few days later, she died from the bite of an asp, smuggled into her quarters in a bowl of luscious figs. She might not have known it was there.

Perhaps that is unfair. In *Antony and Cleopatra* (act 5, scene 2) Shakespeare had Cleopatra die like this, thinking of the Alexandrian wine industry – and Mark Antony:

Give me my robe, put on my crown
I have immortal longings in me; no no more
The juice of Egypt's grape shall moist this lip.

Yare, yare, good Iras; quick methinks I hear
Antony call; I see him rouse himself
To praise my noble act; I hear him mock
The luck of Caesar, which the gods give men
To excuse their after wrath; husband I come:
Now to that name my courage prove my title!
I am fire and air; my other elements
I give to baser life. So have you done?
Come then, and take the last warmth from my lips.
Farewell, kind Charmian; Iras, long farewell.

Pastroudis's is two rooms these days: a cafe and ice-cream shop, and a dining room. A few couples sat with coffee, looking at the passing parade on a slow Friday night.

I decided on the dining room, and heard the waiter tell me, even on a Friday in a seaport, 'no feesh'. No people in here either. This solitary traveller sat with his one bottle of Stella Artois Export, the beer of choice in Egypt. (I had learned quickly to steer well away from Amstel or the cheaper local Stella.) There were ten tables, white tablecloths, prints by Degas. The shouts and the occasional scream from the street penetrated the silence.

I ordered the *specialité* of the house, paella, passing on the 'oriental grill' which is kebab and kofte. Another Stella, because the thought of a whole bottle of Omar Khayam, alone was for me, as for Cleopatra, unacceptable. The paella tasted all right, but there was no action here. No-one. It was embarrassing. Perhaps all Fridays are slow in a Greek cafe in a Muslim city.

I paid too much for the experience and headed off down the street. I had the feeling that I was in the way of a quiet night at Pastroudis's.

One day I set off from the Mecca to go to the area where the major remaining sights of Alexandria were to be found, around the catacombs at Kom el Shogafa, the Hill of Shards, named for the bits of pottery that once covered it.

In 1900 a donkey broke through the crust of the hill and fell down a hole, which turned out to be one of the second century AD tombs in this commercial establishment of catacombs. Alexandrians of the time could bury their dead by renting a niche.

The gods looking after the deceased are a mixture of Egyptian, Greek and Roman forms, as might best serve a cosmopolitan clientele. E. M. Forster wrote, in *Alexandria: A History and a Guide*: 'One must not read too much into anything here. The workmen employed were only concerned to turn out a room that should look suitable for death, and judged by this standard they have succeeded.'

I entered a rotunda on the site and descended, via a splendid winding staircase, perhaps thirty metres to the first level. This central shaft was the way bodies were lowered. On this level was a banqueting hall where relatives gave the dear departed a good send-off, attended by the undertakers. Undertakers: that is literally what they did; they took the dead under the ground to the lower levels, under the feet of the guests.

It was weird and warm down there. There were niches for hundreds of coffins, nearly matched by the dozens of tourists snapping away.

Ten minutes walk from the catacombs through cheerful back streets is the acropolis of the Ptolemies, with the scant remains of the great Serapeum begun by Ptolemy III Euergertes around 230 BC, and sacked by the Christians in 391 AD. A 'daughter' library of the great library and Mouseion downtown was also housed here.

The cult of Serapis was an attempt by the Ptolemies to unite Egyptian and Roman gods in one, using Serapis the Bull as its cult object. Now all that we see of the Serapeum is a great twenty-seven-metre high red granite column, incorrectly known since antiquity as Pompey's Pillar. A few sphinxes, an underground passage or two from the Serapeum, a dusty Nilometer and some column bases complete the scant landscape.

The pillar was in fact raised in 300 AD in honour of the emperor Diocletian, who saved the city from a famine, but the shaft may originally have formed part of the Serapeum. Pompey, on the other hand, was murdered in Egypt in 48 BC, having lost to Julius Caesar in the civil war.

Not far from Kom el Shogafa is Kom el Dikka. This Kom was a hill of rubble for a thousand years until, in 1959, excavations cleared away old houses and a Turkish fort and exposed what had been the Park of Pan in Ptolemaic times – a pleasure garden. The Romans added a small theatre, baths, shops and villas.

It is fortunate, because for the visitor to Alexandria the discovery of the small 800-seat theatre, the only Roman theatre found in Egypt, adds something 'concrete' and Roman to the visit. More than thinking about it or dreaming it, you can actually sit in this pleasant theatre and recite a bit of Catullus or Propertius – if the mood takes you.

Work continues here. I interrupted archeological workmen having a cup of *chai*, while engaged in the task of raising a red Aswan granite column. It's *chai*, not chat they want; a speculative '*Salaam alekum*' is greeted with a grunt.

Archeology has for a hundred years kept a lot of worker–archeologists occupied. Happy is the village with a site and a European or American (or occasionally an Australian) university with funding to pay them.

Another morning, having breakfast in the Mecca. A conversation at a nearby table: Nubians talking bananas.

'English she is funny.'

'How is she?'

'Banana.'

'Oh, bana bana.'

'Ba-nah-nah na.'

'Bananana.'

'Banaananana!'

'Bana nana nana nana!'

After breakfast – rolls and two boiled eggs, honey and coffee – I set off downtown for travel arrangements. This time the taxi driver, who had a veiled lady in the back, dropped me off and didn't want any money. I had to insist: fair's fare.

I wanted to go to Siwa, and searched for the West Delta Bus ticket office. It was around the corner from the Hotel Cecil, not in the middle of the square. Inside, a helpful English-speaking girl listened to my desires in the way of buses. She told me that there was a noon bus the next day 'direct' to Siwa and that it would take between eight and something hours.

As for coming back, that was another story. I would have to buy a ticket in Siwa, and the notion of getting from Siwa to Alexandria and back to Cairo in a single day, however long, was more than a bit dubious.

'Mr Garrie, you must stay another night here.' We were already old friends, so stupid was my idea.

'But the plane for Luxor leaves Cairo at six, maybe at seven at the latest.'

'I know this.'

'But what if the bus is late?'

'Yes. It leaves Siwa at six a.m. If everything is well, it is here at two or three. And?'

'The bus for the airport is at three. Last bus.'

'After that? You are staying here, Mr Garrie.'

'Okay. I will worry about that in a few days.'

'Mr Garrie, I will sell you this ticket to Siwa. Twenty pounds. Tomorrow, twelve o'clock. Not here, behind the train station. But please come back, not so much hurry hurry.'

'Okay.'

'Okay.'

'*Shukrun.*'

'*Inshallah*, Mr Garrie.'

In the EgyptAir office up the road on Sharia Saad Zhagloul, I changed my flight from Cairo to Luxor with the cheerful people there to the latest available: seven p.m. They had never heard of anyone doing Siwa–Alex–Cairo in a day by bus.

'Mr Garrie, you are full of adventure. You will make it. *Inshallah.*'

'And if I don't?'

'There is always another aeroplane some day.'

CHAPTER SIX

MIDDAY AT
THE OASIS

EGYPTIAN BUSES GENERALLY LEAVE on time, but because they stop at even the hint of a passenger and always pause for a half-hour meal break at a cafe (not necessarily with toilet) every two hours or so, they rarely arrive on schedule.

The noon bus from the depot in Alexandria ground out of town in misty rain, and rumbled down the road past El Alamein, and the endless white resort developments to Mersa Matruh.

On this part of the coast, white limestone quarries line the inland side of the road and white limestone resorts are in the process of being built on the seaward side: not just single houses, but developments of hundreds, even thousands of identical apartments. They generally have cute solar hot water panels and tanks on the roof, and collectively resemble a one-coloured Lego-land by the sea.

The bus stopped at the Youseff Hotel, a cement shack with lean-to, halfway between Mersa and Siwa. It was, in the Egyptian style, purpose un-built. A bewhiskered chap tended pots of camel bubbling on a wood stove, with coffee makings and endless *chai*. Three bicycles that looked as if they had been driven around the desert by wayward children leaned on the wall outside. It was a darkening afternoon, getting cold, with bright stars and a scrap of moon already gleaming in the indigo sky.

The rickety bikes did in fact belong to three young people, two German boys and a Danish girl. They had been working on a kibbutz in Israel – 'hard work, verr hard work' – and had taken it into their heads to ride these old bikes to Siwa, catch a four-wheel drive across the desert by the oasis route to Luxor and Cairo, and then take a bus to somewhere else. For now they were going to stay here, despite some trepidation.

'Okay here you sink? No trouble Youseff?'

What could I say? 'I don't think so. But you could always tie the bikes to the roof. Come by bus.'

'No sank you. We bicycle all the way. Is our journey.'

overleaf: Cleopatra's pool, Siwa, Egypt

I thought of Mulga Bill when he caught the cycle craze and left them to it.

Alexander came this way to Siwa in 331 BC, having founded and named Alexandria. He was on his way to conquer the rest of the known world, but first he made a long and dangerous detour to consult the respected oracle at the Temple of Amun in Siwa, which is out in the Western Desert near the border with Libya.

He must really have wanted to go there, because it was a bit of a trek, one that took him away from his direct conquering track. For Alexander on a camel, like me in the bus, it was a 300-kilometre journey from Alexandria to Paraetonium, which is now the town of Mersa Matruh, on the Mediterranean coast, and then a similar distance across the desert to the oasis of Siwa, where the priests performed their oracular tricks.

This journey took about nine days by camel, and for Alexander it involved a couple of miracles: a rainstorm that filled the party's empty water bottles, and then the timely arrival of a couple of crows to guide them through a blinding sandstorm. The only miracle I required was a bus that would make it from Alexandria to Siwa in one piece.

The sealed road from Mersa Matruh to Siwa across the fringing plateau and into the deep caramel-coloured desert has only been open in the last few years. It is very cheap, whatever the comfort level, and however many the stops.

It was dark by the time the bus growled into Siwa, about ten hours after departure. The wild desert scenery, herds of chocolate-brown hairy camels, an incandescent red sunset, a crescent moon in a navy blue sky and a sore behind are no preparation for a night-time arrival.

As the bus turned into the main square, a luminous orange–pink structure came into view. It seemed like a stone city as designed by Gaudi in a dream, or melted by Dali in a surrealist nightmare.

It was the ancient mud-brick fortress, mosque and town called Shali, built in the seventeenth century, and occupied until the middle of the twentieth, when rain, lack of maintenance and a desire for housing somewhat closer to the immensity of palm groves saw people building elsewhere in Siwa.

People still live at the foot of the fortress, which looms over the market square and bus station. Lit by recently installed electricity, it is a spectacular vision, providing an orange glow to aching bus travellers looking for a soft place to stay in the sand-streets around the square.

Sand-streets are romantic by night, less so when you can see the donkey and camel droppings by day. I was guided by a tiny boy who didn't speak a word but took my hand as I tried to orient myself in the town square and led me to the Palm Trees Hotel, a backpacker establishment where a single room, hard bed, blanket (no sheet), shared smelly toilet, not cold (but not hot) water cost just E£5.

With backpack dumped, I looked for food and drink and found a cafe where half-a-dozen faces I recognised from the bus were already getting stuck into fresh orange juice, kebabs, rice and Siwa olives – a large pale-green variety, not too salty – with Siwa dates (big, juicy fellows) to follow and there was spoon-standing coffee. And Siwa water: the Perrier of Egypt.

The soft desert night was all around. No-one spoke much, but the place was welcoming. A couple of Germans discussed the possibility of going further into the desert in a four-wheel drive, of trekking south, then back to the Nile near the oasis of Fayoum. Perhaps Alexander had gone that way when he was here. The waiter had a cousin with a car; they would meet for discussions next day.

I strolled back to the Palm Trees, hung my radio aerial and tried for the news. There was nothing from Australia out there, but a bit of BBC drifted in. I fell asleep.

Early next morning I was woken by Siwa sounds: the muezzin calling the faithful to prayer over a loudspeaker, the roosters crowing at the rebirth of the sun, and the donkeys braying for breakfast.

That morning my search for Alexander around Siwa took me to the one-man tourist information office in search of a map, which is where I found its enthusiastic and knowledgeable proprietor, Mahdi Mohamed Ali Hweiti. Mahdi was a thirtyish Siwan, polite and courteous, and would be proud to take me in his sand-blasted Peugeot 505 to see the sites in the next day or so.

Oasis people such as the people of Siwa are of Berber not Egyptian background, and speak their own language. Mahdi also owned Hassan's English Bookshop and Handicrafts 'to pay for the children's education'. He had Jasmine, four, and Hassan, eight. He was very interested in learning more about English – he read the books before he sold them – but he was also a proud Siwan. 'This is my home.'

In the meantime, I was given the map and directed to the Traditional Siwan House, the Hill of the Dead, the Shali. Mahdi's Xeroxed map had printed at the top: 'Siwa, the world's oldest tourist destination', which, given that the oracle had been attracting visitors for thousands of years, was arguably true. It also noted: 'We ask the women to respect our customs and traditions by keeping their legs and arms covered. Alcohol and affection forbidden in public. Enjoy your stay in our special oasis. Thank you. The inhabitants of Siwa.' 'The inhabitants' comprise about 1700 families.

I walked the dusty streets, watched by bright-eyed children and climbed the Shali, which is quite an extraordinary edifice in the daytime. I then tramped four or five kilometres to the Hill of the Dead, where a guide materialised out of thin air and opened the padlocked and disappointing tombs, in exchange for a handful of baksheesh.

At the top of the hill, though, is a wonderful view of the scattered oasis, the 70 000 olive trees, 300 000 date palms and the shimmering lake. There is a freshwater spring, but the ground water is distressingly growing more salty as the water table rises with the water pumped from the aquifer. Siwa is thirty metres below sea level.

Across the butterscotch desert, high bluffs and cliffs and escarpments rise up, pocked with tombs. Wherever the terrain is suitable, on cliffs and underground, the Egyptians have built tombs. Here they are everywhere.

In later conversation about the water, Mahdi blamed the 'run-off'. He said people dug wells for no reason, and the water went to waste, running into the lake. The more that is pumped out, the more salty it is. 'Too much water in Siwa! Too much.'

We were driving in his Poojoe. A cloud filled the sky, and it began to drizzle. The windscreen smeared: 'Mr Garrie! You have brought us more water.' Mahdi drove by looking out of the side window. He had no windscreen wipers or washers. Some Poojoe!

'This car. You want to know where this car is from?'

'Yes please.'

'A few years ago we all get cars from over there,' pointing west into the desert.

'From Libya?'

'Yes. No tax, very good cars, have wipers, everything. Then Egyptian government say we cannot have green numbers.'

'Libyan number plates?'

'Yes. We must have Egyptian, pay tax. No thank you. We drive to border, throw green numbers over, come back, car does not exist anymore for Egypt.'

'But no spare parts.'

'No wiping.'

Official Egyptian control is a recent and somewhat intermittent innovation of less than a hundred years duration in Siwa. The new road and electricity only arrived in 1988, coming after the oasis area was loosened from military control when tension between Libya and Egypt decreased. The new office building for the coming boom in Siwan tourism would open the following year.

As we drove out past the ever-expanding salt lake, Mahdi said the government could 'spend E£20 million on a road to a village in nowhere,' but could not find E£300 000 for a desalination project.

Mahdi was taking me to visit what Greek archeologist Lianna Souvalezi says is the tomb/temple of Alexander the Great. If true, this would be the greatest discovery in archeology since Troy or Tutankhamun, and the end to the romance of Alexander being buried by his tearful friends in the glass coffin at the crossroads in Alexandria.

It is certainly true that Alexander expressed a desire to be buried at Siwa, near his god–father Amun, but it is not at all certain that he was – probably not.

After his death in Babylon in 323 BC, Alexander was embalmed and laid on a bed of herbs in an elaborate coffin while a huge and wonderful funeral chariot was constructed. It took two years. It was some fifteen metres high, covered in jewels and trophies – including Alexander's war shield which he had taken from Troy – golden statues and paintings of his victories. The whole thing was drawn by sixty-four mules.

One of Alexander's generals, Ptolemy, using the Siwa wish as an excuse, caused the chariot to be taken to Alexandria, where it was put on show and then buried. The Roman emperor Augustus is said to have seen it 300 years later. Suetonius wrote: 'When Alexander's sarcophagus was brought from its shrine, Augustus gazed at the body, then laid a crown of gold on its case and scattered some flowers to pay his respects. When they asked if he would like to see Ptolemy too, "I wished to see a king," he replied, "I did not wish to see corpses." '

The Emperor Caracalla is said to have visited the corpse around 210 AD.

So there is certainly an ancient tradition that Alexander was buried at the intersection of what was then the Canopic Way and the Street of the Soma. But nothing has been found there or anywhere else in Alexandria, which leads to the speculation that Alexander was really buried at Siwa.

There have been other, later, stories. E. M. Forster related one of them: 'A dragoman from the Russian Consulate, probably a liar, said in 1850 that he saw through a hole in a wooden door (beneath the mosque of Nebi Danyal) "a human body in a sort of glass cage with a diadem on its head and half bowed on a sort of elevation or throne. A quantity of books or papyrus were scattered around." '

We arrived at Lianna Souvalezi's speculative dig, about twenty kilometres west of Siwa. A gate and fence keeps idle viewers out; a shed locks away the 'finds'. We must ask permission to see and speak to the archeologist, and walk around.

Lianna Souvalezi has found an interesting site: a circular wall about fifty metres in diameter enclosing the remains of a temple; she says tomb–temple. There seems to be evidence of some Macedonian influence in the carving of some of the architectural elements. Oak leaves, perhaps? Shapes. She says they have even found the seven-pointed Macedonian star (of Vergina) carved on a piece of stone, but this evidence was locked away and I did not see it. Even accepting that it might be an ancient Macedonian site, it still doesn't give you Alexander.

There are, however, many stories of Alexander's visit to the oracle, to the Temple of Amun in Siwa. The temple is built on a large rock some three kilometres from the main square of Siwa. A hundred metres away from the oracle temple is the remaining piece of a wall of the Temple of Umm 'Ubaydah. The rest of it was blown up by a local official in 1897.

Dr Kohlmann from the German Institute of Archeology in Cairo is attempting to discover whether there is a physical architectural connection between the two temples, making it one temple complex. Dr Kohlmann flew over the site in a hot-air balloon and could see that there should be a connection. He then uncovered marble slabs that seemed to indicate a street heading in the direction of the oracle temple.

The locals are not enthusiastic about giving up their livelihoods in exchange for proof of archeological theory, not even if it might disclose something exciting, perhaps to do with Alexander. This conflict between the ancient and the modern is not uncommon in Egypt or course, as attempts to save the pyramids from roads and encroaching suburbia attest.

I walked from Umm 'Ubaydah towards the small citadel, the rock of Aghurmi, where the oracle temple was built first in around 600 BC, in a plain Egyptian style with dressed stone and little decoration.

To enter the temple I climbed through the remains of a mud-brick village and mosque dating back four or five hundred years which had been built in and around the temple. People only gave up this village for comfort and for archeology in the 1960s; the mosque was in use even more recently. The huge wooden door which kept the world out for so long is still there, as is the well which provided water for thousands of years.

The great Egyptian archeologist Ahmed Fakry (revered in Siwa and elsewhere) cleared the mud-brick remains from the inner court of the temple in 1970, and work has gone on since – especially with regard to shoring up the walls of the temple and consolidating the rock on which it stands.

Walking through the outer court for some fifteen metres, I passed into a smaller court, then the sanctuary or cella. The cult statue of the god was in the smaller room within the cella. There was a narrow corridor to the right, with three niches on one wall and, in front, a wall with a gap at the top. The temple would have been roofed, probably with palm tree trunks. In this narrow corridor the priests waited to give their replies.

It is believed that when a high-ranking questioner such as Alexander came with individual private questions, he stood in the sanctuary and asked them directly. The priest would reply in oracular fashion from the other side of the wall, and his voice would float through the opening at the top.

Less-exalted personages had their questions asked for them, or written on a bit of clay, which was placed in a sacred boat – a model of a boat – and carried on the shoulders of purified bearers. Answers were given by the shaking of the boat from side to side, forwards or backwards, as interpreted by the priests. These were, understandably, often less than precise.

I stood in that sanctuary and thought of Alexander. I thought the usual: if these walls could speak. And then thought again: of course, they used to speak all the time.

The oracle at Siwa had been famous for hundreds of years by the time Alexander visited. Among the thousands of consultants was King Croesus of Lydia (as in 'rich as Croesus'), who had asked questions on matters of foreign policy in 550 BC.

And before the games of the ninety-third Olympiad (408 BC) an athlete called Eubotas, from Cyrene on the coast northwest of Siwa, was told by the oracle that he would come first and win the laurel for running. So certain was Eubotas that he took a statue of himself to Olympia in Greece where the games were held, in order that the crowds could see a statue of the winner on the day of the race.

No wonder Alexander, a man of with even more self-confidence than Eubotas, as well as a strong conviction that he was of divine origin, having been tutored by Aristotle and taught by his mother Olympias that he was descended from Hercules and Achilles, wanted to ask a last question or two of the oracle.

What did he ask? No-one knows. Stories have it that Alexander wanted to know whether all the murderers of his father Philip had been avenged, whether he was truly the son of Amun – that is, a son of God – whether he would be successful in his quest to conquer the world, and to which gods he should make sacrifices at particular places around the world.

Alexander never told anyone what the oracle had said, only that what he had heard had pleased him. Looking out across the oasis at Siwa, the sun falling in the Libyan west just thirty kilometres away, I was not thinking that I might be the son of Amun; rather, that in this peaceful and sacred place I felt rather childlike, standing in one of the footprints of history.

I asked a question out loud. 'Will I ever get to Tobruk?' The breeze moaned in the temple. It might have meant yes, it might have meant no.

The six a.m. bus. I had no trouble recognising it, it was the only dirty blue, white and grime-covered bus rumbling at the bus stop in the middle of Siwa. There was nothing else, except the citadel beginning to glow orange in the dawn, the sand, a handful of travellers. I had boiled some Siwa water in my mug, dropped in some Australian powdered milk and instant coffee, and struggled down the sand-street.

As Shaykh Macbeth might have noted, to go back is as bloody as to go o'er, and so it came to pass. I was in a hurry, which is a mistake in Egypt where everything takes the appropriate amount of time.

Only a couple of weeks into the journey, and already I was late. So much to see, so little time. I had to catch the bus. I had to get back to Alexandria by three o'clock in order to catch the last bus to Cairo Airport and the last plane to Luxor at seven o'clock.

Sitting next to me on the bus was a young German backpacker by the name of –

'Guess, please!'

'Okay. Gunther?'

'No.'

'Hans Magnus?'

'No.'

'Bertolt?'

'Nein. No.'

'Heinrich.'

'Yes! please, you got me? How did you do that?'

It was simple. I had just started running through the names of my favourite German writers: Grass, Enzensberger, Brecht … the usual suspects. He was young enough to be my son, and was reading Kafka. How appropriate. In my Sherlock Holmesian way I figured him for the son of educated parents of about my age, who just might have named him after a popular writer around the early 1970s. I had. I explained this bit of mock-deduction to Heinrich.

'So who is it you used? Which Heinrich?' asked Heinrich, 'Heinrich Böll?'

'Ball?'

'Böll,' he said.

'Ah, Böll. Oh no: Heine.'

'Ahh. Heine.'

'That's the one.'

' "Wherever books are burned, men also in the end are burned." '

Wrote Heine. Yes indeed. Quite appropriate, close to the Libyan border, with memories of the army of World War II book burners, burning up and down the coast.

In Egyptian bus style we stopped at a roadhouse two hours out of Mersa Matruh for food and drink. I was eating a dish of hommos and bread, served by a man in a green *galabyia*, when a young Japanese man sat opposite.

'Hello. Can you tell me? Can I change my bus? To Siwa? Is good?'

'Yes, very good.'

'I am on bus, go this way. Now I don't know. Now I go that way to Siwa.'

'Just get on one going west – ask the driver.'

'You Ossie!'

'I am. How can you tell?'

'I am Japanese! Just look Ossie. Where you from?'

'Melbourne.'

'Merbun. I love Merbun. What part?'

'I live in Brunswick.'

'Brunswi'! What stree'?'

'Near Lygon Street.'

'I know, I know! I see you!'

'I've got big palm trees in front of my house.'

'I know, I know, palm tree … I live in same stree' two year!'

'Amazing!'

'You got little dog?'

'Yeah, we've still got Monty.'

'Great meet you, mus' go, bus go! Siwa!'

'See ya.'

Back on the bus, Heinrich said, 'I am going to El Alamein. Where to get off?'

'I don't know.'

Then, 'How much you pay?'

'Twenty pounds.'

'Twenty! I pay only thirteen and a half.'

I had just paid the same as I had to get there, I said.

'Bus man in Siwa put in his pocket. Egyptians! Ptah!'

Germans …

Among other places, the Nazi general Rommel visited Siwa, on 21 September 1942, where he had tea with a number of local dignitaries. The spot is right by the bus station, and is now known as the Rommel Garden.

And Rommel's Afrika Corps came down this road that bisects the limestone quarries and the limestone coastal developments in 1941, motoring to El Alamein, almost at the gates of Alexandria, where the Eighth Army – including the Australian 9th Division – eventually threw them back in July and October 1942.

The 9th Division had been relieved from duties in besieged Tobruk by October 1941. In January 1942 Tobruk was lost to the

Germans, and was taken again after El Alamein in November 1942.

Australia's role at Tobruk commenced with the Australian 6th Division, who captured it from the Italians in January 1941. Tobruk was then defended by the 'Rats', mostly the Australian 9th Division, against Rommel's German forces from February 1941. They were called rats because they were supposed to be caught in Rommel's trap, but wore the badge of the besieged with pride, and still do. (The 6th Division by this time had been ordered to another tragedy in Greece and Crete.)

Tobruk is another shrine for Australians, part of our heritage in the eastern Mediterranean, a kind of World War II equivalent to Gallipoli – another heroic defeat. Tobruk was lost to the Germans in June 1942, though Australians were not there at the time, having been replaced by British and South Africans.

There is a kind of grudging compliment to the Australians at Tobruk in the much-quoted diary of the pessimistic German Lieutenant Schorn. The entry is from 6 May 1941.

Our opponents are Englishmen and Australians. Not trained attacking troops, but men with nerves and toughness, tireless, taking punishment with obstinacy, wonderful in defence. Ah well, the Greeks also spent ten years before Troy.

For someone like me who went to a State primary school in the 1950s, when World War II had only been over for not much more than the length of our tiny lives, an event like Tobruk had a special power. The story was told over the loudspeaker in the classroom, giving it a disembodied power and authority. So were the stories of Singapore and Kokoda, Gallipoli and Simpson and his donkey. Australians were heroes in all these far-off lands, despite the best efforts of British politicians and generals. It even penetrated that it was Labor's John Curtin who had brought the Middle Eastern heroes back to defend Australia. That was the paradox of a 1950s Menzian childhood, when queenliness was next to godliness: the loudspeaker talked about Australians.

Victorian state school education from the 1930s to the late 1950s required the absorption of the Victorian Readers: a set of eight books for the eight grades of primary education. Through these books, generations of children learned to read. Among the stories of the Three Billy Goats Gruff, the Hobyahs and the little yellow dog called Dingo, is the story of Simpson and his donkey (Fourth Book) and 'The Story of Anzac' (by John Masefield). By the time a diligent reader got as far as Sixth Book, stories from the *Arabian Nights*, bits of Shakespeare and Euripides joined the stories and poems of Lawson, Paterson and Kendall. The selection of Australian stories in this uplifting international context was what, I now realise, had the most profound effect on me. By the time we got (if we were so lucky!) to Eighth Book, we read the following as an introduction to a speech by Pericles, placed just before an account of the withdrawal from Anzac: 'More than one writer has found it interesting to compare the influences making for the development of the peoples of southern Australia with those that produced the Golden Age of Athens.' Australia, 'Athens of the South': that's what we were taught. Not a 'new Brittania' as W. C. Wentworth had it, but a new national democracy. And not anymore.

Tobruk joined Gallipoli in the dreamworld of Australian heroism undisturbed by too many facts. Somehow, then, it seemed that the Australian campaign in North Africa was tied up with staying in Tobruk until El Alamein, and then driving Rommel out until he landed in his Mercedes staff car on a lonely road in France, and was strafed to death by a passing Mosquito. Small boys didn't know then that he committed suicide rather than be put on trial for his knowledge of the plot to assassinate Hitler in 1944.

'I haven't got time to go to El Alamein. I hear that the German cemetery is very good – forbidding ...'

'Ja, like inside a big battle helmet.'

'The Australians are in the Commonwealth cemetery, standard issue?'

'Yes, like the others.'

'Different Australians.'

'Ja, all the men are different men.'

I wouldn't be going to Tobruk now, to see Australian football hero Ron Barassi's dad's grave. It had been made pretty clear by the embassy in Cairo that Australians were not being granted visas to Libya, especially, it seemed, to commemorate anything to do with World War II, let alone the Australian Football League Centenary.

I had wanted to go to Tobruk and put a red and blue Melbourne Football Club beanie on Barassi's headstone. It was going to be my way of paying tribute to the men who died there; to the son of an Italian immigrant who died in a part of the world – then called Cyrenaica – that was, in fact, part of Italy. The horribly ironic nature of the Barassi experience was inescapable to me as we drove along.

I didn't tell Heinrich any of this as we rumbled down the road. I saw flashes of the aquamarine sea, and took in the dust of the desert and diesel fumes. But Heinrich was a little surprised when I told him there had been thousands of Australian casualties from the El Alamein battle, the dead buried at the cemetery off the road near here. Like most young German backpackers I met, he was an ardent anti-militarist, yet intensely interested in recovering what he could from his past.

Egypt knows nothing of the 5800 dead Australians from hereabouts. To them a battle fought on their soil was really about one European invader fighting an alternative one, and who was to say which was better? El Alamein is now a tourist attraction for the hordes of Germans and a lesser number of British who simmer along these beaches in the season.

It's a lesson for the antipodean nationalist. Once again

Australians had fought in the eastern Mediterranean defending what? Freedom? And once again the locals had been less interested in *our* freedom than in gaining their own. It seems to me that this was a good enough reason in 1942 for Australians to leave the Middle East and return to defending our freedom closer to home. Perhaps I should have jumped off the bus at El Alamein and gone to see the cemetery.

Heinrich: 'Ohh, I don't know. What should I do?'

I said that if he got off the bus, he'd probably have to find a taxi to show him the monuments, which are scattered.

'Taxi? Ohh no, don't like taxis, they cost so much. Where are you going?'

I explained that I hoped to (had to!) get from Alexandria to Cairo Airport that afternoon and catch a plane to Luxor.

Heinrich looked at me as a miser would a spendthrift. A plane! This contravened backpacker conventions.

'The Islamists are still shooting tourists between Cairo and Luxor,' I said in justification. And added, pompously, that my embassy had advised Going By Plane.

'Ah yes, that is correct,' said Heinrich, 'but you will not make it. Look at the clock.'

The clock on his wrist said it was already two, and that meant trouble; right here we were a long way from River City. Then the bus stopped. Nothing new in that – I had never seen a bus turn down a passenger, no matter how little space was left inside – but this time when the great smelly beast juddered to a stop, it really stopped.

The driver got out for an inspection. Several others got out too. We were on the outer petticoats of Alexandria – and we had a flat tyre. Just then – miracle of miracles – another bus hove into view. It was only half full, which meant that all of us could fit on, providing we didn't mind sitting on backpacks in the aisle or standing and strap-hanging the last forty kilometres.

Heinrich and I climbed aboard, me with more than fingers

crossed, Heinrich muttering that no-one had told him where El Alamein was.

Down the road, more slowly. The tallest spires in Alexandria came into view – not Pompey's Pillar or the Pharos, but the light towers at the soccer stadium. Into the city. I didn't recognise this route. This bus did not seem to be going to the bus station near Masr Station which was the supposed destination. Instead, it was headed for the terminus – an old word meaning end of the world. Now, I thought, I will never make it to the plane on time. The last bus to the airport left at three; it was already three-thirty.

At the Arab Bus Co. The next airport bus was at seven p.m. – when my plane to Luxor left. I couldn't make it. I must make it.

It's funny how travel or that travel deadline feeling prevents you thinking as straight as, in retrospect, you would have liked. Because I had a ticket for seven p.m. I had to get the plane. I wanted to get to Luxor that night so that I could stay in the hotel I had booked. If I missed a night in Luxor, I would still have to get the plane to Israel in a couple of days. The trip would not be in ruins if I didn't make it until the next day, though I had a feeling that if I started from Alexandria next morning I wouldn't be at Luxor till after lunch. Better keep going and get as far as I could that night – at least to Cairo.

That's when I met Ahmed the taxi driver.

At first I asked him to take me to the Service Taxi rank near Masr Station. I hoped to pick up a minibus heading for Cairo. These leave as they fill up, and don't cost much. Even if I missed the plane, I could rebook for first thing in the morning and splash out on a hotel near the airport: a Sheraton maybe. I'd booked into the Sheraton Luxor, I had a voucher – it sounded good.

Ahmed nodded sagely at my accented request: 'Serveees Taxi okay? Masr Station? Okayokay?'

Ahmed was a young man in clean white shirt, pointy shoes, white socks and dark pants, without a moustache but with a bit of light in his eye. We set off. His English was close to nonexistent. I was hoping for the best.

As we approached Masr Station it was clear that this was where Ahmed thought I wanted to get out. I said, 'No, Serrveees Taxi? Okayokay? To Cairo! No more trains! Catch aeroplane!'

Ahmed said, 'Ohhh servieees … servieees, okayokay.' Suddenly his grasp of the language improved. 'Why you go servieees to Cairo. No train?'

'No train. Too late.'

'No bus?'

'No bus, no time.'

'Okayokayokay. I take you. Cairo, quick, quick.'

I thought that this was a possibility. It was four o'clock – three hours for the burn down the Desert Highway. Perhaps there was a way to cut across to the north of Cairo – the airport was on the north side – so that I didn't have to go to Giza and back through the city … 'Yes, maybe. How much?'

'Five hundred.'

'Five hundred what?'

'Five hundred dollars.'

Even by Egyptian standards this was an outrage. 'Cut it out mate, I could fly back to Sydney for that.'

'Oh.'

'Oh, indeed.'

'Okayokayokay. Pounds.'

'Pounds?'

'Egypt pounds.'

Rapid calculation in the head: $225 Australian. 'No sorry, can't afford that.'

'Okayokayokay. How much?'

'Two hundred.'

'Please, mister. Four hundred.'

'Three hundred last price.'

'Okayokayokay. Three hundred. Now we go.'

One hundred and thirty Australian, what a waste! But we went – a little way.

First the car, a Lada, needed diesel oil at a special place only Ahmed knew about. Then we needed to go the wrong way up the Corniche to see a friend of his, seemingly in a top-storey apartment.

'Wait, wait, okayokayokay.'

Twenty minutes later, they came. The friend, snazzily dressed in a Hawaiian shirt and thongs, poked his head in the open window. 'I am friend of Ahmed. He sorry his English not so good. He ask me where you go.'

'Cairo Airport.'

'Yes.'

'I have to be there at seven.'

'Seven! It is now four-thirty. Is nearly impossible.'

'It wouldn't have been –'

'Nearly impossible. You have a price?'

'Three hundred Egyptian pounds.'

'Yes, Ahmed will try.'

'Okay, thank you.'

'Okay, my friend he will do his best and good luck with you.'

'*Inshallah. Salaam.*'

'… *alekum.*'

'Okay Ahmed?'

'Maybe,' he said ominously.

Barrelling down the Desert Highway. A toll road for most of the way. Ahmed, on crossply tyres, pedal to the metal, windows open, cigarette in mouth, concentrated on the road fifty metres in front. Flat out, the Lada topped one hundred kilometres per hour: illegal, but not fast enough by my calculations.

'Ahmed, can we cut across to the airport before Giza?'

'Okay, I drive.'

I looked at the signs. We didn't seem to be making much of an impact on the distance remaining. Time drifted by. Every ten kilometres or so there was a billboard featuring a red Citroën Xantia on it. Just like my car at home, I thought idly. I had never seen a Citroën on the road in Egypt. I said this to Ahmed. He didn't take his hand from the wheel or his eye from the road ahead. It would go twice as fast as this Polish pedal car, I thought. The pink, even light disappeared behind the rows of gums and casuarinas.

Fences: in Egypt developers are very big on fences. It seems that no sooner is a square of land acquired than it is fenced – often an elaborate craftsmanlike stone fence. And then nothing might happen for months or years. The sand builds up on one side, rubbish flies in the other.

It's like buildings – not just in Egypt but in many places in the Middle East. A one-storey flat-roofed concrete house or shop will nearly always have the steel reinforcing wires sticking out through the roof, just in case. It's hard to tell sometimes whether these buildings are half-built or half-demolished.

The most finished structures along the road were the large egg-shaped pigeon houses. These mud-brick structures range from four or five metres high to large pigeon palaces of maybe ten metres, spotted with holes and perches. The most palatial *hammam* houses were the red and white striped ones, like huge conical mushrooms, of the White Horse Pigeon Farm. If there are free range chook farms, why not free flight pigeon farms? Pigeons must be even dumber than chooks.

In Lawrence Durrell's Alexandria Quartet, the luscious Justine used to burl down the Desert Highway in cuckolded husband Nessim's Roller for trysts with the epigrammatic novelist Pursewarden. She crashed it on one trip. I remember the description of the headlights of this Rolls as showing a single baleful eye before burying itself in a dune.

On and on through the dusk, the clock ticking. There was no road across Cairo to the airport from the north, there was no chance. I was never going to make it by seven o'clock.

It was dark as we turned around the back of the pyramids, across the Nile, the Cairo Tower winking, and onto the road to the airport. Ahmed only stopped three or four times to confirm with the traffic policemen that we were headed in the right direction. This was surely the most populous group of officials in Cairo. Black uniformed, with cap and white braid, they are everywhere, waving their arms and having no obvious effect on the slow-moving traffic.

At the airport, Ahmed lost more time working out which of the many scattered terminals I wanted. I finally got close to the main EgyptAir building and paid Ahmed his E£300.

'Baksheesh, Mr Garrie? Baksheesh?'

'No. It's seven forty-five. The plane is already landing in Luxor, just about. Three hundred is plenty.'

Ahmed looked crushed. He'd done his best, but I was sick of the whole baksheesh business. Especially as I'd missed the plane and had to think about where to spend the night.

As it happened, there *was* a later flight to Luxor – much later.

'Is a leetle plane.'

'I don't mind … How little?'

'Just twenty-eight pax.'

'Okay.'

'And it go via Sharm el Sheikh.'

'Okay.'

I hadn't been to this Red Sea resort, so a view out of the aeroplane window would be all right with me. Besides, that would mean arriving at Luxor at dawn or thereabouts and, in a triumph of money and pigheadedness over common sense, I hadn't 'lost a day'.

I landed at Luxor Airport just after six the following morning – twenty-four hours after leaving Siwa.

CHAPTER SEVEN

IN FLIGHT
WITH HORUS

SITTING OUTSIDE THE SHERATON coffee house on the bank of the Nile, I read in the *Guardian* a quote from cyberfiction writer William Gibson that 'Singapore is Disneyland with the death penalty'.

It occurred to me that the temples and tombs of Luxor constitute a sort of eternal Disneyland, but one where the penalty for death had been abolished. This is the place above all others in Egypt where the past is alive, where awe strikes you around every corner of just about every sandy road.

And there are no camel drivers to speak of; instead, obstreperous caleche drivers operating their two-horse carriages along the road beside the east bank of the Nile, and the usual indolent taxi drivers. And the tomb touts – on the west bank as sticky as picnic flies.

A winter's day, clear, in the mid-twenties: ideal bicycle weather. The Sheraton, where I was staying, is a low slung, comfortable, excellent hotel three kilometres south of the 'centre' of Luxor, which is the Luxor Temple.

After the nights at the $2-a-night Palm Trees Hotel at Siwa, educational though the whole experience was, I was glad Mrs Nehad had helped me choose this place. Fifty dollars US off-season rate for Room without a View was fine with me. The sheets were crisp, the water was hot, the dunny was clean. What more could a traveller want – except a beer and an espresso on the terrace, where the View really was.

I met a waiter there who not only knew what coffee was all about, but had a brother in Sydney and a desire to work in a hotel there.

'What she like Sydney?'

What could I say? It was hard to conjure an image, looking across at the gold-plated breathtaking view in front of me: white-sailed feluccas lazily moving down the green river, a cloud of white cattle egrets fishing, the edge of the Western Desert

overleaf: Ram's head sphinxes, Temple of Karnak, Luxor

hovering mauvely in the shimmering light, a man in a green *galabyia* swabbing the deck of a Nile cruise ship.

What was Sydney like? I pulled a picture of my wife and daughters standing at a beauty spot in the Taronga Zoo, framed by a palm. The harbour and the bridge in the background. 'That's what it's like.'

The waiter looked at the picture and said, 'Is beautiful.' I think he was referring to the view.

'Can I go?'

'It is hard to go these days,' I said. 'Ask your brother, go for a holiday and see what it's really like. Not all of it is beautiful.'

Luxor doesn't have the harbour views, it just has the Nile. Luxor is geographically in two parts. The east bank of the Nile, where the town and hotels spread, is the city of the living. It also has the Temple of Luxor and the stupendous temple complex at Karnak. The west bank is mostly a city of the dead, a twenty-square kilometre confusion of valleys carved from the escarpment of the Western Desert as it tumbles down to the flood plain. Temples and tombs are everywhere.

The great Queen Hatshepsut (1490–1468 BC), for whom was built the startling clean-lined mortuary temple at Deir el Bahri, said of this place: 'I know that Karnak is the horizon above the earth, the glorious first ascension, the sacred eye of the Master of the Universe.'

Nineteenth century British Prime Minister Benjamin Disraeli wrote of Luxor in a magazine article in 1832:

Conceive a feverish and tumultuous dream full of triumphal gates, processions of paintings, interminable walls of heroic sculptures, granite colossi of Gods and Kings, prodigious obelisks, avenues of Sphynxs and halls of a thousand columns, thirty feet in girth and of proportionate height. My eyes and mind yet ache with grandeur so little in unison with our own littleness ...

Disraeli said it was useless to try to write about it. It was certainly useless to attempt to see everything in just a few days. I was compelled to be selective.

I took a bicycle ride up the road beside the east bank to visit the Luxor Temple. The Temple of Luxor is magnificent, but it is a shadow compared to the Hypostyle Hall of the Great Temple of Amun at Karnak, another fifteen minutes cycling up the Nile. This place is surely the most extraordinary, beautiful, awesome, sacred-feeling 'pagan' place in Egypt; possibly the world.

After entering by an avenue of ram-headed sphinxes, which leads to the First Pylon or gateway, then a large courtyard with some statuary, a vestibule and then the Second Pylon, you reach the Hypostyle Hall erected by Seti I of the Nineteenth Dynasty, who reigned from 1318 to 1304 BC.

There are 134 columns in a space 102 metres by fifty-three metres. Twelve of them are twenty-three metres tall and form a processional way down the temple. They once held up the clerestory, lighting the other 122 slightly smaller columns made in the form of papyrus – imitating a papyrus forest, if there could be such a thing. They are carved on one side in raised relief, and on the south side in sunk relief and many still have some of the gorgeous colour that must have made the place an especially magical one.

I sat there in the warm sunshine, no-one else around for minutes at a time, and relaxed for the first time since I had arrived in Egypt.

Next day I wanted to spend on the west bank. A stroll down to the Nile will get you across on a punt for E£1. It is the best value boat ride in Egypt, taking about fifteen minutes to cross the sleek green river. And on board you can buy a cake. Flocks of white cattle egrets swarm on helpless fish, or in the hope of helpless fish. Feluccas sail downstream and have to be towed back.

On the other side is a ticket office. A visit to three tombs in the Valley of the Kings costs E£10 plus the same for three camera tickets, plus E£20 to visit Tutankhamun's tomb. One hundred pounds buys fifteen minutes in Nefertiti's airconditioned tomb.

In a taxi or on a bike you will pass and stop at the Colossi – really huge worn statues of Amenhotep III which once stood in front of a temple – look at the ancient graffiti carved in them and perhaps (you can't help it) recall some lines of Shelley's 'Ozymandias'. Shelley only travelled as far as Italy, but perhaps did meet a traveller who had been to Thebes – as the nineteenth century knew Luxor. Shelley's poem does not describe what the Colossi look like today, but it gives a feeling of the Pharonic impulse – perhaps.

I met a traveller from an antique land
Who said: Two vast and trunkless legs of stone
Stand in the desert ...
And on the pedestal these words appear:
'My Name is Ozymandias, king of kings:
Look on my works, ye Mighty, and despair!'
Nothing beside remains. Round the decay
Of that colossal wreck, boundless and bare
The lone and level sands stretch far away.

But elsewhere much does remain. On the west bank are the tombs of about sixty Pharaohs, including the most famous of modern times, Tutankhamun. There are eleven Ramses, for instance.

The Valley of the Kings is a bleak, parched white wadi or dry valley with about two kilometres of walking required to see all the tomb entrances. The floor of the wadi is a formed but unmade road. White, sun-blasted stony hills rise steeply for two or three hundred metres above you. The feeling is one of being at the source of desolation. Archeologists are still finding tombs here, such was the work of thousands of years of subtle digging. Not all tombs are open at once. It would be possible to see eight or nine on one day's visit, though three or four suffices to engender tomb weariness in all but the hardiest Egyptophiles.

'This Ramses. This Osiris. This ankh, mean life. This eye Horus. Look. Look. Quick, flash okay.'

If you are a solo traveller or a couple, rather than in the protective phalanx of a group with its own guide, you will be hassled by the guards inside every tomb, and by some outside it. There is no way you can avoid being 'guarded': 'Me no guide, guardian me!' Having a camera makes you an obvious target. Sometimes I felt positively pushed into taking pictures of things I didn't want to, knowing there wasn't enough light to make it worthwhile.

Then there are the fake antiques. On my way up the steep staircase to see the stick figure paintings in the tomb of Thutmosis III, my sleeve was tugged by a man in a green *galabyia*, white scarf around his head, bad gold-filled teeth, trying to look like a tomb robber. He thrust a corner of a bit of pottery painted with green, ochre and white figures in my face. No-one else was around this far up the valley.

'Meester. Only 150.'

'No, I'm not interested.'

'One-forty. This genuine for sure.'

'If it was genuine you wouldn't be selling it.'

'What you mean? I walk, I look, I pick up.'

'No, I don't want to buy anything.'

He unwrapped something else from a fold in his *galabyia* – he could have had the entire Egyptian Museum in there.

'Piece moomiya … Smell …'

I couldn't resist. I smelled. It smelt foul and old.

'No,' weakening.

'Sixty – two pieces for one hundred.'

He was thrusting them into my hands.

'And this [a badly carved black cat].'

'No.'

'Eighty for three piece.'

'No!'

'And three scarab. All pieces for eighty.'

By this time I was at the bottom of the steps. I wanted to go up, so I paid up: E£70 for the lot, which I carried up the hundred steps, secreted in my coat of many pockets.

I looked in the tomb, saw the Thutmosis mummy case, the fluorescent light, the guardian – he cost another E£10 – and the unusual stick figure paintings. Then, walking out, the same man in the green *galabyia* came up to me – holding out another shard. He didn't recognise me.

'Hang on mate, I've been had once –'

'Just one hundred,' he said.

'*Imshee* … nick *off*!'

I was heading towards the tomb of Tutankhamun.

Tutankhamun was born about 1342 BC, probably the son of Akhenaten, a wild iconoclastic Pharaoh whose principal wife was Nefertiti; however, she was not Tutankhamun's mother, who was probably named Kiya.

Tutankhamun, enthroned in the Temple of Karnak in 1333 BC, was married to one of Nefertiti and his father's daughters, his half-sister Ankhesenamun. He died in 1323. It was a short reign, where he had little real power, but it was marked by much restoration both of buildings and of religion after the destructions of his father.

Tutankhamun was largely forgotten by his successors, and his tomb was later covered up by the larger tomb of Ramses VI, under which it lay intact until 22 November 1922 when it was opened by the archeologist Howard Carter. It was the greatest discovery in the history of archeology, and an extraordinary window on a previously dead and dusty past. The tomb contained everything – most of it now in the Egyptian Museum – needed to ensure Tutankhamun's immortality, which, more than for all other Pharaohs, it has now most certainly done.

Tutankhamun's mummified body, after being unwrapped, X-rayed and examined, was eventually returned to its coffin, where it now lies. The tomb is mostly bare. Only the burial chamber itself has decorations. One guardian of the tomb. No photographs out of respect.

Over in the Valley of the Queens, the elaborate tomb of Tutankhamun's mother-in-law, the fabulously beautiful Nefertiti, is a contrast. For my E£100 I got fifteen minutes in her presence, watched by half-a-dozen guards. There is a little shelter outside her tomb, where cameras and bags are left. Inside, the paintings are indeed exactingly drawn, fabulously coloured, and beautifully restored. Snake-like ducts and fans keep the air inside at the correct non-destructive temperature and humidity.

Nefertiti's tomb is the lowest in the Valley of the Queens, and most damaged by salt. Its restoration is an expensive model of what ought to be done for every tomb. But there is no portrait in the tomb that compares to the serene, strong and modern-looking Unfinished Head of Nefertiti, its sensual mouth and seemingly closed unpainted eyes, in the Egyptian Museum. Perhaps the fifteen minutes in the tomb is enough; you have time to look, you can't take pictures, then you have to get out. I would not have seen half as much in twice the time without that unfinished portrait–image in my head.

Somewhat under the influence of the wine named Omar Khayam, that night I fell prey to the lure of a balloon ride salesman lurking in the lobby of the hotel. I was feeling so peaceful that I agreed to pay US$250 to waft above Luxor early next morning. The price included a preliminary breakfast, followed by a luxury breakfast, and champagne, ferry rides and four-wheel drive back to the hotel.

Flying in the morning sun over the west bank of the Nile,

greeting the sun god Re and the falcon-headed god of the sky, Horus, seemed an appropriately sentimental thing to do, because I would be flying out later that afternoon, headed for Cairo and Israel. In one kind of representation in the west bank tombs, the god Horus is painted a bluey–green colour, holding an ankh (the symbol of life) in one hand, with his falcon head surmounted by the disk of the sun, Re. Horus is thus a symbol of flight.

Looking down towards the Nile that night, it seemed as if Horus himself had been caught in the light from a luxury cruise ship, standing by a felucca, smoking a cigarette and looking back at me. It was a trick of the fading sun; not really Horus, but a man in a green *galabyia* wearing a white skull cap. In Egypt I often had the feeling that things and people were not always what they seemed.

Next morning, just after Nut the mother goddess of the sky (who swallows Re, the sun, each night and delivers him again each morning) had done her job, I was taken by the Virgin Balloon Adventure bus to the river.

Smudges of black and grey birds known as bulbuls flew around the river's edge. The ferryman was wearing a grubby green *galabyia*. Once we'd been delivered across to the west bank, the balloon captain approached our little party and told us that the flight was off. Too windy. Couldn't risk it. Credit card vouchers torn up. Come back another day. The ferryman smirked.

It doesn't pay to believe in omens in Egypt. If you do, the Evil Eye (often shown as the falcon eye of Horus) will surely get you. There was nothing for it but to pack the backpack, have lunch by the pool on the bank of the Nile and wander out to the airport.

The airport at Luxor is small, the terminal inadequate, but it is the heart of the Egyptian tourist industry. Many international charter flights as well as scheduled flights by EgyptAir run from Luxor. Hundreds of thousands of people a year pass through it.

Two flights were scheduled to leave at 3.30 p.m. on 27 March: Flight MS 104, which I was booked on, and Flight MS 138. Both

EgyptAir to Cairo. The terminal was in chaos. There were two plane-loads of passengers of a dozen different nationalities and two different coloured boarding cards with no numbers on them. The departure lounge was packed as tight as a mummy case.

Boys with trollies of soft drinks and nuts pushed their way through the heaving pack. A dozen languages belted out at top voice. Announcements were in a strange variety of Arabic unintelligible even to Egyptians.

'Excuse me what did he say? Which flight is leaving?'

'Sorry, no understand … anything.'

There was a cursory check at the gate, and then on to the tarmac. A couple of airport buses waited to deliver people to the aircraft. But which people? Which plane?

Outside, a harassed official asked a few of us with blue cards to wait to one side. A jabber of Japanese was taken off in one bus to one of the aircraft.

We waited some more. Another bus rolled up and we were pushed on and driven to a different aircraft. As both were headed for Cairo, who cared, I thought.

The system, whatever it was, must have worked. I was on the correct plane, as there was no-one else in seat 38K. I slithered past a couple of nut brown Upper Egyptians with faces straight from a tomb painting. Sitting in front of me was an array of a dozen Americans: big short-haired guys, chatty women and doing-what-they're-told kids with excellent teeth. There was a jumble of Japanese, a medium-sized coterie of Canadians, and an effusion of Egyptians.

The aeroplane eventually took off, twenty minutes late, and swept over the Nile on its way north. I settled back for the trip, eating a piece of dry cake and sipping a cup of Coke delivered by EgyptAir flight attendants in tailored grey and blue. I read the soccer news in the *Guardian* and watched the Nile's dark green stripe, parallelled by another, lighter green band of cultivation. It was quite extraordinary how the line of irrigated land beside the river just stopped, as if drawn with a ruler. Here is life, one step, and there is desert, and death.

Flying inspires meditation. Sitting in that Airbus looking down at the desert and the great green river, I thought that if the Australian landscape from the air looked as if it had been painted by an Aboriginal painter or Fred Williams, then the Egyptian landscape might have been painted by a New York abstract expressionist tomb painter – all stripes in 1950s pastels.

I looked at my watch. We had been travelling for an hour. We should have been descending. Tray tables were locked, seat backs were upright, but we weren't preparing for landing. We were circling. Outside was the dusty mirage of Cairo. Traffic congestion perhaps. I watch the mud-coloured outline of Cairo emerge now and again from the haze in the soft light of the late afternoon.

After an hour of circling, my reverie was cut short by a rippling feeling of annoyance. Surely there wasn't that much traffic in Cairo? More circling. What else could it be? An accident on the ground? Equipment problem in the plane? Maybe we had burst a tyre on take-off and are burning fuel. A quiver of anxiety fizzed through my body.

It was now some two hours since we had left Luxor. The passengers were sick of sitting still. They looked questioningly at the hostesses, who walked up and down the aisles saying nothing.

Just then a burst of Arabic came over the intercom. It was not the captain's voice. It was high-pitched, fast, perhaps hysterical Arabic, like static interference. There was a dim awareness at the back of the plane that something was going on at the front.

I didn't understand most of it. But I did recognise a few words which brainwaves automatically translated. '*Inshallah*' – if God wills it. '*Amman*' – capital of Jordan. '*Libya*' – a country to our left.

It was now evident that the plane was not circling but flying on a level course. I looked out the window. I was flying with Horus, god of the sky, and his evil eye. The sun, Re, was setting in the west, swallowed by the mother of night. Shadows on the wings. We were heading west, not east: Libya, not Jordan or points east of it.

Even at that moment it did not really sink in. Hijack. The plane's been hijacked. The words reverberated in that room in my brain I keep full of newspaper cuttings. I might die! Anything might happen.

One of the American crew-cuts in front of me said, 'I think we have a serious situation here.'

But what kind of situation was it? Peering down the aisle, I could not see what was happening in the cockpit. The curtains separating us from the first-class section of the plane were drawn. Perhaps that was a figure moving across. Could have been a hostess … or a hijacker.

That was one of the disturbing feelings at that time: something was going on but we were not personally and directly involved. We were not threatened physically, but an emotional battering by silence began; we were not told anything by anyone. That is the Standard Operating Procedure: don't tell the passengers anything, they might do something.

Some people were standing by then, peering down the aisle. Hostesses looked worried and shooed us back into our seats.

There was the captain's voice in Arabic for many seconds, then, in briefer English, 'Please sit down. Please lower your voice. It is for your own safety.'

The dawning fact of the hijacking caused some whispered conversation between the Americans in front of me. They were doubly agitated. Being hijacked is one thing, but going to Libya is quite another. They remembered the tribulations of the hostages in Iran twenty years or so ago. We all thought of the hostages in Lebanon.

But who had hijacked us? Presumably it wasn't Hamas, the Palestinian group that had blown up buses in Israel in the months before this, or we would all be in pieces over Cairo already. Who would hijack a plane-load of tourists and go to Libya? It didn't seem to make any political sense. Hezbollah had thus far stuck to their own neck of the woods in south Lebanon. The Kurdish separatist group PKK had a grudge against Turks and also Germans, and had set bombs for tourists in Turkey, but this was a bit far south of their range.

An Egyptian fundamentalist group such as the one that had been shooting up buses and trains for the past few years in the region of Luxor, and was determined to crack the tourist industry, the backbone of the Egyptian economy, seemed the most likely bet – which was not very heartening, because they did kill people, and they had threatened suicide missions on the Hamas model in recent months.

I was enveloped in the womb of the aeroplane. Without seeing any physical violence, without being individually and personally threatened, I just went with the flow, and found myself getting annoyed that I was not more afraid.

I read a book for a few minutes. It happened to be Amin Maalouf's *Samarkand*, a romance about Omar Khayam and the original Assassins. A few paragraphs about Hassan in his mountain fastness ordering the deaths of those who opposed his brand of Islam was not very reassuring, but was at the same time distancing. It had all happened before.

The plane hummed along. It did not sink violently and there were no flames. It was now 6.15 p.m. An announcement over the intercom asked all foreign passengers to hand their passports to a hostess. There was a breeze of anxiety. Who were they looking for? Obviously not Egyptians; any Americans? Israelis? Non-Egyptian Europeans? Australians? Surely not.

But it was time for a bit of Australian anger at the system. I held a hissed conversation with a hostess who, while clearly frightened, was trying hard to follow orders. I didn't want to lose my passport. Losing your passport is more than losing your identity. If the worst occurs, it is losing the possibility of being quickly identified.

No-one knew I was on this flight. I doubted whether there was an actual detailed flight list. No-one had asked me my nationality in Luxor. Perhaps I would simply become a paragraph, 'Aussie tourist disappears', with a follow-up paragraph a week later: 'Aussie tourist one of Egypt hijack dead.' Wrong place at the wrong time.

After an hour's flying we landed, at 8.05 p.m. It was a smooth landing as the sinking sun illuminated the twin runways and single control tower. As we hit the tarmac I saw there was nothing else around; no people, no buildings – just desert.

I had wanted to come here, and here I was. In Libya. What an irony. They had tried to keep me out, and now I was their unwilling guest. Looking out into the desert night, a faint glow of moonlight on the runway, I saw the winking of orange lights as a vehicle, perhaps a jeep, buzzed on my side of the plane.

I wondered what it was that the hijackers wanted. If, as seemed most likely, these were Islamists, perhaps Egyptians, with a grudge against the government of Egypt, and its tourist infrastructure, what could they possibly want? Perhaps it was to be a demonstration that the tourist infrastructure could be 'taken' by them at any time. Perhaps they had comrades in an Egyptian jail who could be released.

Up front there was some agitation. A rush of passengers came down the aisle, including an Egyptian woman in her forties, wearing a white crocheted cap under an orange headscarf, and a black coat. She was sobbing hysterically. These appeared to be first-class passengers forced from their seats, and sent down the back to cram, five to a row, with the sweating economy passengers.

A burst of Arabic over the intercom, in an hysterical tone. The voice of the hijacker. The non-Egyptians looked around. No translation. Perhaps that wasn't possible.

More people hurried down to the back end of the plane. Necks craned into the aisle to see what was going on. We couldn't see anything but shadows. The captain's voice advised us to relax.

I wondered again what the terrorist's demands might be. A good one would be to close down Luxor Airport, I thought. Demand that. Put an end to the Hollywood of Egyptian tourism, the Babylon of modern Egypt.

Or else.

Or else what? One passenger at a time, or the whole lot of us at once?

An hour passed. I read the in-flight magazine *Horus* again. I was bored, and felt a rumble of real annoyance work its way into my mind.

Another hour. Occasional stabs of staccato Arabic punctuated the rhythm of a stationary aircraft. It was getting humid, and a little smelly. An aircraft is like your own bedroom, comforting and familiar, but it is also like a dream, a magic carpet, which could at any moment simply take off and return to our original destination, and it would then be as if nothing had happened, just a longer flight than expected.

Or it could just blow up.

The captain's voice confirmed that we were 'somewhere in Libya' and asked if would mind sitting still and move to the toilet only if absolutely necessary. At this reminder of not having visited the toilet for some hours, everyone on the plane felt uncomfortable – but nobody moved.

We were in both physical and mental transit, trying to think of the future, or the past. We would do as we were told and hope for the best. I thought of the Jews on cattle trucks rumbling through Germany on their way to Bergen Belsen or Auschwitz, and of the armchair criticism that had been made: 'Why didn't they do something?' What can you do? In my case I did nothing because I was afraid. Or perhaps I wanted to believe I was asleep, or just on a flight delayed by engine trouble – anything but what was really going on.

Another hour. And another. Then the curtain at the front of the plane parted and a vision emerged. It was the captain, and he looked just like a young Omar Sharif. For some reason I found this comforting. We *were* in a movie.

The captain's name, I found out later, was Imhotep Shehata Mohammed Nasser. Such names! All Egypt's history is in those names: Imhotep the engineer from Saqqara, Mohammed the name of the Prophet, Nasser the nationalist hero.

Captain Imhotep walked down the aisle and spoke to passengers on either side. The hijacker's demands were 'small'. He exuded confidence and the smell of travel in Egypt, lemon cologne. They had messages for the world. They were broadcasting them: to Israel, to Egypt, to the United States, to Palestine, to Syria, to Sudan.

One of the small demands, I discovered later, was 'to put pressure on the Egyptian government over the imposition of sanctions against the Sudan, after the expiration of the notice for the handing over of the defendants involved in the attempted assassination of President Mubarek'. I took it to mean that the hijackers also wanted Mubarek assassinated and objected to Sudan being penalised for the non-handover of the assassins. Not to mention the pre-Israeli-election shelling and bombing of Lebanon and the blockading of the Palestinians in Gaza and the West Bank. This seemed a pretty fundamental list of objections to what was happening in the region, and not easily solved.

The major hijacker's name, I also discovered later, was Mohammed Mahmoud Hemid Selim, a 43-year-old cafeteria owner from Luxor, perhaps originally from the Arabian tribe of Beni Hilal. Many Egyptians are of 'Bedouin' background. With him were two teenage boys, Khaled Mohamed Mahmoud Hemid Selim and Ahmed Hussein Kamel Selim. They had with them 'explosive materials' – ammonium nitrate, potassium chlorates and black powder.

I did not find the account of their demands particularly comforting. But at least there was action – if not by us.

An hour passed. And another. And another.

'*You are free!*' The curtain parted suddenly and a dark head with shining eyes poked through, followed by an arm in green and black camouflage carrying a black automatic rifle. He smiled and said, 'Welcome in Libya! You are free!'

Captain Imhotep's voice said in Arabic and English, 'The hijackers have left the plane peacefully.' The hijackers shook the hands of the crew, thanking them for their kindness, and were driven off by the Libyans.

The soldier, just a kid, said to us again: 'Welcome in Libya!'

The aircraft erupted in cheers and clapping, and chants of 'Allah! Allah! Allah!'

People stood up. The soldier smiled, but he did not move. It dawned on me that we were out of the hijacking frying pan into the Libyan fire. We were in Libya, but we were not yet free.

Captain Imhotep made another entrance. People clapped, took photographs. A gust of cool air breezed in from the desert outside, and washed into the back of the plane. There was what could only be described as a physical wave of relief. I am not dead yet. Hooray for me!

We were told by Captain Imhotep that we were at a military airfield near Tobruk called Martubah. Tobruk! I had actually made it to Tobruk. But, like the Rats, I was confined and couldn't get out to look around.

The captain also mentioned that we didn't have enough fuel to get back to Cairo. Nor was it safe to take off in the dark. This airfield had no lights, as we could see for ourselves. We were there for the 'duration', at least until the middle of the next day, or longer, however long that might be.

Some more time passed. We got our passports back. The

crew-cuts looked especially pleased. Their passports were covered in gooey white stickers with messages in Arabic, which a woman said they had acquired 'in Saudi'. They were military personnel from the big American base in Saudi Arabia, holidaying in civvies in Luxor. No wonder they were worried. They carried Official, rather then standard American passports.

Then, early in the black morning, an agitation of Libyan soldiers came down the aisle and ordered us off the plane. They were excited and gestured with their weapons, but I could not say that they pointed them at anyone. I grabbed my precious camera bag, stumbled into the aisle, staggered down the steps (where did they come from?) and onto the tarmac, which was lit by the headlights of perhaps twenty trucks, jeeps, buses and Japanese sedans with flashing orange lights.

We were told to get on a bus. I chose the closest, a smaller sixteen-seater rumbling to one side of the queue. On my bus were pale faced crew-cuts and their exhausted children. Confusion reigned. Where we were going, no-one knew. We started, stopped, backed up, parked, started again. After half an hour of this, we formed up in convoy.

The driver, cigarette in the side of his mouth, wearing a black and white scarf twisted around his head and a greenish *galabyia*, drove us into the chilly night accompanied fore and aft by military police (in civvies) in their sedans. We passed a barracks of more soldiers. They appeared at the side of the road in the orange security lights and stared and waved guns at the circus passing by.

We came to a crossroads, and most of the buses went left. Our bus turned to the right.

After a few kilometres the driver pulled up – at a service station. He got out, closed the door and had a conversation with the attendant. Plenty of petrol, you would think, in this part of the world. Watching the driver and the attendant talk and gesticulate, it's easy to imagine what they are discussing.

'Who's paying for the petrol?'

'Look, I got woken up in the middle of the night. I went out to that airstrip, picked up these people, and now I have to take them to …'

'Okay, but someone has to pay.'

'This is a matter of national urgency. Colonel Gad …'

'Don't give me that.'

'What if I write you a note?'

'My boss …'

'Colonel Gadaffi.'

'But …'

'There are blokes with guns …'

We finally filled up, the driver signed a docket and we headed off. The other buses were waiting at the crossroads. We drove through the night. I was aware of the desert on one side, and it seemed to me that the sea was on the right. That meant we were not going to Bardia or Sallum one hundred kilometres or so away on the border with Egypt. We were driving, like Rommel, deeper into Libya.

I mentioned this to a crew-cut in the bus. He was not at all happy. He said we'd been hijacked a second time.

None of the bus drivers wanted to be last to wherever it was we were going. They jockeyed for position as if it were the Melbourne Grand Prix, looking for passing manoeuvres under brakes at corners, and planting pedal to the roaring metal on the long straights.

Compared to Egyptian commercial bus drivers, my standard for fast driving on desert roads, these guys were more reckless by a wide margin. We hung on, and watched nameless dark villages rush by.

I thought of the names of towns west of Tobruk, knowing them from the battles fought in World War II, the stuff of childhood reading. Derna. Cyrene. Bardia. Benghazi. It was a very long way to the capital of Libya, Tripoli. We were likely to be going to Benghazi, about 300 kilometres from Tobruk. An air-field would be there. Maybe a plane. Maybe not.

Suddenly we were in a town with lights but no people. Half an hour through the modern but mean-feeling streets, we jerked to a stop outside a hotel.

There was an eruption of TV lights and cameras flashes, and the door opened. I was out. Our bus driver had won the race. Like the Australian 6th Division, I was first into Benghazi. A hand emerged from the glare, then a sweating face, dark hair plastered on shining forehead, a moustache, a grin. 'Welcome in Libya. You are free! Welcome to the best hotel.'

The hand pulled me away from the bus. The other passengers got out, and we were ushered into the foyer. The manager, for that is who it was, wanted me to say a few words for the TV cameras. I had no words. I was tired. I was unhappy at being there, wher-ever it was.

'Where are we? What's going on? Who is in charge?'

Later, when I slumped into a white leather couch in the foyer of the hotel, I knew I should have said, 'Take me to your leader.'

The rest of the buses unloaded their passengers. They stag-gered into the foyer where a copse of microphones was sur-rounded by an excited group of Libyan notables, including the hotel manager and a man dressed in white robes over a suit. He looked like a Shaykh, and he stepped up to the microphone and made a speech.

'Welcome in Libya in the name of Allah and freedom-loving peoples. In the name of the messengers of peace, the enemies of terrors. On the anniversary of the liberation of Benghazi by the British. We are feeling that you are tired but we all suffer, suffer from terror, like you suffer hours ago. We as people suffer years of terror and unjust resolutions. We have more feeling of terrors. We are victims of terrors. We are very happy to see you in the peace city of Benghazi. You are suffering. We hope you can see with your own eyes the country of peace and suffering. We are for freedom and liberty. I hope to chance to meet you. Please, please send a message to your families. You are in Libya. You are welcome.'

This speech, in fluent lengthy Arabic and fractured translated English, was greeted by tired applause. The Shaykh, dressed in a seemingly last minute ensemble of tea towels and sheets over yesterday's shirt and pants, looked as tired and emotional as we did. The translator was a young man in a crisp white shirt who seemed to know what the Shaykh was going to say before he finished saying it.

The Shaykh sweated in the dozen or so TV lights, as did those of us in the front row. I felt a growing resentment at our liberators. I didn't get hijacked so they could get hours of TV propaganda showing how wonderful their country was. A few days ago they didn't even want me here, and now I was among the heroes of the anti-terrorist Libyan freedom loving people's Green Revolution. Give me a break.

'You are welcome in Libya. Thank you thank you thank you.'

The TV director had got enough footage. The lights went out and we were ushered upstairs to a function room for dinner. It was now about seven a.m.

Tables groaned with hotel food. I bumped into a Canadian girl in a queue who told me she had been near the front when the hijackers left the plane. She thought they had thanked the captain and crew for their cooperation. I wondered what had happened to them and whether they were in cahoots with the Libyans.

People were slightly hysterical with tiredness, relief and apprehension in the dining room. We heaped plates with lumps of lamb, piles of carrots and some mystery vegetables. What I would have given for an orange.

I chatted to a couple of young American nurses, Michael and Krystal. He told me he 'works out' and she drinks 'gallons of water' for her rather taut but very clean facial complexion. They were on holiday and had been working in Saudi Arabia. Krystal said she was most furious with the Egyptians' security lapses at Luxor. 'How did these guys get on with their bombs? The scanner was out of order, an electrical fault – come on!'

The captain worked the room, reassuring anyone who spoke Arabic. We learned that the Egyptian Foreign Minister Amr Moussa was in Benghazi negotiating our 'release' from the Libyans.

I recognised the hostess from our flight, Dalia, with whom I'd had terse words. She smiled wanly and said, 'I can tell you now what happened. I was so frightened. A man and a boy, they pushed me aside. I thought they wanted to go to the bathroom in first class. I stood in the way, but they pushed me into the seat, and went into the cockpit. Thank God I did not die of a shock. They had bombs. They told the captain, "If you make one move I will blow up the plane." He opened a plastic bag and sprayed things on the floor.'

The Captain said that their first demand had been to be taken to Libya to talk to Colonel Gadaffi. He said that is why we had landed at Martubah near Tobruk – to give us time. The captain told the hijackers that there wasn't enough fuel to get to Tripoli where Gadaffi was. They would wait for him at Tobruk, where the negotiations would continue with their Libyan brothers. On the ground there the Libyan brothers said over the walkie-talkie, 'We will exert all our efforts to meet your demand.'

The hijackers supposedly belonged to no terrorist group. They were said (by the Egyptian authorities) to be 'deranged and mystified persons who believed in scruples and black magic'. They were also alcoholics and drug addicts – anything but Muslim fundamentalists; anything but that.

I decided to take up the offer of a free room in whatever hotel this was and take a shower. Down at reception the sleepy attendant handed over one of those coded plastic card-keys, which fitted a modern room on the fifth floor. Two beds, three lights, hot water, a view of a grey city that could have been anywhere.

I had a flash of inspiration. I looked in the wallet of informative material that hotels provide: guest services, postcards for the hotel, letterhead paper. It was printed in green. Arabic at the top, and seals with some script and the symbol of Libya: two green hands holding a keyhole shape – a mosque, perhaps – that contained a palm tree. Down the bottom of the page, some English. 'TIBESTY Hotel. Jamal Abdelnasser St Benghazi.' That's what the manager had said: not the best hotel, but Tibesty Hotel.

The Australian 6th Division captured Benghazi on 6 February 1941, in the defeat of the Italian forces in Cyrenaica, the contemporary name for this part of Libya. Back then it was an Italian backwater, a redoubt against the fractious Berber tribes, on Mussolini's 'fourth shore of Italy'. It was part of the Italian Empire, as were other bits of the eastern Mediterranean, such as the island of Rhodes. Libya was granted independence by the UN in 1950, and in December 1951, after further negotiations with the Italians, became an independent kingdom under King Idris el-Senussi. Colonel Gadaffi overthrew the king in 1969, and nationalised oil. Libya was part of the short-lived United Arab Republic idea with Egypt and Syria in 1971.

From being something of an early seventies favourite with some of the loopier anti-American left in Australia and elsewhere because of his promotion of so-called 'revolutionary' terrorist groups around the world, Gadaffi has moved somewhere beyond anathema into a nostalgic celebrityhood. He is an icon of times past, a superannuated but still-living Che Guevara.

Failing to find a toothbrush (it was still in my backpack on the airstrip at Tobruk) I tried to tune my little Sony shortwave radio, part of the survival and self-entertainment material in my camera bag. There was nothing on the BBC World Service. Did that mean we were not even news? Surely the Libyans would have beamed their freedom-loving pictures out by now …

Later. I dozed off, woke up, grey light streaming through the curtains. I went downstairs to see what was going on.

The Green Revolution was in full swing. There were exhausted hijackees slumped all over the foyer beneath little green tickets fluttering in the air conditioning. They had maxims on them in English and Arabic from Colonel Gadaffi's magnum opus of the revolution, *The Green Book*: 'The House is to be served by its residents', 'Committees everywhere', 'Who have neither family nor shelter society is their guardian', 'The social, i.e. national, factor is the driving force of human history', 'In need, freedom is latent'.

I liked that last one. I needed to get out of there in order to be free once again.

I toured the shops in the hotel atrium. They were few in number and sparsely visited by customers. I wanted a copy of Colonel Gadaffi's bestselling children's book, which is all the rage in Cairo.

There was no bookshop in the Tibesty Hotel. Shirts and slacks yes, but newspapers and postcards, no. I spoke to my new friend the hotel manager on the first floor of the atrium. By then, he was looking like Basil Fawlty searching for a rat. I mentioned the absence of the Colonel's book. His eyes literally widened. 'But we haven't had a tourist here in four years,' he said. I don't know that the Colonel would think that was a reasonable excuse.

In the foyer, below, a commotion, a crush around the front door. Speak of the devil, it was the Colonel himself! He was being mobbed like a film star. In close-up he looked like one – a man who had woken up too early in a tent, went to make-up for a long day's appearances on TV. His pancake was thick. He wore a sporting white jacket and horizontally striped shirt. It was the uniform of a decaying playboy or Mediterranean yacht owner on the rocks.

Gadaffi appeared among a loose scrum of uniformed security men, unfortunately not the famed Revolutionary Virgins, for the Libyan TV cameras. He chatted with a few star-struck hijackees. I could not get close enough to hear.

Having made his appearance and demonstrated his commitment to anti-terrorism, Gadaffi went, and we waited some more. The day wore on. I drank some coffee with an EgyptAir pilot. He said that he had flown an Airbus to Benghazi twelve hours before. He told me they were waiting for the 'negotiations' to conclude. But when are we leaving? He didn't know. The Egyptian Foreign Minister was still in discussions with the chief of Libyan security.

This was the doldrums of captivity. We were free in Libya, but there was nowhere to go. Travelling alone I was without the company of a network or group of any kind.

I wandered around the hotel, looking out the doorway across a road to Benghazi's shipless harbour, seeing a poster of Gadaffi's smiling face, fists raised in his typical pose – like a man flexing his biceps – surrounded by colourful children.

Looking out of the doorway again, I saw a bus pull up. Then another one. A tremor passed through the crowd, who stood and started to move. No announcement had been made, but somehow everyone knew: it was time to go.

On the plane as we approached Cairo an announcement was made: great dignitaries were waiting for us, and would like to greet us all personally and individually. The dignitaries were the Egyptian Ministers for Tourism and the Interior, and the Chairman of EgyptAir. Lights, more cameras, action: a party.

We taxied to a stop at the EgyptAir terminal. I'd been here before, and was supposed to be here again yesterday. I suddenly felt very tired. As the plane came to a halt, the voice on the intercom asked 'our Japanese friends' to rise and walk forward, tell the attendant on the door their name, and be announced to the waiting throng.

I looked out the window: lights, cameras, buses, dignitaries. 'Yukio … [cheers and applause] Yoshiko … Akira … And now for the Canadian friends.' There were forty of them. 'Our very good friends from Britain … from France … and our American friends.' A dozen get up and make their way forward. 'And now for the Egyptians.' I soon realised that there was no-one left but me, two South Africans and another European type person I'd never noticed before – probably a Belgian.

We were noticed by a hostie. A minute later: 'And now ... the non-Egyptian Europeans!'

That was us. We walked out, and were not greeted by name or by our ambassadors. Our names were not called out, nor were our nationalities. We did not have our hands shaken by a Minister. But we got on the bus to take us to the terminal building. The Third Secretary of the British Embassy was debriefing a sobbing compatriot. He looked up and drawled, 'British are we?'

'I am not British! I am an Australian!'

He didn't care. 'Righteo cobber,' he said. 'Best of luck.'

At the terminal, a wild tea party was in full swing. Four tables groaned with cakes and Cokes. Water and stale ham rolls were being downed at a rapid rate. The Americans were taken to a room of their own; so were the Canadians.

We non-Egyptian Europeans ran a gauntlet of hosties, and were presented with a pink carnation and a rolled up bit of papyrus. It was from Dr Hassan Ragab's (famous) Papyrus Institute, and was not the worst painting I've seen of good old Horus. It had to be him, of course.

I just wanted to get out of Egypt, but I wasn't leaving without my luggage, which, as far as I knew, was sitting on the tarmac at Tobruk. I called the Australian Embassy and left a message on the answering machine. I had a conversation with a general of the tourist police about it. He advised me to wait and see if the plane was leaving Tobruk that night or the next day. I had a room at a nearby hotel. Why didn't I wait there?

Ahmed, the tourist policeman detailed to look after me, came back with the news that the luggage 'might' come in tonight. They were still checking the plane in Tobruk for bombs. I decided to go to the hotel.

My room wasn't the best, but it had beer in the fridge. It faced on to some sort of courtyard, and at midnight they were still partying around the barbecue listening to Pussyfoot loudly on the outdoor stereo. I watched sumo wrestling on the TV; that Akibono is huge. I bought a toothbrush from the hotel shop. I fell asleep.

I was awoken by a call from Michael Smith, Australian Ambassador to Egypt. He'd got my message, had phoned every hotel in Cairo, had found me. When the hijack had been on, he explained, the airline had denied there were any Australians involved. There were Canadians, Americans, Japanese, British and some non-Egyptian Europeans, but no Australians. He had been surprised to hear that I was there, and happy I'd made it. He would come around for breakfast.

I bought yesterday's London *Times*. There was no mention of our adventure in the paper, but there were sobering stories about a German gunman holding seven hostages at Leienkaul, the British mine clearance expert captured by Khmer Rouge deserters in Cambodia, the unrepentant assassin of Yitzhak Rabin haranguing the court in Israel, and seven French Trappist monks abducted by the Armed Islamic Group in Algeria. I thought once again how lucky I had been to be hijacked by either a professional who had had second thoughts, or an amateur who hadn't actually gone off half-cocked.

(I later learned that the hijackers had been extradited to Egypt from Libya for trial. The ambassador faxed me a news report of the sentences they received. Mohamed Mahmoud Hemid Selim, forty-three, was given a life sentence. His son, Khaled Mohamed Mahmoud Hemid, seventeen, received ten years. Ahmed Hussein Kamel Selim, three years. Abdel-Wahab Mukhtar Said, who supplied the explosives to the hijackers, was sentenced to seven years.)

On the way out of the foyer I spotted my familiar blue backpack propped in a corner. I had a toothbrush, I had new cleanish clothes, I had an ambassador to look after me and help get me out of the country, I was alive. *Inshallah* indeed.

The Ambassador, slightly chagrined at missing an Australian in trouble (not that he could have done the slightest thing about it) squired me around the backblocks and vacant offices of the airport, trying to change my ticket. Not much security there.

To catch up with my schedule, I would have to give Israel and Beersheba a miss and go direct to Jordan. This proved more difficult than it should have, but eventually was successful. Having a fluent Arabic speaker at my elbow proved surprisingly decisive in the EgyptAir bureaucracy. They eventually made me first class. That was the least they could do, I thought.

Next day I walked into the EgyptAir terminal to catch a flight to Amman in Jordan. My backpack was scanned. Thank goodness, I thought. I walked through the other scanning device, which I somehow activated. The security guard, a young man with a friendly moustache, asked whether I was carrying a gun.

'No, no gun,' I said.

'Okay.' He motioned me to go through.

That left me weak at the knees.

CHAPTER EIGHT

TO THE KINGDOM, COME!

I MADE MY FIRST-CLASS escape from Cairo, flying over the Suez Canal to Amman in Jordan.

In World War I, the Australian Light Horse regiments and the other units of the Egyptian Expeditionary Force crossed into Sinai in August 1916, beginning the campaign to beat the Turks back from the canal at Romani on the coast.

In 1916, the Light Horse – at least those men who had survived the holocaust of the charge at the Nek, were back from Gallipoli, reformed and reunited with their horses, and part of General Harry Chauvel's Australia and New Zealand Mounted Division.

The action against the Turkish and German forces holding the whole of the Middle East – from, Suez to what was then Palestine and Syria and through to the Turkish border – was under the overall command of the British generals Phillip Chetwode and, from June 1917, Edmund 'Bull' Allenby. Harry Chauvel (he became Sir Harry in January 1917), had command of the three divisions of the Desert Mounted Corps, comprising all the mounted troops: Australian, New Zealand, British and Indian, horses and camels. Also in the picture was the Arab Army under the guidance of Lawrence of Arabia. They harassed their way north and inland from the desert of the Hejaz in Arabia; the conventional troops fought along the coast and up the valley of the Jordan River towards Damascus and Aleppo.

Australians, particularly Chauvel's Light Horse regiments, were prominent in the successful battles fought in this very successful campaign, beginning with Romani in August 1916, followed by several battles at Gaza in March and April 1917, the charge at Beersheba in October, the battles around the Jordan at Es Salt and Amman in April 1918, at Megiddo in September, and culminating in the taking of Damascus on 1 October 1918. It was Chauvel's strategic and tactical sense added to the bravery and elan of the Light-horsemen that won these battles and created new legends in these most legendary lands.

overleaf: Al Khazna (the 'Treasury'), Petra, Jordan

Chauvel was, with Sir John Monash, one of the two great Australian commanders of large forces in World War I, which makes him one of the greater generals of history. In this part of the world that is the highest praise, because these battlefields have tested the best light cavalry for 5000 years. The Australian charge at Beersheba was the last successful cavalry charge in warfare, and Chauvel's very Australian order 'Put Grant straight at it' a fitting culmination of the spirit of cavalry action.

Compare this to the fate of the British Light Horse Brigade in their sacrificial charge in the Crimean War (not that far away) in 1854. This was, in Tennyson's poem, all about sacrifice for queen and empire, about officers who 'blunder'd' to the supreme cost of their men.

Their's not to make reply,
Their's not to reason why,
Their's but to do or die:
Into the Valley of Death
Rode the six hundred.

The Australian Light Horse already knew all about official blundering and about sacrifice. They had experienced it at a horrifying level in the dismounted charge at the Nek, at Anzac in 1915. But at Beersheba, under Australian command, and on their Australian horses, the Light Horse joyfully, it seems, defied military wisdom, and with swords in hand and Adam Lindsay Gordon on their lips, stormed the Turkish defences.

This is how Harry Gullett, Official Historian of the Palestine and Syria campaign describes what happened in the *Official History of Australia in the War of 1914–18, Volume VII, Sinai and Palestine*:

At Beersheba the usual tactics of the Anzacs, though exercised to the full, were found inadequate to overcome the opposition; and the

Light Horsemen, appearing in a new role, threw caution and cunning to the winds and snatched victory at the last moment in a blind, wild, headlong gallop.

The day was on the wane, it was now neck or nothing. There was a brief but tense discussion, in which Fitzgerald and Grant pleaded for the honour of the galloping attack which was clearly in Chauvel's mind. Fitzgerald's (British) yeomanry had their swords and were close behind Chauvel's headquarters; Grant's Australians had only their rifles and bayonets, but they were nearer Beersheba. After a moment's thought, Chauvel gave the lead to the Light Horsemen. 'Put Grant straight at it,' was his terse command ...

It was a great success. For the cost of thirty-one Light-horsemen dead and thirty-two wounded, a Turkish division was captured, along with the vital wells.

Something of the rush and vigour of the charge can be seen in George Lambert's painting at the Australian War Memorial: the power of the horses leaping over the stunned and dying Turks, the dust, the confusion, the closeness of stinking battle, man to man, horse to man. Lambert's battle paintings are not romantic; they are active and athletic, and perhaps there is enjoyment in that, but they are also full of dying.

T. E. Lawrence, fighting with the Arab irregulars further east, noted in *Seven Pillars of Wisdom* that the Light Horse regarded war as a kind of 'point to point race'. That would have been taken as a compliment by Chauvel and his men.

Bypassing Israel meant I wouldn't be able to go to the cemetery at Beersheba to pay my respects to Tibby Cotter, Australian fast bowler, and the others, which I very much regretted. Tibby's story was an individual one, but somehow for me it typified the character of those Anzac crusaders.

Albert 'Tibby' Cotter was a smallish fast bowler from Sydney with a slinging action a bit like Jeff Thomson and a reputation for breaking stumps and bails. Before Beersheba he demonstrated his prowess by hitting the stumps 18 out of 24 times with mud balls, and saying to his mate, 'That's my last bowl, Blue; something is going to happen.'

Joining the 12th Light Horse, Private Cotter was distinguished at the second Gaza engagement, and in action known as a man without fear. Acting as a mounted stretcher-bearer in the Beersheba battle he was 'shot dead by a Turk at close range' according to the *Official History*. He wasn't even supposed to be at the charge; he was supposed to be back at headquarters on guard duty. His cobber 'Blue' told the story later.

Tibby was a great scrounger, 'liable to turn up in the middle of the desert with a bottle of champagne'. On the morning of the charge, he told Blue, 'I've skittled a Turk in one hit; and what do you think he had on him? Here it is – a yard of ling.' After the action he promised his mates a fish supper. Tibby was shot by a machine-gun while riding next to Blue, who went back after the charge and found him still alive. 'Blue,' said Tibby, 'you can have the fish supper on your own.' He died shortly afterwards.

That is so Australian it makes you want to cry, and what came to mind as I was flying close by Tibby's grave at Beersheba.

Ross Smith's is another Australian story from this region. Ross, later Sir Ross, was the legendary Australian airman, and a machine-gunner with the 1st Light Horse at Romani before he volunteered for the Australian Flying Corps in 1917. He learned to fly flimsy aircraft such as Biggles flew: the Bristol fighter and the Handley Page bomber. Ross Smith won a pair of Military Crosses for Biggles-like actions, including landing in the desert and rescuing a mate. Towards the end of the war, in 1918, he helped destroy the remaining German aircraft in the area on the ground at Der'a, which brought thousands of recruits to the green flag of Lawrence of Arabia and the Arab Army. Der'a is now just across the Syrian border, on the road between Amman and Damascus.

It would be a nice gesture on the part of EgyptAir, I thought, if it named one of its aircraft flying from Cairo to Sydney after Ross Smith, because it was he, in November 1918, who pioneered the route out of Cairo as far as Calcutta. In 1919, with brother Keith, he won the £10 000 prize for flying from London to Australia in less than thirty days. Ross Smith died in a flying accident in 1922, a long time ago, but this was his pioneering sky, right here high above old Palestine.

I landed at Queen Alia Airport in Amman. It was a clear black night. No-one knew I was coming tonight. I had the element of surprise, unlike the Light Horse who attacked Hill 3039 and the dug-in Turkish defenders of the village of Amman in March 1918, in the rain.

There are over 1.5 million people living in Amman. It is an unexpectedly modern city, with quite un-Egyptian buildings. White apartment blocks and substantial white houses spread up the hills the Turks defended in 1918. There is no sand on the streets. In fact, Amman looks a little like a landlocked Sydney.

Amman has one similarity to Cairo: rapacious taxi drivers. I met my first at the bus stop. The airport bus stopped in the city somewhere, I didn't know where, certainly not the place I later found to be the main bus station. I got off and was like a bit of meat chucked in a dam, attacked by these nipping yabbie-like taxi drivers. They all knew me, they all knew where I wanted to go, which was something of surprise as I didn't.

'I take you, my friend.'

'America my friend.'

'Welcome in Jordan.'

Amman was once the city of Rabbah Ammon in the Bible, city of the Ammonites with whom King David had much trouble and felt obliged to subjugate in the tenth century BC.

Ammon–Amon–Amun. I had met this god before: in Egypt, with Alexander at Siwa, and in the great temple at Karnak. In

Egypt an inscription at Luxor says Amon-Ra was 'the father of the gods, the fashioner of men, the creator of cattle, the lord of all being': a god of substance, deserving of a city. I liked the idea of the city of Amman owing its name to Ammon, the pagan-named capital so close to the range of the first Christians.

The Egyptian ruler Ptolemy II Philadelphus (reigned 285–246 BC) conquered the area, and the city of Rabbah Ammon, and changed its name to Philadelphia. This is the name the Romans knew when they later absorbed it into the Roman empire as part of the province of Arabia. The Ammonites melded with the Arab people of the region.

On the street, my backpack was thrown off the bus and grabbed by a small man with a big moustache. That was his way of ensuring I became a passenger. I got in the front seat. A pal of the driver's was in the back. We went down the well-lit streets, up and down hills. Amman is built on seven hills, they say; we did three of them.

The taxi stopped, the driver got out, the mystery mate also got out, and they went up the stairs of a very cheap hotel, obviously another mate's place.

'Stay here?' the driver asked when he came back.

Not likely, I thought. I repeated the name of my preferred hotel: Hotel Tyche. 'Titch? Tykee? Titchie?' He had never heard of it. My Arabic pronunciation was still Egyptian flavoured.

I wrote the name down, and we went into another brightly lit hotel with a name in Arabic script. Nicely dressed chaps in bow ties stood behind a marble desk. I showed one of them the piece of paper, and he shouted a blast of Arabic at the driver, who looked sheepish. My place turned out to be a well-established tourist joint not far away. If only I knew to how say 'Tyche' – that is, 'Tykee' – properly.

At the hotel the meter, which had been ticking away all the time, showed 2.362. I handed over one of my precious five

Jordanian dinar notes (universally called JDs) and got two JD change. Change! I felt like a winner.

The ramshackle Hotel Tyche was 40JD a night. It had a fax machine, a bar, a bed, and what sounded like either a wailing wedding or a funeral going on not far away.

I was tired. It had been a long stretch of days. In Australian mode, I rang the embassy, received the recorded message, left one. I rang the tour operator who was supposed to have met me at the Jordanian end of the Allenby Bridge the next day to bring me to where I already was. 'I am already here,' I told him. We arranged to meet at his office. The Ambassador called back. I explained my business in Amman to her and told some stories: mine and the Light Horse's. Anzac Day was coming up, and the information about the Australian relationship with Amman was useful.

At the end of March 1918 the Australian Light Horse, the Camel Corps and the 60th Division (the 'Londoners') forded the flooded river Jordan to raid the Hejaz Railway at Amman. This bloody episode, the most costly of all the actions in which the Light Horse participated, is best described in Harry Gullett's *Official History* volume on Sinai and Palestine.

Harry Gullett was a former *Sydney Morning Herald* journalist. An Official War Correspondent in World War I in France, he returned to Australia, enlisted as gunner and returned to England in 1917. Charles Bean recruited him there for the beginning of the Australian War Museum, which became the Australian War Memorial. Gullett was its first director. Bean then recommended him to be the war correspondent for the Palestine campaign. He arrived in 1918 and covered the events of that year.

Gullett had a role in the reconciliation process after the Surafend incident in 1919. He persuaded Allenby to praise the overall great achievements of the Light Horse and the Anzac Mounted Division, assuaging the bitterness felt by the

Australians who believed they had been scapegoated by faint praise. What the Egyptians felt is another matter.

Gullett had a varied career after the war. He wrote the *Official History*, was director of the Australian Immigration Bureau for Billy Hughes, and in 1925 became a Nationalist member of federal parliament. He was Minister for External Affairs in the 1939 Menzies government and was killed in an air crash near Canberra in 1940.

Gullett's *Official History* was a primary source for the Light Horse part of the Anzac legend. Gullett was one of those plain-writing Australian journalists of his day who, apparently artlessly, was also one of the most evocative writers we have had.

Here is Gullett on the 2nd Light Horse riding to war in the land of the Bible after Beersheba. They rode into Jerusalem, just across the Jordan River from Amman:

Riding past the olive groves to Ramleh, the Light Horsemen followed the main road to Latron, a very gay and eager column; for although heavy fighting might be ahead, they would before that be seeing Jerusalem, and perhaps Bethlehem, and every mind anticipated the crossing of the Jordan on the way to the land of Moab. They rode with the strong purpose of old soldiers, but still with the sharp expectancy of happy travellers venturing into a famous land touched with mystery and hallowed by religion, history and tradition, all more or less familiar to them since their childhood. On either side of them was the glory of a spring day on the rolling maritime plain, with its thousand crazily-shaped little patches of crops illumined with wild flowers. Overhead was a blue sky flecked with occasional light clouds, larks sang their sustained song, and in the long column of horsemen there was a note of joy and youth rare in that exhausted old land of suffering and ruins.

The men of the 2nd Light Horse Brigade at Jerusalem and the Camel Brigade at Bethlehem were for the first time in the Holy Places; careless of what awaited them east of the Jordan, they explored the cities with the zest of pilgrims ... The curiosity of the men was boundless; and their diligent reading of the Old and New Testaments, combined with a true reverence, strangely broken by sceptical challenges and even lapses into daring, good-humoured blasphemy, imposed a heavy strain on the physical endurance, the biblical knowledge of the regimental padres. From daylight to dark these good men walked the many ways of Christ at the head of successive parties of troopers, who enjoyed nothing so much as 'to take a fall' out of their guides. Full of significant suggestion was this spectacle of young Australian Light Horsemen, led by churchmen in military dress and emu feathers, heavy boots, and clinking spurs, proceeding along the Via Dolorosa or gathered round the traditional Stations of the Cross.

One of these padres, the Rev. Maitland Woods, once shrewdly, if romantically, said in a Thanksgiving service after victory, 'I would describe the Light-horseman as a man who, while denying he is a Christian, practises all the Christian virtues.'

Across the Jordan, the Hejaz Railway, from Damascus north to Constantinople, and south to Medina in Arabia was the only line of communication and supply for the Turkish forces in the Great War. Destroying it, or cutting access to it, was a way of shortening the war in the area and keeping the Turks occupied. Lawrence and the Arab Army destroyed sections of the line, but the Turks always repaired it; however, if the tunnels and viaducts through the hills around Amman could be destroyed they would not be so easily repaired.

The March attack was focussed on Hill 3039, the Jebel Amman, the main hill in the city where most of the embassies are now concentrated. It guarded the Hejaz Railway tunnels and viaducts to the east, which still exist, although the railway is now only used for freight. It was muddy, the attack was undermanned, and it was perhaps too ambitious. There was little or no artillery to help clear the Turkish machine-gun defences.

Despite the usual heroics, Gullett said, 'Adverse weather conditions and the opposition encountered prevented these objects [destruction of the railway, the viaducts, Amman station] from being completely obtained.' He went on, 'Damage was trifling and of very little embarrassment to the enemy. The failure was expensive.'

The Anzac Mounted Division lost 118 officers and men killed, 551 wounded and fifty-five missing. It was the 'blackest day' of the Light Horse campaign in Palestine. Wrote Gullett:

Troops feel some failures more sharply than others, and the measure of regret and resentment has very little to do with the previous prospects of success. Amman was almost a hopeless enterprise and all ranks might have accepted defeat without any suspicion of reproach. But the Australians and New Zealanders felt their reverse on the bleak tableland more deeply than any other reverse in the long war, with the single exception of Gallipoli ... every Australian and New Zealander who fought at Amman prayed for the day he would fight there again ...

Amman was not taken until 26 September 1918, when the Australians and New Zealanders showed great dash and courage on their horses and with the bayonet. The old Roman citadel was taken by elements of the 5th Light Horse and New Zealand's gallant Canterburys. Turkish resistance, already wavering, collapsed on the appearance of the Queenslanders of the 7th Light Horse.

Others captured the Amman railway station and cut off the Turkish forces to the south, which were concentrated in the vicinity of the railhead at Ma'an, moving north towards Ziza, now Al Jiza where the Queen Alia Airport is situated. These Turks were threatened by 10 000 of the Arab Army, and would not surrender to them or to a small group of Anzacs.

An advance guard of Light Horse galloped to the Turkish position and into one of those wonderfully improbable Australian moments in the war. It was decided to 'join forces' with the Turks for the night of the 28 September, and, taking two Arab sheikhs from the Arab Army with them, the Light Horse detachment entered the Turkish camp. They told the Turks to keep their weapons and maintain their positions, and told the sheikhs that if they were attacked the first people shot would be them.

Here is how Gullett described it:

> The sheikhs sent out messengers to inform their followers of this threat, and the Turks and the Australians proceeded, after years of bitter fighting, to bivouac together. They gathered about the same fires, exchanging their food, making chappatis together, and by many signs expressing reciprocal respect and admiration. The Australians, although outnumbered eight to one, had no concern for their safety, and the confidence with which they moved about the armed lines was a tribute to the honour of the Turks. Perhaps in all their campaigning the Light-horsemen were never so richly entertained.

Next day the Australian contingent was reinforced and everyone marched back to Amman. This time the campaign casualties in capturing Amman were light: twenty-seven killed, 105 wounded, seven missing.

One morning I tuned in my radio to the unmistakable tones of Tim Lane, Melbourne ABC's sport calling legend. Football was mentioned in the wavering long waves of Radio Australia, which I imagined wafting over the Himalayas towards me like a floating punt kick, but, as usual here in the Middle East, the signal disappeared before I got the scores.

Outside the hotel was a row of three old, red befinned American cars, Chevrolets and an Oldsmobile, sitting in the cold sun. An overweight driver with bad teeth and wheezing, fitful English offered to take me to the office of the tour operator.

I thought I'd go to Jerash, another fabled Roman town up in the Jordan Valley, after making the stop. The driver tried to start the Chevvie but it wouldn't start with the key. He pushed it with one foot out of the door and rolled it down the hill. The engine caught. The suspension rolled like a waterbed. The brakes screeched to a stop at red lights. The driver offered to do 'full tour'. 'Amman, Jerash, castle. Full tour. You want? 40JD. I wait.'

I said that I didn't want him to wait. I might be some time. The car was dangerous, not fit for a big trip. He said, 'No pay me. I wait.'

Inside the tour office, Abdeen, a young Palestinian Jordanian, told me I was very lucky that I had come direct from Cairo to Amman. He said that very probably I would have been stopped from entering Syria if I had gone via Israel. I had been told that it was okay as long as you got your Israeli passport stamps on a loose leaf of paper. You can even get your Jordanian entry stamp on a loose leaf.

'What you say is true,' Abdeen said, 'but at the Syrian border they will want to know how you got into Jordan without a stamp.' Ahah. It was like the dog who did not bark – a vital clue for Sherlock Holmes and me.

'At the border with Syria they look for proof of entry, which you now have, before they let you in. Otherwise, sorry, and you have to have another nice time in the kingdom.'

We talked a little about his background. I told him that Australians had helped liberate Amman from the Turks in 1918. His sense of history didn't encompass World War I; it was a thousand years old and ten or twenty years old, with not much in between.

Abdeen said, 'Israelis are no angels and the Palestinians are no angels either. Most people on both sides don't want the war to go on, but some people on both sides might be defined as fanatics. They like to fight. They want to fight! They will always fight.'

On the phone, he found me a taxi to go to Jerash.

I thought of this driver as the 'the Singing Defective'. He drove an early eighties Corolla and provided entertainment with non-stop singing in Arabic and bad, dirty jokes.

'What country are you?'

'Australia.'

'But where are you from?'

'Australia.'

'Where is your father from?'

'England. He came to Australia sixty years ago.'

'Ah. You are English.'

'No, I was born in Australia.'

'And your mother?'

'She was born in Australia. Her family has been in Australia for 170 years.'

'So long. But she is English also?'

'They came from England, yes. But she is Australian.'

'So how long is Australia?'

'Aborigines, 80 000 years; Europeans, 200 years; one nation, ninety-five years.'

'Ah.'

'Australians fought here in 1918.'

'Here? Why?'

'World War I.'

'Ah, English war.'

'Well …'

'I Palestinian. No, I am born in Jordan. My father, my mother Palestine. I am Jordan. Like you, English, Australia. Now Jordan. Have passport.'

To Jerash, the olive green hills, white spring blossom. Jerash was a small trading town from the time of Alexander in the 300s BC which prospered in the next-half dozen centuries, especially in Roman times, along with Petra to the south and Palmyra to the north. Pompey may have dropped in around 63 BC – he visited Petra. The emperor Hadrian stayed for a month or so in 29 AD.

Today the ruins of Jerash are terrifically well preserved and renovated, perhaps the best Roman ruins in the region. It's a fairly compact site, standing beside the modern village of Jerash, on the road to Damascus.

There are two theatres being restored, a beautiful elliptical colonnaded forum, and some nice long streets. I walked the empty site – there was just a handful of visitors – watched the archeologists at work on the north theatre with cranes, and picked a few red poppies.

Wherever there are traders, you'll find the mother of goddesses and patron of the city, Artemis, and the splendidly preserved temple at Jerash is some indication of the arrangement, if not the scale, of the Temple of Artemis at Ephesus, the ancient wonder.

On the way back we drove singing into the hills to Ajlun, where there was an 'anti-Crusader' castle. High on a spur, it dominates local access to the Jordan Valley. Like all castle builders, Saladin's nephew, Izz as-Din Urama bin Munqidh, knew where to build in the twelfth century. That day it took twenty minutes of careful driving to get to the top. Walking the stones up with horse or donkeys would seem impossible. How did they build it?

Damaged by Mongols, rebuilt by Mamelukes, garrisoned by Ottoman Turks, the castle was damaged further by earthquakes and was abandoned in the seventeenth century. Now restored, it has a spectacular view down the Jordan Valley. I stood and looked, but my peace was interrupted by a loud German tour leader who commenced a long speech, and chattering, disdainful Frenchmen of a certain age, wearing pastel jumpers jauntily on their shoulders.

Next day, waiting for the bus to Petra, I read the *Jordan Times*, one of the better English-language newspapers in the region. Coming from Cairo, I thought the traffic in Amman was very civilised, but not a letter writer named Al Ghaserian, who wrote, from the heart, that drivers should note the following points:

Stop signs: watch out. These are death traps. You better drive fast to avoid any surprises. Yield signs: don't yield. Drive through and the rest is God's will. No entry signs: in pure English, you can drive through but in reverse or if you own a special car – a Mercedes or BMW. Speed limit: don't bother. Have fun. Police cars do! Traffic lights: never ever in your life be the first one to stop at a red traffic light. This is a cowardly move. Can you hoot loudly? The minute the light turns green, you must hoot the car in front. This is a sign of manhood.

Consoling thoughts as I boarded the bus south to the fabled lost city of Petra, made famous by intrepid travellers and Indiana Jones, who galloped round the corner of the wadi and was confronted by the astounding sight of the pink Treasury building.

Petra was rescued from literary neglect by E. M. Forster as much as anyone. He was the one who recalled the obscure poet Dean Burgon's line about Petra 'the rose red city half as old as time' in a story about literary immortality called the *Celestial Omnibus* in 1911. Indiana Jones and E. M. Forster: that was enough to make me lust to see the ruins for myself.

In the *Jordan Times* I had read the boast that a million tourists had visited Petra in 1995. A million! Not so long ago it was one of the hardest places in the world to get to, the handful of visitors bringing back tales of the wonderful rock-cut tombs and temples of the Nabataeans, and the roaring flash floods that would occasionally catch and drown visitors in the narrow wadi known as the Siq. Jacob Burkhardt, a Swiss traveller, was the one who rediscovered the place in 1812, after it had been hidden from the world by the locals for 1500 years.

Now there are bus-loads of daytrippers from Amman, and JETT-bus-loads of people who stay a night or two in the village clinging to the hillside of the crevassed moonscape outside the entrance to the site.

It was rocky and green until the bus approached Wadi Musa,

the village and valley nearest Petra. Wadi Musa was a long building site with a dozen or more hotels in various stages of construction.

Wadi Musa, or Petra-the-village is built mostly on the up-slope from the road of the valley, the stream below a repository for building materials and other rubbish. The road into the town is dusty with the Middle East's universal solvent: cement. There are a few souvenir shops with Bedouin paraphernalia, fax and post offices, soft drink and even 'lamburger' sandwich store-fronts.

I was staying at the Treasury Hotel, which turned out to be back up the steep hill. The small hotel, recently renovated, was clean, white, and had a view from the room of the side of the hill. But from the foyer and dining room there was a spectacular view across the valley towards Petra, which looked like a crumpled grey and brown blanket.

I walked a kilometre downhill to the entrance, where the Petra Rest House and the visitors centre are set in a little no-go-for-buses area. The visitors centre is sponsored by the Noor el-Hussein Foundation. Queen Noor is King Hussein's wife. The local ladies auxiliary was selling handicrafts, like a state school stall.

It costs 20JD for a day ticket to the site – about A$45. There were T-shirt, trinket, cap and card stalls around, and surly guides buying wads of tickets with bricks of money for their bus-loads, thinking they could queue jump the solitary traveller. Not likely.

'There's a queue.'

'Eh?'

'I'm next, brother.'

'I've got fifty people on the bus.'

'You'll have to wait two minutes more.'

'Why should I?'

'Because … because … I'm an Australian and I'm not going to be pushed around, okay?'

'Australian, Australian, okay, okay.'

Inside the gate, on the left, is a stable area for hundreds of ponies and donkeys, complete with tin-roofed shelters. This is the Brooke Hospital for Animals, paid for by a lady disturbed at the ponies broiling in the sun. The Bedouin pony boys gallop up and down Wadi Musa raising dust and having a whale of a time. I was happy to see that the blanket-saddled ponies used stirrups, as I had read somewhere that the Nabataeans had introduced the stirrup to the West: a technological innovation that had changed the face of warfare and laid the way for the Light Horse. The Nabataeans built and lived in the best bits of Petra from around 600 BC until 100 AD, when it was Romanised.

The pony boys ask, politely by Egyptian standards, whether you'd like a ride or not, and are especially solicitous of overweight older ladies, sometimes offering to fetch a donkey and cart. Given the numberless tourists who now trudge down the pebbly track, they must get enough replies in the affirmative to make the whole thing worthwhile.

The four-legged transports have their own pony-track, separated from pedestrians by a low stone wall, but they do their beseeching on the walking track. The pony track is also used for spectacular galloping back to the start from their destination.

As a dedicated walker, I trudged for the half-hour or so to the entrance to the Siq. It was like walking down a street towards a big football match, there were so many people.

Down the highway of Wadi Musa, the butter-coloured sandstone rises round and soft into a pale blue sky. A donkey stands on top, a morose silhouette. The Snakes Tomb and the Obelisk Tomb are cut into the rock. These are eroded by wind and water in a preview of what has happened to most of the tombs further in.

The wide expanse of the wadi (and the ponies), stops at the fissure of the Siq. Those who have ridden down seem a little surprised that their 10JD or 15JD only gets them to the beginning of the difficult walk. Only the oldish and the infirm are allowed to be carried further, in 'off peak' periods.

There is a sign telling us that a diversion dam and tunnel had been built, where the Nabataeans also had had one, to prevent the flash flood carrying off tourists as one did in 1963, killing twenty-three. It didn't feel like rain anyway.

Now the bus-loads form into single file and trudge down the narrow defile of striped reds and ochres, narrowing in parts to a metre across and rising to over 1000 metres high.

This is one of the most quietly exciting walks to be had anywhere, despite the hordes doing it. For Australians it's a bit like the Standley Chasm with ruins at the end of it. The ground is sand mixed with pebbles large enough to slip on and roll an ankle, which of course I did.

The track through here seems a long way. It is a twisting couple of kilometres, in parts with Roman paving exposed, views coming into and out of focus, the sun slanting across the top, photographers lined up at the points where blue sky and red rock make a pattern, or a tomb is carved in deep shadow.

Along the way I was passed by a group of eight or nine shaven-headed English youths, shirts off, white skins set to go a painful puce, singing what seemed to be a soccer song. They elbowed their way past the faltering line of slow tourists, looking neither left nor right, up nor down. They seemed set to 'do' Petra by marching in and marching straight out again.

The whole area is mysterious and, with heightened anticipation accompanying each painful step, it is through an opening that you first glimpse the Treasury, the famous al Khazna.

From within a dark shadow you see the sun glowing on the rock. It *is* rose-red; a dusky orange–pink glowing carving thirty metres high emerging as you walk around the last corner. I stopped, said 'wow' under my breath, and noticed that everyone else had stopped as well. This single glimpse had made the walk – hell, the whole trip – worthwhile. This place went on my list of wonders that were still wonderful.

I leaned against the cool rock of the Siq and just watched, and said under my breath: 'Match me such a marvel save in eastern clime, A rose red city half as old as time.'

The last five or ten metres around the corner then revealed the carved building, in all its contemporary glory. In the basketball-court sized opening were a dozen trinket sellers, a camel or two, other sellers flogging bottles of coloured sand – were those the sands of time? – and 500 people jostling for the single spot from which to take the perfect pic. The impression was an unhappy one: that vista! Those tawdry salesmen!

The Treasury is protected from wind and blowing sand much better than virtually every other building in Petra. It is about forty metres high, 2000 years old and carved directly from the sand-stone. Visitors climb the steps up, to find a dark and completely empty chamber hewn from the rock, with two side rooms; empty, that is, save for the scrawlings and carvings of a hundred years of visitors determined to leave their mark. It's called the Treasury because, despite the evidence of one's eyes that it is solid rock, a local legend has it that there is treasure hidden 'inside' it, perhaps in the urn-like carving scarred with rifle and cannon shots near the top of the monument.

I then watched with incredulity as a scarfed teenage girl asked her mother to wait while she carved her initials on the entrance to the chamber. She didn't pause while I took a picture of her in this act of desecration.

But what are Nabataean ruins to modern Jordanians – for that is what I took this girl to be – except soft sandstone as ripe for a graffitist as it has been for the abrasion of the wind.

I walked outside and on into the widening wadi, past a collection of tea and cola counters with chairs and a shady tree which I marked as a place to stop at on the way back.

The weather has had an effect on the more exposed carved tombs, such as the theatre which now looks as if it were made of chocolate poured by Salvador Dali on a hot day. It once seated around 8000 Nabataeans for shows and speeches.

Five hundred metres further round on the right-hand side were three spectacular tombs: the Urn Tomb, later used as a Byzantine church, which was well worth the climb up, and the weathered Corinthian and Palace Tombs. There were more spectacular views up there, sitting on the edge of the terrace in front of the large, empty chamber, looking out into an amphitheatre the size of the MCG.

One thing I did notice very quickly was that the local Bedouin, who had been relocated to another village twenty years before, were back there with silver trinkets in all the most inaccessible places. It was slightly disconcerting to have climbed 740 metres up steep and dangerous stone steps to find a stall and a persuasive saleswoman at the top, accompanied by a couple of sharp-eyed scallywags.

From up there the whole of 'Roman' Petra spreads out below at the bottom of the continuation of Wadi Musa. It is beautiful, forbidding and inhospitable country, folded away to each side like a meringue moonscape. It is very difficult to understand how anyone got here, let alone spent hundreds, nearly a thousand years there. The ways in would have been hard to find and water intermittent unless stored in massive cisterns, which I didn't see in this part of Petra.

I was now about four hours in, and felt compelled to keep going. I skirted the excavations behind the Qasr al Bint (another temple, of the Winged Lions) and climbed behind the camp used by the Department of Antiquities (with public toilets) to a small museum. It was on a high path around a massif between the end of Wadi Musa and two other wadis which converged there.

There was very little in the museum, testimony either to years of looting or years of little digging. But among the few exhibits were two small carvings of horses in a glass case in the middle of the room. They were of Nabataean vintage and seemed to have stirrups. I was chuffed by this little discovery, even if my stirrup theory is disputed.

Outside the museum the path continued precipitously around the edge of the massif, past more amazing views of cliffs and valleys, a circular fort, which was full of kids whooping to the echo, and the remains of what is said to be a twelfth century Crusader (some say anti-Crusader) fortress.

I limped back towards the theatre and the Treasury, stopped for a cola under the tree, and listened to the Bedouin boys charm an elderly American lady into more tea plus a ride back in a donkey cart to the entrance. I stumbled further, stopping only to gawp at the Treasury again, knowing, like Indiana Jones, that I would not pass this way again.

In the Siq I was passed by the old lady in the cart looking as pleased as the Queen of Sheba. At the exit I stopped for another restorative Coke at the aptly named Rest House.

Sitting in the fading sun I watched the English soccer lads sitting over at the edge of the terrace. They had obviously arrived there quite a while before me, as the ground was littered with beer bottles. They were red-raw now, offensive and looking for trouble.

Whatever their view on wearing the veil might have been, or on Western women's mode of dress at this tourist resort, no-one deserved the abuse by these yobs hurled at any passing female who declined their invitation to join them. It was a measure of the tolerance of the local people that the yobbos lasted as long as they did. Only when they dropped or threw a couple of bottles did a posse of waiters emerge and start cleaning up. One of them suggested the lads should move on before anything else happened. One of the party dropped another bottle before a wiser, or more sober, member of the party said, 'Lessgo soomwhr they like our money, lads' and off they went. I wondered why they had come to Petra at all.

By the end of the next day I was back in Amman after a ride in a 'local' bus. As usual the bus dropped passengers on the outskirts of town. I caught a taxi to the bus terminal, and waited. I watched a bus leave for Baghdad. No thanks. I waited some more and then went around the corner for a quick plate of *fuul* and a coffee. 'Things very bad Jordan,' said the man next to me. He was Mr Hassan who worked for the Jordan Oil Refinery, supported six children 'and their mother and her mother. Things very bad Jordan.' He earned 450JD a month, and received one month's bonus every six months. He owned his house and a car and insisted on buying lunch. 'You come again to the kingdom, come! Show you everything. Bring wife, children. Things very bad Jordan. How to come to Australia? Australian visa very hard for Jordanian.'

A spontaneous act of kindness. I promised, 'next time in the kingdom' and caught the bus that travelled the road to Damascus.

CHAPTER NINE

ON THE ROAD THROUGH DAMASCUS

HIGH WITH ANTICIPATION, I approached the border between Jordan and Syria sitting in the back of the bus fending off a dozen children who had, since leaving Amman, wanted to practise English.

'Hello. What your name. Ho ho ho,' each child chortled in turn.

'My name is Garrie. What is your name?'

'Hello Mr Garrie. Ho ho ho. Goodbye. Mr Garrie? What is my name? Ho ho ho.'

It was hard to maintain concentration on any potential trouble ahead in the face of an hour's verbal gymnastics involving the same few words and the same joke. I was distracted from the task at hand, and breezed through the Jordanian exit procedures and, a few kilometres further on, the Syrian entry system with little bother. A few of the kids accompanied me to the desk, laughing at me some more as I stood in the wrong queue. I wasn't Jordanian was I? I was 'tourism, there, there'. Fill in the yellow form, stamp, stamp, okayokay.

There were pillboxes and guard towers, and there were armed Syrians in uniform who got on the bus between the border crossing point and the inner perimeter to check that the right stamps were in everyone's passports. They were cold and not interested in conversation, not even with the kids. There was no obvious interest on either side of the border in either customs or the security checking of baggage.

After the nervous anticipation of the border, the ride to Damascus was uneventful. Along the road there were strange sights in the dusk, such as winking lights at intersections in Der'a like Christmas trees, and pictures of President Assad and his late son Basil set in a whirligig frame of bright coloured lights. There were tank and aircraft bunkers and radar installations swinging in silhouette. The Golan Heights and Lebanon were not far away on the left. Nothing is very far away in this part of the world.

I got out at the bus station in Damascus. As usual, I was assailed by taxi touts and, as usual, I picked the wrong one.

overleaf: Bedouin on the road to Palmyra, Syria

Despite the out-of-date guidebook information that you have to change heaps of money at the bad official rate at the border, no-one at the border had asked me. I explained this to the taxi driver. 'Change money. *Cambio.*'

'Okayokayokay.'

He was a thin, desperate-seeming man, always chewing. He parked in the dark behind a swank hotel, the white marble interior glowing into the night. It was a Marriot – not my scene, or his. We walked in, and he conducted me past a bevy of businessmen in tight-fitting suits, strutting around the foyer like self-satisfied pigeons. We headed out the back to where the money-changers hang out. All is in darkness. No money! The taxi driver looked even more furtive. I asked at the newsagent. The boy inside laughed: buy a paper in dinars, get change in Syrian pounds? Ho ho ho. What did I think this place was? A tourist hotel?

We scuttled out and drove in silence to the Hotel Internationale de Damasc where I had booked a room. All I had on me was a 5JD note. I gave the taxi driver the 5JD, a small fortune of about S£500 (A$10). No change. He shrugged. I delivered a small lecture on the ethics of taxi-driving for tourist suckers. He left.

The small foyer was full of Germans. They moved about like a squadron of panzers; nothing could stand in their way, not even a weary, limping backpacker. They didn't even see me, pushing and demanding service of the many apparently blind and deaf chaps behind the counter.

'You with group?'

'No, I am alone.'

'Alone?' A raised eyebrow. Alone!

The hotel was oldish and without much in the way of the Gallic charm suggested by its name. It did have Beethoven piano sonatas on the room radio and a great big gum tree out the front. The restaurant was closed, but a man delivered a chicken, a potato and a bottle of the local beer, which, as they say in Adelaide, is cloudy but fine. This was Barada beer, named for the once-sparkling stream that watered this great city. If a beer in Melbourne were named Yarra … You get the picture? It was chewy, but it did the job.

Next morning, I took a taxi to the embassy, which was a quick way of becoming completely disoriented in Damascus. There were long wide streets, great squares, the great enclosing hills of Mt Kassioun, and no clear sight of the famed River Barada or the orchards in the huge meadow that once extended along the river to the west.

We found the embassy after asking directions of various groups of men in civilian clothes – some with automatic weapons slung over a shoulder – hanging around the intersections. These men are not gangs of unemployed, they are the (not so) secret police, the Mahabaret. Naturally they know where things are.

In the olden days, travellers sat in shaded coffee houses out on the meadow by the Barada. In 1617 a traveller named Henry Maundrell, watched Turks 'regaling themselves in this pleasant place; there being nothing which they behold with so much delight as greens and water: to which if a beautiful face be added, they have a proverb, that all three together make a perfect antidote to melancholy.'

The Australian Embassy is not set in such a meadow, but is adjacent to a great field of what seemed to be prickly pear. The ambassador, Jim Dolymore, took me out the back of the embassy to the Commonwealth Cemetery, which is set in this strange cactus environment.

Over 300 Australians are buried in that peaceful spot: 139 from 1914–18 and 172 from 1939–45. The Damascus Cemetery is designed along standard Commowealth War Graves Commission lines, but is no less powerful for that reason. It is comforting that all over the world there are places like this, meticulously and lovingly cared for by the War Graves Commission's local workers.

I mentioned to the ambassador that places like this one were possibly the main reason left for there to be a Commonwealth, but he remained diplomatically silent on the subject. 'You can't forget the Commonwealth Games,' he said.

There are others from the Commonwealth, when it was an Empire, buried here. There are Greek names, Hindu names, pre-partition Muslim Indian names, British names. There's a memorial to the Indian soldiers buried here. Many of the Australians seem to have died from typhoid and dysentery between 11 and 29 October 1918: after they had defeated the Turkish enemy.

Lunch was at a local cafe with a couple of other people from the Australian Embassy, and the British Military Attaché, Colonel Dick Clarke, a big, bluff, balding ex-soldier with a passion for the military history of Syria, especially in World War I. We had a spirited chat about who was first into Damascus in 1918. I stuck to the official Australian line: we were. Colonel Clarke made the not very strong case for Lawrence of Arabia, and we all agreed that the local Damascenes had taken matters into their own hands before either of our liberating forces arrived.

The ambassador said he had read about a Syrian woman's reaction to to the liberating Australians; that she, at first, thought her city was suffering another unwanted invasion, but that in the next breath she talked about how wonderful the Light Horse looked on their big horses with their emu-feathered hats, and how free she felt.

On the night of 30 September 1918, Turkish rule had virtually ceased in Damascus. All night the streets and bazaars were in a tumult of excited crowds as the Arab populace thronged the streets. They carried the Hejaz flag and fired rifles in the air, exulting in what they deemed their new found nationalism and threatening the fearful but expectant Christians. Allenby's capture of Jerusalem had seemed to the Christians the answer of providence to their centuries of prayer; the news of Chauvel and the Australians' rushing approach to Damascus was a miracle of divine dispensation.

Harry Gullett wrote in the *Official History*:

> The city has always endured as the home of a rich and numerous people ... nature intended this ancient haunt of men for an enduring homing place ... The torrential Barada River, fed by the ever-flowing springs of the Lebanons, bursts from its gorge at the very gates of the city and, over the rich but thirsty plain, creates and sustains a wide and prolific garden ... The traveller comes suddenly on the great city set in a beautiful forest of orchards and plantations, brilliant with the vivid flowers of subtropical climes ... Damascus, with all its easy wealth, built up by water, rich soil and strong sunshine, has always been an open town to a resolute invader.

None of this exists now, except the city. The river is a drain, the orchards are built over by modern Damascus.

The Australians were coming from nearby Duma, where the day before there had been a terrible battle, a slaughter of Turks caught in a narrow gorge. General Wilson of the 3rd Light Horse found, wrote Gullett:

> The passage through the gorge was restricted to a walk by the terrible effects of the previous evening's slaughter. The roadway was heaped up with over 370 dead and wounded Turks and Germans, vehicles and killed and maimed teams of cattle and horses. A flock of sheep which had accompanied one of the columns were all dead upon the road, and even dogs had been shot ... But though the scene was grim, and they as yet knew nothing of the sporting enterprise ahead, the Western Australians, long seasoned alike to the horrors and risks of war, rode with light hearts through the early morning shadows of the winding pass. The train at Dumar (taken with 480 prisoners) had contained besides great wealth in gold and

silver coin, a store of German cigars; and as the troopers passed out of the gorge, and the sun-touched minarets of the city rose above the beautiful tangle of green gardens splashed with ripening fruit and gay with flowers, they blew forth clouds of smoke, and seemed to have no thought beyond their keen relish of the moment.

They bowled along beside the Barada into the city, not knowing what might be waiting. This is the picture of them, galloping into Damascus in H. Septimus Powers' painting *Into Damascus* in the Australian War Memorial: swords at the ready, hats firm on head, solid in the saddle, emu feathers fluttering, the blue Barada a creek beside them, the walls of the wadi rising behind, a blue sky; 200 Australians about to invade the most ancient city.

The Light Horse rode past the Orient and Victoria hotels, and the Palace Hotel (now Al Quaitby Street where the National Museum stands), swinging around the railway station to what was then the town hall and along the northern wall of the Old City, past the tomb of Saladin himself.

At the town hall, Lieutenant Colonel Olden of the 10th Light Horse told Emir Said, who seemed to be in charge, that he was surrounded by thousands of Chauvel's troops and that resistance was impossible. He demanded that the Australian troops not be molested. Emir Said agreed and said, 'In the name of the civil population of Damascus, I welcome the British army.' Olden was too polite to point out that this was the bloody Australian Light Horse. The Emir formally wrote out these assurances, and Olden left on the Homs Road, chasing more Turks.

Harry Gullett wrote:

The Australians on this wonderful morning were the only calm purposeful men in this clamorous city. Years of campaigning had moulded them into reserved men of the world, and the streets of old Damascus were but a stage in the long path of war. They rode with drawn swords, dusty and unshaven, their big hats battered and drooping, through the excited people of that ancient city, with the same easy casual bearing, and the same quiet self-confidence, which marked their bearing on the country tracks at home.

They ate their grapes, and smoked their cigars, and missed no dark smiling eyes at the windows; but they showed no excitement or elation. And their lean long-tailed horses, at home now like their riders on any road in the world, found nothing in the shouting mob or banging rifles of the Arabs, or in the narrow ways and vivid hues of the bazaars, to cause them once to shy or even cock an ear.

Wilson, too, rode off chasing the Turks with 'every man in his brigade'. After Wilson had cleared the streets, Lawrence rode into the town with a few Arab horsemen on the heels of the advance guard of the Indian 14th Cavalry Brigade. The Arabs believed they shared with the Indians the honour of first entry, and made a melodramatic demonstration.

Twelve-thousand Turks surrendered that day, sick with typhus and other diseases. 'The Turkish tragedy was culminating in Damascus,' wrote Lawrence. 'They had been ill cared for, there was little food in the city, and there were problems feeding Allenby's army as it poured into the city, let alone the Turkish prisoners.'

The three cavalry divisions rejoiced in their pleasant surroundings. They had arrived too late for the apricots, for which the orchards of Damascus were famous, but (Gullett again): 'The wide vineyards were laden with grapes of rare quality, and the city stalls glowed with pomegranates and other luscious fruits. After their long summer ride over the bare plains, the men delighted in the widespread plantations, and rested and slept within sight and sound of cold clear running water. Damascus seemed indeed to have been worth the winning.'

The Barada, such as it is, still runs north of the Old City and the famous *souk*, one of the splendours of shopping anywhere in the world. Colonel Clarke told me that if I were to buy anything in the *souk*, I should first look at Mr Hassahn Zahabi's, just by the entrance to the Omayyad Mosque.

I set off for the entrance to the main shopping street of the whole bazaar, the Souk al-Hamidyah. This is a wide, covered way selling bolts of vivid damask silk, those ill-fitting black suits, Damascene inlaid mother of pearl boxes, brassware, whistles, jewellery, pots and pans. Damascus is not exactly overrun with tourists – there are hardly any compared to Khan el Khalili market in Cairo – and as a consequence must sell a few things that Damascenes themselves want to buy. Al-Hamidyah is the retail commercial part of this *souk*; around a corner are narrower and darker lanes and streets selling nuts and figs, spices and saffron. I bought a big handful of vivid orange saffron threads for S£50.

Accosted by hopeful, cheerful and friendly salesmen (no women), who hurtled from their shop fronts on seeing the shadow of a tourist, I wandered down al-Hamidyah looking for Mr Hassahn's emporium.

It was perfectly obvious: just to the left of the two sizable Roman columns which once were part of the western gate of the old city and the tourist entrance to the mosque.

Mr Hassahn was one of the most charming salesmen I had ever met. He didn't want to sell anything. He had no prices. He had wonderful things, including nineteenth century French prints of Islamic art. He gave me tea; I looked around; I heard him switch from English to Danish to German. I bought a tablecloth and some of the prints. I would have bought the entire stock and not noticed, but Mr Hassahn tired of 'not' selling me his things, and sent me to the mosque.

The Omayyad Mosque is one of the most holy places in the Islamic world, on a spot which has been holy for 3000 years. A temple to Hadad, the Aramaen god of thunder and the sun, had stood here. Hadad became Jupiter under the Romans, and a big temple was erected in the 100s AD, the remains of which are the light bulb draped remains of the western gate outside the entrance and Mr Hassahn's shop. In the Christian era it became a church, dedicated to John the Baptist. It remained a church even after the Arab conquest in 636, and was appropriated by Caliph Walid I in 708. He demolished the church inside the Roman walls, and built an elaborate mosaic-paved courtyard. Fires destroyed the prayer hall in 1069 and 1893. It has since been rebuilt.

Saladin's tomb is behind the northern wall of the Omayyad Mosque, in a grooved domed building within a small garden surrounded by trees, including – yes – a trailing gum tree. There was a caretaker sitting on the front step of the verandah; he nodded. I began to take off my shoes; he indicated that I needn't bother. I did anyway, thinking that it was proper to be respectful of the great man. An inscription thanks Saladin for liberating Jerusalem from the 'blemish of the unbelievers'. I wondered briefly what Saladin would think of the present situation in that city, and felt he would have been a vigorous proponent of the peace process. And, he might well have given thought to Jerusalem once again becoming an interfaith city, an international city for Muslims, Christians and Jews. After all when *he* captured Jerusalem in 1187 he wept at the sight of the Christian widows. Because he liberated Jerusalem from the Christians and prevented its recapture by the Third Crusade, Saladin is the greatest of all Muslim heroes.

Born into a Kurdish family with good connections in 1137, he became Sultan of Egypt in 1169 after very complex military and dynastic moves. Between 1174 and 1186 he gradually brought all the Muslim countries of the Middle East under one command and launched a jihad against the Christian kingdoms along the coastal strip. He was remarkably fair-minded and virtuous.

Saladin died in Damascus in 1193, aged fifty-six, after concluding a handshake peace treaty with the Crusaders that was to last for three years, three months and three days. My image of Saladin is from a childhood reading of Sir Walter Scott's novel,

The Talisman. Saladin, in a test of chivalry, swordsmanship and strength with Richard Coeur de Lion, cut a falling veil in two with his Damascene edged scimitar. Richard clobbered a lump of iron in two.

Saladin has two coffins, both with funeral turbans at the head. Kaiser Wilhelm II, in 1898, visited when the Germans were cuddling up to the Ottoman Empire, and provided a gross and ornate coffin, replacing the simple and elegantly carved one. The body is in the Kaiser's coffin. Saladin's spirit is in the decrepid wooden coffin. As it says on this coffin, 'O God receive this soul, and open to him the doors of paradise, that last conquest for which he hoped.'

The caretaker said, 'Picture okay.' I snapped away, barefoot on the worn carpet. I bought some postcards from the caretaker because there had been no charge to get in.

South of the mosque, through spice- and perfume-selling *souk*s, and one with cubbyholes filled with black, brown and cream fleeces, is the 'Street called Straight'. This is where the house of Ananias, where, nearly 2000 years ago, the one-time murderous persecutor of Christians, Saul of Tarsus, sought refuge in the house of Judas after he had been blinded by the light on the road from Jerusalem to Damascus.

Jesus told Ananias to 'Go into the street which is called Straight, and enquire in the house of Judas for one called Saul of Tarsus so that he [Ananias] might touch him and restore Saul's sight.'

This Ananias did, and the scales fell from Saul's eyes. He was baptised, took food, and his strength returned. After his conversion Paul, as he was later known, had to escape from the forty Jewish men who were said to be after him for preaching the Christian 'heresy' in Damascus, and was lowered from the walls in a basket. That event is supposed to have happened at the end of the street called Straight (it isn't straight at all, it's crooked). A small chapel to St Paul stands on the spot.

I walked up the street called Straight, known to the Romans as Via Recta, and turned left into small, pleasant Hananyia Street, lined with antique and brocade shops. At the end is the Ananias Chapel, which might have been built on the site of Judas's house. Downstairs is a cool stone cellar four or five metres under the ground, a chapel, a lot of memories. Maybe it was the right spot after all. A nice man let me in. I left some money in the collection box and walked back up the stairs. I was locked in. The caretaker 'tsk tsked' me in a French accent and let me out. I walked down the dusk-darkening street again, back into the *souk*.

In the National Museum, which I visited one morning, is a very old synagogue taken from Dura Europos, an ancient town out beyond Palmyra on the banks of the Euphrates. The Jews who chased Paul out of town were in turn forced to find refuge on the frontiers of the Roman Empire after their suppression in the second century AD. It is 1500 years old and has some wonderful naive frescoes painted on the walls. These are the only pictures of biblical events in a figurative style from this entire region. They are rare treasures for having survived after Islam forbade this kind of art. The stories include that of Esther, a depiction of the Temple, the flight from Egypt, Solomon receiving the Queen of Sheba, Samuel anointing David and, on the ceiling, a pattern of wheat, food, centaurs and faces.

The synagogue was originally a converted house and bears the inscription (in Jesus's language, Aramaic): 'This house was built in the year 556, this corresponding to the second year of Phillipos … Kaisar, in the leadership of Samuel, priest, son of Yed'ya.' The equivalent Christian year must therefore be around 244 AD, not long before Dura Europos was destroyed.

Most inspiring, for a writer anyway, was a small clay tablet with the Ugaritic alphabet from the fourteenth century BC on it. It is just about the world's oldest alphabet. I bought a plastic replica on the way out.

Next day I met my dragoman, Mohammad Muslli, and set off for Palmyra, three to four hours to the north-east, in the direction of the Euphrates, eating nuts bought in the *souk*. Mohammad had a bag of white beans.

It is possible to drive yourself around Syria or to get about by bus, but I was in a hurry, and I wanted to start out from Damascus and drive to the border with Turkey and see some of the places I had dreamed of: Palmyra, city of Queen Zenobia, the great crusader castle of Krac des Chevaliers, the city of Aleppo. It would be easier with my own dragoman and guide.

Mohammad seemed a bit reserved and annoyed that morning. He was a small plump man in a denim shirt. After a little while, having consulted my watch, I found out why. I was late! When Mohammad had rung from the lobby of the hotel, thinking him an hour early I had brusquely said I'd be there in another hour, and he had taken offence. But I was an hour out! No-one had told me that it was daylight saving time in Syria. No wonder things had always been closing down on me the day before. What a dope!

'Mr Garrie, you should be looking at your clock.'

'I'm sorry, Mohammad, I was on travel time – no need for a clock.'

'You say it true.'

After this temporal breakthrough, we shared our nuts and figs and beans and got along. Mohammad spoke very good English and had driven Australians before.

I asked him about Basil, son of President Assad, formerly the anointed one, still seen in dark glasses and beard flapping on flags around Damascus.

'Ahh, Basil. He go too fast to airport. Road divide. He not see. Yes, in Porsche. Boom. Seventy-five metres he travel over and over on top. Friend with him. Only Basil is kill. Friend okay. Our God say when he waiting for you, this is your time. Was time of

Basil. Father Assad has two other sons, one daughter. Plenty. But no Basil. He love him.'

The cult of Basil is okay with Mohammad. Basil was a kind of James Dean, cut down in his prime. Only the good die young, even in Syria. But it did feel a bit strange to me. When Basils were Byzantine emperors the name meant 'equal of the apostles', nearly but not quite a son of God. I suppose Basil was one of those Basils to President Assad, despite his playboy ways. Basil was an apostle of a newer Syria. What will happen in this ancient, basically tolerant, diversely religious but still authoritarian country after Assad is anyone's guess.

The subject of the Gulf War came up. Mohammad took a wicked pleasure in the defeat of Saddam Hussein and the role of Assad in supporting the victors. He told me that there is a great deal of oil out near the border leaking in from Iraq. It is 'a present from Saddam Hussein'.

The road to Palmyra stretched 400 kilometres through a flat stony valley. It was not exactly desert – the ground was sprinkled with green. There were huge massifs streaked with dark brown chocolatey stripes; Bedouin tents, tiny in the distance, pitched away from the roads; sand-coloured sheep; small villages with flat roofs. Mohammad said that some of these buildings are central depots for wandering Bedouin, who store furniture and even old trucks in them when they are off with the sheep and the tents in the spring. In the winter they pitch their tents beside these storehouses.

There were checkpoints at every crossroad, where the secret police loitered. There was a sign at one crossroad – 'Baghdad 800 kilometres' – but the road was blocked off. Mohammad, who travels these roads a lot, stopped and was waved through without much of a glance. I wouldn't care to drive myself through here, however. We passed evidence of large phosphate mines, a railway, and roads off into the mountains.

Two English travellers, Robert Wood and James Dawkins, came across Palmyra in 1751 – the first 'European' sighting:

> All at once the greatest quantity of ruins we had ever seen, all of white marble, and beyond them towards the Euphrates a flat waste, as far as the eye could reach, without any other object which shewed either life or motion. It is scarce possible to imagine anything more striking than this view: so great a number of Corinthian pillars, mixed with so little wall or solid building, afforded a most romantic variety of prospect.

And so it was as we pulled in round a long valley to see the palms of the oasis, then strange square tombs like squat chimneys on a green hillside, then a castle on a crag and the spreading apricot-coloured columns of Palmyra. Beyond it was the modern village of Tadmor.

Driving into Palmyra, we passed a building hiding in the palms with a gateway complete with loitering men. Mohammad said, 'Chief of secret police live here.' Further around the road, which passed the large Temple of Bel on the right, was the Hotel Zenobia.

This hotel was a real surprise; a cool marbled building of about twenty rooms, with a small restaurant and a garden, right in the middle of the ruins. Agatha Christie stayed here in the 1930s. At last I had a Room with a View – I could see Palmyra's columns and the Temple of Baal-Shamin through the window.

The hotel is named for Queen Zenobia, Palmyra's most famous daughter and one of the most remarkable women of any age.

The oasis has been known as Tadmor from the earliest times, being one of the cities King Solomon built in the wilderness, and mentioned in clay tablets as long ago as 2000 BC. The Romans took over Tadmor, by then called Palmyra, at the turn of the millennium. There was an imperial visit by Hadrian in 130 AD around the time most of the ruins were built. But at the height of

Palmyra's success, a threat from the east arose in the form of the Sassanids (Persians) who captured outposts on the Euphrates, including Dura Europus, in the 250s AD, defeated the Romans at Edessa in 260 and captured the Roman Emperor Valerian. This had a catastrophic effect on trade up from the Red Sea and by camel caravans through Persia. Something needed to be done.

A local Palmyrene, one Septimus Odenathus, Governor of Syria, helped the Romans at this time fight the invading Persians, but he was killed in 266. His wife Zenobia may in fact have done it. Zenobia then ruled on behalf of her son and proceeded to conquer Egypt, and parts between, with the temporary acquiescence of the Roman Emperor Aurelian.

But Zenobia had larger ambitions, and proclaimed herself Augusta (Empress) as well as proclaiming the independence of Palmyra and its possessions. Aurelian was obliged to reconquer Palmyra. The decisive battle was at Edessa. Zenobia lost and was captured crossing the Euphrates. Palmyra surrendered. Aurelian garrisoned the city, but these Romans were slaughtered by the locals soon afterwards, prompting Aurelian to massacre the whole population. That was the end of Palmyra, but not Zenobia.

Aurelian wrote of Zenobia: 'Those who say I have only conquered a woman do not know what that woman was, nor how lightning were her decisions, how persevering she was in her plans, how resolute her soldiers.' He paraded her, in golden chains, through the streets of Rome in the 274 AD victory parade, and she lived happily, perhaps, ever-after in a villa in Tivoli.

Evidence of Zenobia in the streets of Palmyra is scanty, though she features heavily in the souvenir shop at the Temple of Bel and on Syrian banknotes. There is a head, perhaps of Zenobia, lying on the ground near the crossroads of the ancient city.

Mohammad and I walked from the huge Temple of Bel, a satisfyingly pagan ruined temple compound, beneath the big Monumental Arch, past a nice theatre and baths, under the Tetrapylon – a restored four-columned archway straddling the crossroads –

and past the scant remains of the residential suburb. We stopped at a temple complex and the ruins of the so-called 'camp of Diocletian'.

The whole site is wonderfully romantic, but nothing more so than the elegant small temple of Baal-Shamin. We took tea with the Bedouin selling bits of silver on the temple steps. The Bedouin used to live in and around the site but were shifted to the modern village a decade ago, to allow for the partial excavation and restoration of the place. They told us they regretted the move, although they appreciated the increase in customers.

Later that day we drove over to the weirdest part of Palmyra, the Valley of the Tombs. These are brick 'tower' tombs rising four or five storeys high, with up to 300 family members stacked inside, like so many railway lockers. The setting sun made these structures glow against the darkening green of the hills. The whole effect was quite strange. I climbed inside one, and saw a skull in another. The towers were built in the first and second centuries AD, and were superseded by the fashion of stacking the family in an underground chamber called a hypogeum, with each locker adorned with a stiff, formal Palmyrene portrait of the deceased. The hypogeum of the Yarhai family in the museum at Damascus is a more accessible example.

At sunset, Mohammad and I drove up to the Arab castle which dominates the skyline above Palmyra.

Mohammad wound the car carefully up the steep slope of the hill, perhaps 200 metres high, and parked on the edge of the precipice. I gingerly walked around the edge and discovered that at the top a very deep moat – about ten metres wide and thirty deep, dry as bones – had been excavated. Over it a creaky wooden single file facsimile draw-bridge, with a minimum of rails, had been constructed.

As I suffer from a touch of vertigo, I had to overcome a fear of falling backwards over the edge or forwards into the moat. Not wanting to appear a wimp, I strode straight across, pushed from the rear by an American crone with an umbrella who was saying, 'I gotta get the shot of the sunset. I gotta.'

The Arab castle was built in the 1600s by an Emir Fakir al-Din, probably on the site of earlier fortifications. Fakir al-Din ruled here on behalf of the Ottoman Turks. It seems he grew too powerful, was defeated, taken to Constantinople in 1635 and strangled. It was said he was so small in stature that an egg falling from his pocket would not break. He left behind the ruin of the most spectacular sunset viewing site I'd seen.

The castle itself was just walls and shaky stones, but the view over Palmyra and the Valley of the Tombs was incredible. West over the ruins, the last rays of the sun picked out the shine of a few sheep among the tower tombs before the orange orb slid into the purple haze. Jetstream trailed white in the lighter blue; behind, the blue black night of stars, and a narrow Arab moon.

I thought of Omar Khayam, and of the trains of camels coming from the Euphrates bringing silk and spices to Damascus. This was such an extraordinary site, the sort of place he might once have visited. Perhaps he would have been thinking of an escape from the Shia sect of the Assassins, dreaming of a tulip-cheeked houri, a jug of wine …

I thought, too, of the Lebanese novelist Amin Maalouf, and his post-modern historical romances: particularly *Samarkand*, which I had just read, built around the conceit that Omar Khayam, Hassan Sabbah, founder of the Assassins, and Nizam the Grand Vizier all knew each other. Hassan did build his terrible fortress in a place not unlike this, at Alamut, from where he insinuated his Assassins into the *diwan* of those whom he decided were deserving of death, those who had transgressed his version of Islam. That was a thousand years ago – not long in this part of the world – but the spirit of Hassan Sabba and the idea of Alamut is still alive – as the multitudes of victims of terrorism have known. I had just had my tiny brush with it.

The sun in the west was sinking, the moon in the east rising.

Mohammad told me over dinner that after he had finished with me he would be getting ready to go on the haj, the pilgrimage to Mecca, for twenty-one days. He was very excited about it. His wife was going with him. It was like an ecstatic holiday. He was going to buy the special *galabyia*-type robe, white with gold piping, in the *souk* at Aleppo when we got there. When he came back he would be entitled to wear the white skull cap of a haji, and would be greeted with greater respect all over Syria. I admired his faith, which was purposeful, honest and personal. He was going on the mass pilgrimage, but in his daily life with me his faith was a quiet, individual, somewhat ascetic activity. There was nothing of the rage against the unbeliever you sometimes find in 'fundamentalists' of any religion.

Fundamentalism is obviously out there – I had, after all, just escaped from a few of them – but I failed to come across it, in Mohammad, or any other Muslim (or Jewish, or Christian) person I came across and managed to talk to. It made me wonder, not for the first time, why we all couldn't just rub along together – even in Jerusalem.

Next day we drove from Palmyra to an even greater castle, the beached Crusader battleship the Krac des Chevaliers, commanding the only pass through the coastal mountain range from Tartus to the interior cities of Homs and Hama. From the castle, Lebanon is visible just to the south, to the north is the next castle, at Margat.

The geography of this spot has meant that there has been a fortress here for thousands of years. The present castle was begun by the Knights Hospitallers in 1144 and expanded over the next hundred years. It fell, to a stratagem in 1271, when the 'bone stuck in the throat of the Muslims' was finally removed.

No other castle I had been in, in Britain or Japan or the Middle East, has the stature of the Krac. It was for 161 years the force of

Christian Europe being 'projected' into the Middle East, like a foreign military base today.

Inside the passageways it feels as if a clanking knight was about to come looking for his horse in the massive stables, or a stir of cooks was about to work the cauldrons and ovens in the huge kitchen to put on dinner for 500. Wandering inside the pitch black walls I did smell chicken cooking, but it was the kebabs of the cafeteria wafting though the ventilation.

Krac des Chevaliers was never taken by force. It was lost when the wily Mameluke sultan Baybars, having besieged the castle in 1271, sent a forged message to the Knights Hospitallers suggesting that perhaps they might consider surrendering because they were surrounded by the mighty Baybars; signed, Count of Tripoli. The knights surrendered, were given safe passage out, leaving their five years supply of food, and never came back.

'One-eyed Baybars' was another extraordinary individual. He had been sold as a slave in Damascus in 1230, but by 1260 had risen through the Mameluke ranks to be the general who routed the Mongol invasion near Nazareth and threw them back across the Euphrates. The world would have been a different place had he lost that battle. (The Mamelukes were originally mercenary slaves in Egyptian employ, who came to take over control of Egypt between 1260 and 1516.)

As a reward Baybars asked to become Governor of Aleppo, but the sultan Qutuz refused. Baybars killed him and became sultan himself. Among other things, he built a road from Cairo to Damascus so that he could play polo in Cairo on Saturday and lead the prayers at the Ommayad Mosque in Damascus the following Friday. He died in 1277 after drinking too much *kumiz* – the Mongol drink made from fermented mare's milk.

We left Krak and drove down the mountain and across the plain to Hama, a city sunk in a valley of the Orontes, where eighteen great *norias* or waterwheels used to pitch the water up to the fields above. Now they are just for show, and the river is like a sewer. Hama was the scene of a fundamentalist Muslim uprising against the government of President Assad in 1982, which was put down with great ferocity.

North onto the road to Aleppo, we passed pistachio groves and bright green fields being worked by women in extraordinarily bright clothes: astounding pink and turquoise and royal blues, like jewels or reef fish in the fields.

Near Aleppo, Mohammad stopped outside the small Commonwealth Cemetery, next to an open rubble-strewn field. I looked over the fence at the green oasis, studded with headstones. There are ten Australians buried here from the 1939–45 war. Australians from the 7th Division and the RAAF had played the largest part in the hard fighting against the Vichy French forces who were allied with the Germans in June and July 1941. The Australians, along with Indian, free French and British forces captured Palestine, Syria and Lebanon from the Vichy, just as their fathers had done just twenty-three years before.

A lady in a bright blue and pink scarf was taking her brown and cream sheep for a walk along the street outside the cemetery. The sheep seemed happy for the exercise, and bleated softly.

Mohammad took me to a hotel, a pleasantly pokey two flights up place in the middle of downtown Aleppo. It didn't cost much, but it wasn't the one I had booked. Even a dragoman has to do a deal.

I walked with Mohammad to the *souk*, with its thirty kilometres of covered streets and many great *khans*, or large 'squares', some surrounded by specialist shops, others more like warehouse spaces. Some of the *souk* has a renovated and touristic feel, with handicrafts on sale in neat stalls, but the other twenty-nine kilometres is like what a medieval market must have been. Mohammad bought his haj gear; I bought some dark moulded soap.

In the maze of streets we found the Great Mosque, built on the garden of older agora of the ancient Greek city, which became the garden of the Cathedral of St Helena. The mosque was founded in about 717, and is as beautifully peaceful as the mosque in Damascus.

Mohammad prayed. I sat. Nearby is the Halawiye Madrasa, or Halawiye school, founded in 1124, which is actually in the sixth century Cathedral of St Helena, named for the mother of the Emperor Constantine who passed through on her way to Jerusalem in 326. Inside the octagonal-shaped building there were Corinthian columns, and a Byzantine cross, and one of the teachers, who sold me a few Roman coins from a great box full.

After eating delicious kebabs and drinking bright red freshly squeezed orange juice, we walked past a strawberry seller on the way to the Christian quarter. He was selling his big punnets of strawberries for S£40. Shoe salesmen, sock salesmen, shirt salesmen plied their wares in the street. Mohammad told me that flip-flops, what we call thongs in Australia, are called 'zenobias' in Aleppo. An Armenian school band pounded out the national anthem. Further on was a cluster of Christian churches down narrow cobbled streets. There was a Gregorian Armenian Church, a Greek Orthodox Church and a Syrian Catholic Church, all going full swing. It was Easter. On the way back, the strawberry salesman was changing his sign from S$30 to S$20. It's a trading town.

Not far from the *souk* is the famous Baron Hotel. The hotel is small and slightly down at heel. I looked in the sitting room, and there on the wall was T. E. Lawrence's unpaid bill from 8 June 1914. It was for S£76.20. He must have eaten well back in those days.

Another visitor had stayed at the Baron Hotel. It was Lawrence and the Australians' principal opponent Mustafa Kemal, who, in October 1918, was finally in command of the retreating but still fighting Turkish armies.

Kemal was ill with a kidney complaint and was in bed at the Baron one afternoon late in October when a commotion outside caused him to get up. A crowd of local Aleppans was storming the hotel in anticipation, it seemed, of the arrival of the Australian and British forces as well as the Arab irregulars. Kemal drove the rioters out with his riding crop. Aleppo was under attack.

Kemal then surveyed the situation from the balcony of the Baron and said to another officer, 'Certain inhabitants of Aleppo, whom I wish to defend, are throwing grenades at me from the roof.' He ordered a machine-gun attack on the rioters.

Soon afterwards the Turkish army withdrew from Aleppo, fighting a number of stiff rearguard actions. It was because of one of these actions, fifteen kilometres from the city centre on the road to Bab Salami, that a stone memorial was erected. It was covered in election posters when Mohammad took me to see. The names of a number of members of the Imperial Cavalry Division are recorded as dying here on 26 October 1918. This must have been one of the last actions of the war in the area.

The monument stood beside a road that was being widened from two lanes to four, and was under threat of demolition. It sat next to a shabby, dusty shop selling soft drinks, bread, tinned foods and a few vegetables. We stopped and looked at the monument, with the names of the dead – Indian and British, Muslim, Hindu and Christian – and soon attracted a crowd of tea-drinkers from the shop. They were voluble in their defence of the monument against the road wideners. It was what passed for a tourist attraction in the street – weren't *we* there? – and to shift it would be a crime. What would I do about it? An old man in the white skull cap of a Haji and a tea-coloured *galabyia* was very steamed up.

The prospect of confronting President Assad over a British monument to a long-forgotten incident in a war that was not even really part of Syria's national story did not appeal. I said I would let the Commonwealth War Graves Commission know that it was under threat. My audience didn't seem to take in this sop to their interests, and kept yapping away. Eventually Mohammad said we should drink tea and go.

Mohammad drove me to the border next morning, after a breakfast of champions: full-on *fuul* with very big beans, hommos, onions, tomatoes, bread, water. No coffee. The *fuul* set like concrete after a few minutes and I couldn't go on, but Mohammad attacked my share as well as his with relish.

Formalities on the Syrian side were minimal, but rude and slow. I said goodbye to Mohammad and promised to send him a Sydney 2000 T-shirt. I gave him the last of my Syrian pounds and some dollars. From the fiscal point of view, things were looking a bit tight. I knew I would have to confront the cash problem once I was in Turkey.

Mohammad drove off; I started walking. It turned out to be a five- or six-kilometre hike to the border and then on to the Turkish customs and police post. There was no sign of a bus. A truck driver gave me a lift, but after a kilometre I abandoned him because he was jammed up against the next truck waiting to be cleared. Trucks in convoy from Europe, customs cars fore and aft, stream though Syria on the way to Jordan and Saudi.

There was nothing to do but walk. My pack was heavy, my book bag heavier. By the time I had walked to Turkey I felt like death. I felt like giving up. Instead I found a car to take me to Adana.

CHAPTER TEN

THE COLOSSUS
OF ROADS

ADANA LIES UNDER A hot, wet blanket in ancient Cilicia, an old market town serving the steamy plain of the Seyhan and the Çeyan rivers. The Tigris or the Euphrates these streams are not, but the effect is similar. You could grow anything out of season here, and they do, beneath the barrier of the Taurus Mountains, the mountain chain that descends from the eruption of the Anatolian Plateau to the Akdeniz, a stretch of brilliant aquamarine known in English as the Mediterranean. Adana is not 'ancient' anything, but ancient Tarsus is just up the road, and has been since before Saul walked in the other direction to ancient Antioch and Iskenderun – and Jerusalem.

This was a part of the defeated Ottoman Empire that Mustafa Kemal fought so hard to keep as part of a new Turkey after World War I. It is geographically part of Hatay, that part of Turkey around Alexandretta given them by the French in 1939 to ensure Turkey's neutrality in World War II. The Syrians still consider it to be their territory. Mustafa Kemal might have lost the battles to Allenby and the Australians when commanding armies in the area in 1918, but in the Turkish war of independence between 1920 and 1922 Kemal defeated the Greeks and maintained the Anatolian integrity of Turkey, adding another chapter to the longest continuously running border dispute between Europe and continental Asia.

Perhaps Kemal wanted to keep this part of the world Turkish because he liked tomatoes in winter.

I stayed at the Surmeli Hotel, an empty modern pile haunted by American servicemen. They lurked speechless in the bar. And sat morosely in civvies in the dining room. The air base used to keep an eye on the Iraqis and the Kurds is some distance from here, but perhaps there are no other facilities closer by. Perhaps Adana is the closest bit of civilisation.

I don't know if it was the exhausting walk across the border, or the phone call home (the first since Amman) that revealed finances on the home front were not progressing as planned, or

overleaf: Site of the Colossus, Mandraki Harbour, Rhodes

somehow feeling that I had done the hardest part of the trip, but I suddenly felt flat. I decided to chop a week off the end of the journey and not spend as much time travelling in Greece as I'd planned. Olympia seemed less relevant than it had in the planning. I felt very tired. It was all I could do to go downstairs to look for a bus that was going around the coast to Antalya. Then Marmaris and a ferry across the old wine-dark sea to Rhodes. Then Kos maybe, Bodrum, to Kuşadasi, Selçuk and Ephesus … this was starting to sound good again … and Gallipoli, Istanbul, the train to Athens.

I walked around Adana at sunset and saw what had to be the world's biggest mosque in an advanced stage of concrete construction: four huge minarets, a gigantic dome, shining like wet cement in the sun.

I began to feel happy about being in Turkey. There was a certain familiarity about the place, a more open, European sort of bustle compared to the languid and secretive Syrian streets. There were not so many women dressed all in black, or in potato sacks, in this part of Turkey. Although there are over 1.5 million people in Adana, the people seemed to be small-town provincial, commercial types: modern Palmyrenes it seemed to me, on the basis of conversations with cake sellers and enthusiastic English-practising boys in a stationery shop.

There were no European newspapers to be had. The Turkish *Daily News* was a day late, and people wondered, out loud, what I was doing in Adana at all. 'Nothing to see, nothing here Adana,' said the lady in the bus company office. 'You go to Antalya shopping, swimming – is beautiful,' as if paradise were to be found after an eight-hour bus ride further up the road.

The sounds as well as the smells are not Arabic in Adana. It was difficult to get my brain and tongue around saying *merhaba* instead of *salaam alekum*. I retreated to the hotel, drank beer and ate nuts in the bar, slept, watched TV. It was Good Friday. The news showed fundamentalist Christians in the Philippines nailing each other to crosses. 'Ha ha,' smirked the newsreader, saying in Turkish something like, 'You'd have to have a really crazy religion to do that!'

Next morning I checked out. My credit card didn't work for the 'extras'. Extras! What extras? I was in a hurry to catch the *servis* to the *otogar* (bus station) and the bus to Antalya. I didn't argue, but I felt ripped off. There was something not quite right about the number of noughts. It was hard getting used to the idea of 80 000 of anything to the US dollar.

Eight a.m., and the little *servis* bus took me to the *otogar*; quite a big one, with connections to Ankara and Istanbul as well as points along the coast.

By this time I was quite addicted to nuts and figs as pleasurable survival rations, and bought half a kilo of same at the *otogar* for 300 000 Turkish lire (TL). The boys giggled as I pointed to pistachios, almonds, white beans, various seeds, a bottle of water. They gave me a tulip glass of free tea.

Half-a-dozen shoeshine boys with smudged faces, bright eyes and blackened brass cases of polish and brushes worked the crowd. A surprising (to me) number of people accepted their offer. There seemed to be a Fagin in charge, because one of the boys ran tearily to him, indicating that a mousey, moustachioed bloke hadn't paid enough. The bloke shrugged and handed Fagin another note.

Ah, the sounds of the *otogar* as the bus company reps sing the names of destinations: 'Iz*mir* Izmir Izmir …', 'Is*tan*bul Istanbul Istanbul …' I love Turkish buses. Egyptian buses can be painful, Jordanian buses offhanded and Syrian 'hop hops' inaccessible, but half of Turkey is aboard a bus at any given moment, and half of them are singing. The other half are splashing themselves with lemon cologne.

Provided you buy a ticket the day before you want to travel, you can (except at the height of summer) get on a bus to go anywhere in Turkey, on any day. And they are cheap. This trip from

Adana to Antalya, about 550 kilometres in twelve hours through some of the most picturesque and spectacular coastal scenery, cost TL 700 000: less than US$10.

This road is truly the colossus of roads: twisting, turning, up and down, narrow, slow, views of ocean, valleys, coves with white hotels perched on the end, glasshouses of tomatoes and strawberries, lemon trees, even a plantation or two of bananas. There are pine trees and pink and white flowers wild in the verge. Daisy fields. It's up and down the echidna spines of the Taurus mountains as they drop into the sea, like the Great Ocean Road in Victoria, only more so.

After about five hours, the bus emerged from the mountains onto a flat and straight stretch of road and headed into Anamur, the most southerly point on the Turkish coast. There were more seaside resorts, honey, more bananas. A Crusader castle flashed by at Manure Kalesi.

I talked to Mehmet. He was in his early twenties, and had about twenty words of English.

'Hello, you American?'

'No, I am an Australian.'

'Oh really, Australian. Fren'.'

'Okay friend.' (We shake.)

'Turkey, you like?'

'Yes, I like very much. Second time.'

'Oh really?'

'First time, Istanbul, Izmir, Erzurum, Çoruh.'

'Oh really? Army me, Bayburt.'

'Bayburt near Trabzon? Erzerum?'

'Oh really yes, yes!' (We shake again.)

'We had army up on river – guarding, dancing.'

That was in 1993. I remember a night, after an arak or two, wandering from the tented city of the Rafters to the fire and the music of the company of soldiers guarding us from the allegedly threatening Kurds. Wouldn't have done for a bunch of sports lovers to be blown up by the PKK when Istanbul was bidding for the 1996 Olympics, would it? They welcomed me with dancing boots. A big circle, around the sparkling fire, the pounding of the music from a *souk*-blaster, clapping hands, big boots and sandalled feet. Three hours later, the arak wore off.

'Oh really, not love army but I am Turkish.'

'I am Australian.'

I reflected for a moment that this Mehmet was doing what he thought he should do, and had to do, for his country in this day and age, while I had made quite a different choice thirty years before for my country. He had acquiesced in the Turkish draft; I had resisted the Australian version. And I was heading for Gallipoli, where the choices for the 'Mehmets and Johnnies', in Mustafa Kemal's phrase, had been clearcut for them too. I felt a wash of fellow-feeling. The modern Mehmet and I shared figs on the roadside.

We roared through Alanya, a go-getting resort town, and saw tourists lolling in the sunset, the wistaria out, yellow acacia blossoming. Hundred of Otels going up, block after block after block of them. Along ten kilometres of coast, bananas were being uprooted to make way for banana loungers. There was an uninviting grey tough sand beach.

Nearly twelve hours after leaving Adana, the bus pulled into Antalya, another go-getting seaside resort. I bought a ticket to Marmaris for the next day: TL 750 000, ten a.m.

'Big bus?'

'No leetle bus.'

A detailed study of my Lonely Planet guide gave me a strong feeling that I should stay at something called 'Abadotel'. Sounded good to me.

A taxi provided me with an eastern Akdeniz first – he turned on the meter. It cost TL 100 000 from the bus station to the hotel, through winding little streets with discreet signs for *pansyon*s, bars and carpets. This was the old town in Antalya, where the madding crowd were waiting to descend once it warmed up a bit. I handed over TL 200 000 because the driver was so honest.

Abadotel was a small *pansyon*, at the end of a kind of cul de sac, and it had a room with breakfast for US$20. I was too bus-lagged to think of bargaining. It was clean, had a shower, but had no food. The proprietors had a private dinner party in full swing in the dining room. I decanted my pack, threw water around, and stepped outside.

I decided to walk towards Hadrian's Gate. Antalya is named after an Attalos II Philadelphus, a ruler of the kingdom of Perga-mum, making it the capital of the region of Pamphylia in the 100s BC. The Romans took over in 133 BC, Hadrian building some strong walls, of which Hadrian's Gate remains. It is at the end of Hesapçi Soçak where it meets the main street of Antalya, Atatürk Caddessi. It was dark. There were few people around. I needed a walk after the day on the bus.

In that mysterious way that happens when you 'just walk' in a new city, my feet directed themselves to the lights at the end of the soçak, past bars and carpet shops, half lit and half open. Later in the season they would spring into action at the slightest sign of interest, but now the air had a bracing chill to it, and they'd all rather continue hibernating inside, watching the soccer on TV. My feet took me up the steps to pass beneath Hadrian's Gate, just another ruin in the streetlights: marble, three arches, big towers – then down Atatürk. The beautifully fluted, or half-columned, slender brown tiles of what I took to be the Yiovli Minaret speared up into the night sky.

Atatürk Cadessi boasted a familiar looking row of Canary Island date palms just like a Melbourne boulevard. It was abuzz with two lanes of traffic on either side, restaurants and cafes. After a quick survey, I dropped into the place with the most people.

A waiter took me to a table. A dark-haired, pale young woman was sitting there. There were a couple of empty tables, but the waiter winked and put me opposite the girl.

Beer, chicken, rice. The girl was eating very carefully. She looked up warily after every three or four nibbles. This could be interesting was one idle, passing thought. Alone in Antalya – why not?

'Hello, are you Turkish?'

'Oh! No! Turkish no, speak little English.'

'You are from?'

'Oh! Azerbaijan me.'

'Holiday?'

'Yes. Shop, shop, shop.'

'Yes. Bus?'

'Oh! Bus. Yes.'

'Baku?'

'Baku. Know how you?'

'Just a wild guess. Only town I know in Azerbaijan.'

'Not you American?'

'Australian.'

'Oh! Australia. Ver hard understand you English.' (And I thought I spoke with a civilised accent.) 'English, America okay. Australia English …' She made circling cuckoo gestures in the air near her ear. 'No more talk. Go now. Goodbye.' And with that she got up and left.

I had another beer and walked slowly back under Hadrian's Gate. I remembered St Paul. He had come here with Barnabus and Mark but he couldn't have seen the gate because it wasn't built then. He was martyred before Hadrian's reign. It was the traveller's lament in reverse: he shoulda come here next year.

Antalya might be a pleasant place for a holiday, but out of season I was happy just to be passing through. I wandered down an even less populated soçak and up to the tiny room.

Notes, radio, sleep, breakfast. I couldn't get used to the idea of olives and cheese for breakfast, but gratefully wolfed the coffee and warm bread. I took a taxi back to the *otogar* (same price) and looked forward to another day on the bus.

The Isuzu thirty-six-seat bus climbed out of Antalya and headed for the hills. The trip was not around the coast, but across a range of mountains, rejoining the coast road near Fethiye. Wildflowers lined the roadside and ran like confetti into pine plantations. There was a yellow gorse, a pink scatter of flowers on a low stem and tall yellow flowers. Near the top of the first ridge, almonds were in blossom. Olive trees dripped and small graves in Islamic style could be seen between the trees. Past Korkuteli there was a garish red and white striped minaret with a blue tip.

Snow topped the mountains. The road traversed a wide flat green valley surrounded by brown cloud-shadowed hills. Tractors plied the tracks, carrying things of stone and wood. Thin rows of poplars served as fences around small fields of wheat. At Bekçiler, men were spring ploughing with horses, while women took their sheep for a walk on leads.

We stopped in the high valley for cup of 'Nes' and some more nuts. The air was crisp and clean, the cafe by the side of the road empty, kettles of water already steaming, stolid bus caterers behind the jump waiting to serve. A man outside herded his fat sheep, which looked like woolly chocolates.

It was a Sunday. A girl and boy in their best clothes hailed the bus and climbed aboard, travelled for ten minutes and got off next to a grove of gums. Rain fell, the bus buzzed on and on. People got on wet, smoked, misted up the windows. We pulled into the Marmaris *otogar* at 5.10 p.m., 590 kilometres and nine hours from Antalya.

The *otogar* was 500 metres from the spot where my first choice hotel was supposed to be. I set off, my feet following my nose across a little bridge, and through the maze of a half-open bazaar.

Asking a few sleepy stallholders where the Hotel Begonya was made me realise that I was still not attuned to Turkish, or Turklish, as the pidgin might be called. They couldn't understand me or me them. On failing feet I emerged on the promenade, named (again) Atatürk Cadessi. I walked around on the seafront past the tiny 'fortress' to the harbour. Restaurants spilled onto the roadway. Builders' vans buzzed about. Further up is a private marina, with hotel and tourists, and beyond that the ferry terminal. I banged on a few doors, and found a pleasant gateway into a courtyard of the Hotel Begonya. 'But sorry,' said a laughing woman, it was being fixed up 'for the season'. Bad luck.

She showed me out the back gate and pointed at the white three-storey building on a corner twenty metres away. I staggered over there and was admitted by a small bright-eyed boy with a great line in patter: 'Good clean room shower hot in afternoon breakfast okay for you only one million come look yes bring your bag you want towel okay.' Okay! I'll take it.

Marmaris, like most Turkish resort towns, has grown from backpacker favoured fishing village and Atatürkian outpost to fully blown five-star German tourist venue in a decade or less. The ancient history of Marmaris was mostly as a town called Physkos, a dependency of nearby Rhodes. Which is why I was here: to catch a ferry to the site of the Colossus. It was late in the afternoon and I walked out looking for a ferry ticket office.

A ticket to Rhodes was US$35 next day, no bargain compared to a Turkish bus. I was back in the land of that morning's English newspaper, which I read at the Restaurant Mona Titti, where the owner told jokes to roaring Germans along the lines of the name of his restaurant. I liked his fish, but not his jokes. Marmaris must be something in the summer.

At the Otel Lahti after dinner, I sat with the patron, various cousins and children, a steady supply of tea, and watched TV: a strange science fiction epic in Turkish with girls in bikinis, flashes of light and rubber-headed aliens. The family sat around in a semicircle, respectfully watching me rather than the TV. A cousin spoke good English. He translated for his uncles. Conversation with this young Turk began with Atatürk and history.

'You not respect him, he beat you.'

'Only at Gallipoli. We beat him in Syria.'

'You beat Atatürk?! Is true?'

'Yep, 1918.'

'I tell my uncles.'

Furious discussion about the national hero ensued.

'They say he was coming back to prepare for revolution. Not lose, come home.'

'That's okay by me. But Australia and Turkey ... we have a lot in common.'

'Yes, Gallipoli. You lose.'

'Gallipoli was a step in making of Turkey. It was a step in making Australia, too.'

'Why you invade our country?'

'It was the war. We were on the side of the English.'

'English!'

'You were on the side of the Germans.'

'They help us.'

'But there was not Turkey, that was the sultan.'

'I know, I know that.'

'But Australians know Mustafa Kemal was an honourable man.'

'You say true.'

'Both our countries were born at Gallipoli.'

'Yes.'

The other men nodded in agreement. We shook hands. We understood each other, maybe.

After a breakfast of *ekmek* (bread), honey and coffee at the hotel, served by a bevy of the patron's daughters, nieces and sisters, I took the ten o'clock ferry to Rhodes. I had my ticket, I had my passport, other of my fellow passengers seemed not to have either. Ticket agents scurried about, shouting. Altercations in a number of languages broke out. Queues disassembled and reformed in different places. Already eyes were on the duty free shop; luckily, it was not yet open.

Eventually we were allowed to depart Turkey, and stepped outside into the cool breeze blowing from the Greek Islands.

It hadn't been too bad. I had heard of worse situations involving travel between Turkey and Greece, but at the time there was a little bit of international tension going on between the two countries regarding islets and rocklets and flags being raised, gunboats and warplanes being scrambled. But these modern incidents based on ancient grievances could not, in the end, be allowed to interfere with the greatest god worshipped around here: Turizm. It speaks all languages and eventually overcomes all difficulties.

The *Kometa II*, an enclosed hydrofoil, rumbled into the wharf, flying a Greek flag. We stepped aboard. A crewman took my passport: 'Get back after.' A ferry to Greece: Asia Minor to Europe Major. I had been looking forward to this little journey for years and years. Pity it wasn't a proper ferry.

The voyage owed nothing to Ulysses; no Sirens, just the curving arrow of a wake past islands and headlands and sparkling sea. Beautiful of course.

A disappointingly short time later the *Kometa II* bumped into the commercial harbour of Rhodes. Passports were retrieved from the Greeks and stamped. Outside the passport control, at the wall of the old town, were a few hopeful shops. The day trippers from Marmaris lurched off, getting their land legs straightaway. A hulking American boy said, 'Great, they have beer' and got some. A family of Greeks were greeted and ushered into a small car. A Citroën! Here must be civilisation. There might even be telephones that work.

There was a gate in the wall, the Marine Gate. Inside was an

incline and the pension I was looking for, called the Kava d'Oro.
It was supposed to be an 800-year-old house built into the walls
of the old town.

Five minutes later I was in a white room, more like a whitewashed tunnel, with a shower that dribbled warmly on a sunny
day, the promise of a washing machine below – and directions. I
was happy. I was going to search for the Colossus.

Rhodes today hardly needs a landmark attraction or symbol
like the Colossus to bring people here. Today's Colossus of
Rhodes is shopping. The old town is one large market, set in a
medieval museum, which has obliterated the mystery of where
and what the Colossus was.

I walked to the Mandraki Harbour, which is outside the walls
of the Old Town. The Old Town was mostly built for the activi-
ties of the Knights of St John, who arrived here in 1309 after
Jerusalem was taken by Saladin. They stayed until 1522.

Down at the harbour, a sweep of grandiose Italianate buildings line the promenade. (Rhodes was Italian between World War
I and the end of World War II.) Perhaps the buildings erected then
might be called 'Mussoliniums': the post office, the town hall
and the police station all had aspects of the heroic architecture
beloved of fascist dictators.

The two arms enclosing the Mandraki Harbour end with small
towers on which green bronze statues of a roe deer and a stag
have been placed. One arm terminates in the St Nicholas Fort and
lighthouse and stag. The other arm ends in the round tower with
the roe deer. There is a fifty-metre gap between the two arms of
the harbour which is where the Colossus of Rhodes is supposed
to have once stood.

Ancient technology would not have allowed a forty-cubit,
forty-metre high statue to bestride this gap. The Colossus most
probably stood where the fort is now. There are large stones of
the correct period there, and some inside the fort are said to be cut
to a shape that would form a large round pedestal. But that's it,

nothing else. As little remains of the Colossus as I had found of the Pharos in Alexandria: a few stones.

The Colossus, however, is perhaps the simplest of all the ancient wonders to imagine, because whatever the exact shape of the statue was, New York's Statue of Liberty, an even bigger she-colossus, is built in its image. She has a flaming torch with the radiating beams of the sun god spiking from her head like some bronze punk. I built her in my mind's eye on the location of the fort, and saw the Colossus.

To build bigger, taller, higher is both an ancient and a modern desire. Ancient Egypt and modern America were both built with 'coloss-optimism' as part of their artistic, religious and national-ist bags of tricks. The Greeks were not bad at it either. For them, in many cases, bigger was also better – a bigger temple was a better temple.

Australians are not immune. We have the world's biggest rock, pineapple, banana, motel shaped like a crocodile, earth-worm. And even now the big men from the big end of town are plotting the world's biggest building, to be placed right where a colossus should be built: dockside in Melbourne.

In another respect, the Colossus of Rhodes could be consid-ered a modern phenomenon; it was part of the PR campaign of Alexander the Great – the first politician to invent and nurture an image.

Quite a few of the ancient wonders were made, rebuilt or ordered in the century of Alexander: the Pharos, the Temple of Artemis, the Mausoleum and the Colossus. The Colossus was made by Chares, a student of Alexander's chief image-maker, Lysippus. The sculptor and image-maker Lysippus was the one who perfected the 'classic' image of Alexander: the natural wide-eyed look, the long hair, the heroic pose.

Sam Goldwyn used to say of movie stars that it didn't matter much how tall they were, as long as they had a big head, one that filled the screen. Lysippus had a different point of view; he wanted a big muscular body and a smaller head to impress the people of his day in the most effective and permanent medium: sculpture.

In the museum at Rhodes is a head of Alexander as Helios the sun god, with holes for the sunny aureoles. There's quite a good case for believing that the head of the Colossus looked something like this one: staring upward, expectant, mane of hair, mouth slightly open, eyes looking to the future. This was how Alexander wanted to be seen and remembered.

Alexander was happy about becoming the son of a god and a Pharaoh in Egypt, and, as the greatest man of his age, would also have been pleased to be immortalised in the image of Helios, the most fundamental god of humankind, in the largest statue ever built.

The inscription of the Colossus survives:

To you, Helios, yes to you, the people of Dorian Rhodes raised this Colossus high up to heaven, after they had calmed the bronze wave of war, and crowned their country with spoils won from the enemy. Not only over the sea but also on land they set up the bright light of unfettered freedom.

This tells us something of the reason why the Colossus was built. The why and when is pretty straightforward. Rhodes the city was founded in 408 BC, by the union of three other cities on the island, to take advantage of the harbours and the site in the north of the island. Its street plan was designed by the best town-planner of the day, Hippodamus of Miletus, who favoured the grid system with 'zoning' for special uses, such as temples.

Rhodes was part of various alliances with Athens, but withdrew in 356 BC at the instigation of the Carian leader Mausolus (of the Mausoleum and Halicarnassus), who garrisoned the city. Caria was a kingdom situated just across the sea around Marmaris. Rhodes sided at first with the Persians against Alexander but switched when he became the man of the hour. After his death in 323 BC, his generals divided the world among themselves, but fought each other for the rest. Rhodes allied itself with Ptolemy of Egypt against Antigonus the One-eyed, Governor of Phrygia (the north-east area of the mainland across the strait, north of Caria).

Antigonus attacked Ptolemy and his allies in 306 BC, but could not defeat him, and demanded Rhodes join him against Ptolemy. The Rhodians refused, and Antigonus's son, Demetrius, undertook the consequent siege. Demetrius acquired the name Pliocretes – 'the besieger' – because of his diligent, though unsuccessful, effort at Rhodes.

Freedom-loving Rhodians – the freedom they most loved was the freedom to trade – fighting an absolutist monarchy with all the high-tech siege equipment is a stirring story. Rhodes held out against 40 000 soldiers, 30 000 sappers, 200 ships and a huge siege engine: a thirty-metre high armoured tower made of stone, with protective armour of iron and leather, complete with water tanks, catapults, battering rams and bridging gear. It was a *helepolis* – a 'taker of cities'.

After a year, even with this most formidable engine, Demetrius was forced to give up and make terms. Rhodes then became an ally of Antigonus against all except Ptolemy. Demetrius was so impressed (or tired) by the Rhodians that he left them all his great engines and catapults. The free-trading Rhodians promptly sold these for a huge amount of money, with which they commissioned an enormous bronze statue from Chares, pupil of Lysippus.

Chares worked for twelve years, between 294 and 282 BC, erecting the seventy-cubit high monument. But it only stood for seventy years. The Colossus toppled in the earthquake of 226 BC, cut off at the knees. According to one source (Strabo), Ptolemy III offered to pay for its re-erection but the Rhodians had been advised by an oracle to leave it where it lay, which they did for

900 years. In 654 AD Arab raiders sold the bronze to a 'Jew from Edessa' who transported it to Syria on the backs of 900 camels.

During the time it lay on the ground, many visitors poked about, and remarked on the mass of stones and iron fixings that were inside.

While scholarly disputation has bubbled along these 2000 years about the shape and method of construction, it is obvious that the whole seventy cubits (thirty-five metres) was not cast in a piece. And the idea of Philo of Byzantium that it was cast in sections, starting at the feet, also seems unlikely as the bronze pieces would be difficult to 'fuse' together.

Philo said, 'The artist fortified the bronze from within by means of an iron framework and squared blocks of stone, whose tie bars bear witness to hammering of Cyclopean force …'

Pliny the Elder wrote in his encyclopedia *Natural History* that 'Few people can make their arms meet around the thumb of the figure, and the fingers are larger than most statues; and where the limbs have broken off, enormous cavities yawn, while inside are seen great masses of rock with the weight of which the artist steadied it when he erected it.'

The archeologist John Romer has pointed out that other colossal statues, such as the Zeus at Olympia, were made of a diversity of materials and often 'plated' over a stone base. For something the size of the Colossus, it would seem that the best way of erecting it would have been to fasten castings of pieces of it to a stone interior, building gradually higher in the manner of a skyscraper.

Perhaps the arm or head might have been done in a single piece, but the method of construction indicates that this was a feet-together statue, a Helios with a hand raised at the elbow carrying a torch, and maybe steadied by a spear. If it wasn't in naked form, possibly the folds of the garments reinforced it on the ground.

So here in the harbour was where the Colossus stood, and fell down. I suppose if it was really an image of Alexander, Shake-speare did get it right. In the 900 years he lay on the ground, 'Petty men did crawl 'neath his huge legs and peep about.' And Alexander did 'bestride the narrow world, like a Colossus'. Alexander was a 'wonder man', appropriately enough dying at the site of another one in Babylon.

In search of a ticket to Kos I found a travel agent near the inter-section of 28 October (which becomes 25 March) Street, and America Street. Hoping that the lady behind the desk spoke Eng-lish, I said, 'Hello, I'd like a ...'

'G'day!'

'G'day? You're?'

'I'm from Bundaberg.'

'Pleased to meet you.'

'And you?'

'Brunswick. You haven't lost your accent.'

'Neither have you.'

'How long have you been here in Rhodes?'

'Eighteen years. My accent is getting stronger. And you?'

'One day. Mine is too.'

Twenty-five March Street is named for Independence Day, commemorating the day in 1821 when Bishop Germanos first hoisted the Greek flag at Aghia Lavra in the Peloponnese to begin the war of independence against the Ottoman Empire. Greece's independence was recognised by the Ottomans in 1832.

The date might also be regarded as the beginning of the modern friction between Turkey and Greece, conflict that has been going in different ways since the Trojan War, and through the centuries when the Byzantine Empire, based in Constantino-ple, was Greek.

In 1914, at the outbreak of World War I, there were two ideas about potential participation by Greece. One, represented by King Constantine, was to remain neutral. Greece had just gained territory in Macedonia, as a result of two Balkan wars, from the Ottoman Empire (Italy gained Rhodes, and Britain annexed Cyprus in 1913–14). Prime Minister Venizelos, however, was the arch-proponent of the 'Great Idea', which was to re-establish the Greek territories in the Ottoman Empire: a new Byzantine Empire with its capital in Constantinople. Initially King Constantine agreed to commit troops to the landing at Gallipoli. He later changed his mind, to the chagrin of Venizelos. The king was influenced by the resignation of future dictator Metaxas, then chief of staff. The upshot was that there was no repeat of the Trojan War in 1915; however, in the carve up of the Ottoman Empire Greece was given Smyrna in 1919.

In January 1921 the Greeks invaded newly established Turkey beyond Smyrna, getting to the gates of Ankara before being defeated by Mustafa Kemal. Smyrna became modern Izmir. Mustafa Kemal was of course born, like Alexander the Great, in the now Greek city of Thessaloniki, when it was an Ottoman Turkish town.

Smyrna was burned at the time Greeks departed, and the biggest bit of ethnic cleansing (before World War II) began when the Turks of Greece left for Istanbul, and the Greeks of Turkey left for Athens. A million and a half people left Turkey for Greece after the war ended in 1923, many of them settling in Macedonia, changing Mustafa Kemal's birthplace from 43 per cent to 89 per cent Greek.

The street named 28 October tells more modern history. This celebrates *Ochi* Day ('No' Day) in 1940 when Prime Minister Metaxas, despite being a fascist, wanted Greece to remain neutral in World War II and said 'no' to Mussolini's request to traverse troops through Greece. The Italians then invaded, but only got as far as Albania where they were defeated by the Greeks. Metaxas also said *ochi* to the British who wanted Greece as a base to attack the Germans, but he died in January 1941. His successor said *ne* (yes) to the Brits, the Germans invaded and, as a consequence, many Australians, British and New Zealanders died on mainland Greece and on Crete over the next few months.

The Greeks also suffered extraordinary privations during the war against the Italians, and then during the German occupation, and then fighting against each other.

Rhodes became part of modern Greece in 1947.

This ancient but fluid ownership of islands and people, and the massive migration to and fro is difficult to get used to. Australia does not have a land border with anyone; it occupies its very own continent. This unique confluence of history and geography is one of the major forces contributing to our sense of self and our place in the world. Our connections with the rest of the world have had much to do with the problems and opportunities arising from this 'tyranny of distance'. Only in recent years have the opportunites been seen by most of us to outweigh the problems of distance from Europe and America.

Travelling outside the country I felt more strongly Australian than ever, and secure in my connection to post-1945 multiculturalism, 1901 federation, the 1788 colonisation and the 80 000 plus BC settlement by the first Australians.

Here in Rhodes was a different brew of emotion, history and culture, and one's attachment to a place, to the idea of a place. To think of oneself as a Rhodian in a modern Greek nation must require a leap of imagination through time, back beyond the days of Alexander the Great to some civilisation that perhaps never really existed. It is a romantic notion that must overlook the last 3000 years of migration, ethnic cleansing and invasion.

Rhodes is what it always was, a tourist trading town, from the days when sold the siege engine to build a Colossal tourist attraction. Now the Old Town is just a Plaka, a tourist precinct of bewilderingly arranged narrow streets selling everything a tourist could desire – except an accurate map.

Having bought my ferry ticket in the New Town streets of 25 March and 28 October, I walked back to inspect the shops of the Old Town.

The main street of the Old Town is called Socrates (Sokratous). It is wider than the others. On one side of Socrates Street, a prose poem of Rhodian commerce revealed itself to me. This was the essence of Rhodes:

Carat gold by weight, cash travellers cheques no credit cards; Nikos Byzantine jewels and silver picture frames; gold; Mad Stuff – vests, chrome belts; Stephanie Boutique – frilly things; Christochios gold; handmade sandals; Tzivelek jewels; ΘΕΟΥΛΑΚΙΣ jewels; furs and carpets; Freeshop sunglasses and polo shirts; Rhodian handcrafts – T-shirts; Lukas gold; Paradise gold; Pegasus old guns, swords, eggs, chess sets, stamps, brassware; Benetton; Kasiotis gold; Kambouropolis Brios textiles – flokati rugs, bath mats (1000 drachma), towels; toys and dolls; Elegance Centre – leather and furs; ice-cream shop; Stefanos Stam. Gazokatis handmade Rhodian and Lindos popular arts – brass crosses, copper plates, statuettes; Lindos Tourist Shop; Pelz Leder Haus; more Lindos souvenirs – kebab skewers; Allegro gold; gold; gold; pelz; gold; coffee beans; Look jewellery; Kir. Hartofils 'A name to trust' embroidered tablecloths, lace; Kaba Kava bottleshop – Borzoi Vodka 1050 dr; beer hall (shut); pottery house; photo market; Pesmatzagalou (closed); Eros gold; Cash Point and Telephone (today 238.5 dr to US$1, 187.5 to A$1); Pizza (spinach pie piece 340 dr, donut 250 dr; Pansion Appolonia (upstairs); John Cornapolus jeweller; J Frantzis gold; Stergios Corner Greek salad 900, Moussaka 1000, Gyros plate 1500, Souvlaki 1500, Swordfish fillet 1800; across the road at 114 Sok. rusty guns 15 000, fridge magnets, bronze mask 9500, skewers 150, perfume bottles 500, statues of Colossus 3800, coins, stamps, backgammon sets, wool, woollen jumpers, embroidered blouses, reproduction vases by a professor any period; Maxim leather; Michael Karaotis leather; Leather market – shoes; gold; gold; Kaloudis; T-shirts; CDs; cassettes;

gold; shoes; sandals; leather (closed); Eleas gold; T-shirts; Liquor Store Nikolas Ouzo 1400 1 litre, Ouzo miniatures 2150, Rhodian wine 450; Mogiolu Pelzhaus; gold – grandma sits in front; Gregory Travel and Exchange; Economou photo and postcards, leather; Chris gold; site of excavation of a mosque; plates and pottery; cushions and carpets.

In discussion with shopkeeper one:

'This museum piece. Quality. Made by a professor.'

'It's very nice, but too expensive.'

'Oh not so expensive.'

'How much then?'

'For you 50 000 drachma.'

'Fifty thousand! That's $300 Australian.'

'Cheap.'

'For a reproduction?'

'You want to know how much an *original*?'

As this was a shop in Europe, not in Syria or Egypt, he shrugged his shoulders and didn't even offer me a cup of tea.

Shopkeeper two had 'genuine' white fishermen's jumpers Made in Rhodes.

'You like?'

'Very nice.'

'You buy?'

'Ah, no. We have plenty of wool back home.'

'Not Rhodes wool.'

'True, but good wool. Australian wool.'

'Australian wool, ptah!'

'Ptah?!'

'You buy?'

'Not with that attitude.'

'Good price.'

'Okay. How much?'

'Twelve thousand. All right 11 900.'

'Sixty dollars.'

'Not in real dollars, American dollars.'

'Ptah!'

It was time to talk Turkey with someone else. Next morning I caught the ferry to Bodrum.

CHAPTER ELEVEN

LIFE AT THE MAUSOLEUM

I TOOK A LAST look at the space the Colossus had once bestrode. As the ferry pulled out of Rhodes, I was sailing first to Kos, and then to the Turkish town of Bodrum, once the Carian city of Halicarnassus. There I was going to visit the site of another ancient wonder, the tomb of king Mausolus, the Mausoleum.

It was a big, white rumbling ferry with an empty stern deck. Its outdoor slatted furniture was bolted down and it was covered by a green fibreglass roof. I climbed to the next deck and sat with my own private view of the wake, the Greek flag fluttering, the passing islands.

The coast of Turkey was extraordinarily close. The ferry sailed past Cape Crio where there was a lighthouse and a Turkish flag blazoned on a rock. The lighthouse was appropriate because around the corner from Cape Crio is Cnidus (or Knidos), an abandoned ancient port where Sostratus, architect of the Pharos of Alexandria, was born.

The Cnidians were famous for trying to protect themselves against the rampaging Persians in the 500s BC by turning the peninsula into an island, through digging a channel across it. Many locals had their eyes damaged by the splintering rock and someone sailed across to Delphi in Greece to consult the oracle. The oracle told them to give up, with the excellent advice: 'If Zeus had meant for Cnidus to be an island, he would have made it so himself.'

Zeus must have been the only being who had any idea about what was going on with islands, islets and rocklets in that part of the Aegean. Since Zeus's fabled time they have been matters for dispute between a long list of peoples from Western Europe to Central Asia. The Franks of France, Greeks, Italians, Venetians, Romans, Pergamenes, Carians, Lycians, Persians, and Turks of different kinds – everyone has liked and coveted the islands and the coastal towns.

Early in 1996, border disputation between the modern Greeks and the modern Turks nearly bubbled over again. Gunboats were

overleaf: column detail, the Mausoleum at Halicarnassus, Bodrum

dispatched, sabres rattled, fishermen raised flags and took them down, and another storm in the nationalist/tribal teacup blew up. The quarrel was part of the story that began perhaps with the Trojan War, when 'mainland' Greeks raided the 'mainland' occupied by the Trojans. This part of Turkey was famously Greek for thousands of years (before it was Italian, or Roman).

It's a very mixed-up history. Perhaps Zeus himself might have sorted it out, except his 'Greek' subjects are now, for the most part, adherents to another God. Perhaps he has washed his hands of the whole business.

I was talking to a French lady in her fifties. Paulette was from Lyons, and had spent many years in Lebanon studying Arabic. We were discussing Maalouf: their Amin Maalouf, not our David Malouf.

'Oh no *Samarkand* too romantic *n'est pas M'sieur Garrie?* Too French. His book about the Crusades from the Arab side is good – *Leo the African*. Such stories! You have read Ibn Battuta – the Arab Marco Polo? Well, he could travel very much … The war is *fini* in Lebanon, but in the Middle East war is all they understand, *n'est pas?*'

But not, I hoped, in Greece and Turkey.

I struggled down the steep stairs and out of the jaws of the ferry, when a busy ticket tout saw me, rushed up and said, 'Bodrum yes! Why not. Okayokayokay. Quick.' He pointed to a hydrofoil lying by the wharf, engine turning over. 'Five minute.' We rushed to the passport and ticket office, handed over 5000 drachma for the ticket, 5000 drachma for the port tax, had passport stamped, on the boat. Fifteen minutes later I surged into the romantic harbour at Bodrum. A Turkish destroyer rode at anchor below the walls of the Crusader castle of St Peter, ready to put to sea at the drop of a flag.

While waiting in the passport queue, I noticed an Englishman and retsina-breathed girlfriend struggling with six plastic bags of clinking bottles. They needed to get a visa, and I looked at their passports as they handed them in at the window. They seemed to have made the duty free grog run to Kos about once a day for twelve months. The Turks didn't seem to mind the ruse. While I was waiting with the girl holding the bags, she asked me where I was staying.

'Don't know yet … a pension …'

'Don't shtay with him,' she said blearily, looking at the Lonely Planet list. 'He's a *crook* ahahaha.'

I found the advice friendly, but it didn't help. I staggered past the castle, looking for a street name I recognised from the map. Atatürk (of course) was supposed to run parallel to the sea, one block back from the larger bay east of the castle …

'G'day,' said a bloke wheeling a bike. 'You're an Australian.'

I had stopped to tie a shoelace. 'Is it that obvious? How could you tell?'

'You just look like an Aussie.'

Thank Zeus for that, I didn't look like an Englishman or a German for once.

'I'm an Australian, sort of. Married to one,' he said. 'Come and stay at my *pansyon*.' He put my pack on his bike handlebars and off we rolled. 'I want to come to Sydney to open a fish restaurant.'

'You will have a bit of competition.'

'I'm sick of Bodrum. It was just a village ten years ago. Now it is all traffic and tourists (sorry!). We came from Istanbul to escape. Now the mountain has come to Mohammed. Sydney is nicer, yes, than Bodrum?'

'Don't know. Bigger, like Istanbul. Younger, more expensive …'

'What sort of business should I begin? I want to be my boss.'

'I don't know.'

'Something *turistik*: import–export?'

'Better than fish.'

'Yes, maybe fish.'

Elvan Pansyon: half a million a night, not far from the castle or the Mausoleum.

I walked back through the whitewashed narrow streets of the market area, the shop owners dozing in the weak pre-season sun. A few blue evil-eyes for sale, postcards, British newspapers. Waiters patrolled the seafront, hooking in weak strollers for a beer, a coffee and a sandwich. I caught up with what was happening in English football, wrote a postcard to the *Guardian* requesting publication of AFL results and silently toasted the city, birthplace of Herodotus. There were fresh fish for sale on the dock, Bodrumanians purchasing enough for dinner. Schooners made of orange wood, white and blue stripes rocked at the waterline. The owners were swabbing and scraping, but ready for a sunset cruise if there were any tourists within boathook's reach. Bodrum was like a cat after a nap: stretching itself, licking itself, getting ready for a summer's action.

The mole where the ferry pulled in, and where I was drinking a beer and looking at the Castle of St Peter, was probably where King Mausolus had his 'private' harbour, built inside the protective natural harbour and beside his palace. His tomb, the famous Mausoleum, was up the hill, so that it gleamed impressively to viewers entering the harbour.

Mausolus was married to his sister Artemisia ('the younger') as was the custom in his dynasty. Mausolus made this place, Halicarnassus, his capital and moved here around 370 BC. Mausolus governed Caria, part of the Persian dominion of Lydia, between 377 and 353 BC. Carian domains included a few offshore islands, Kos and Rhodes among them.

Artemisia the Younger completed her brother–husband's great Mausoleum by about 350 BC, when she died. In medieval Europe this Artemisia became the epitome of wifely devotion because she was said to have taken a drink each day of some of Mausolus's ashes mixed with wine.

Mausolus selected the impressive site for his tomb. He seems to have been a considerable town-planner and architect, as tradition has made many of these ancient rulers.

Vitruvius (70–25 BC), the Roman writer on architecture, was impressed by the palace, which was decorated with fine marble though made of brick. 'These walls have maintained their excellent solidity up to the present day; they have been so finely burnished that they are as translucent as glass to look at.' This was because they were covered in very thin slabs of marble, a process first developed in Caria, according to Pliny the Elder (AD 23–79).

Vitruvius wrote of Mausolus's 'shrewdness and skill in preparing for building'. Halicarnassus 'was curved like a theatre, so the market was positioned at the bottom along the harbour. A broad road was constructed halfway up the curving slope along a recess in the hill, and in the middle of this road the Mausoleum was built with such extraordinary skill that it is numbered among the Seven Wonders of the World.'

Mausolus built a city wall seven kilometres long around Halicarnassus, placing the Emporium or international trade market outside the wall on the eastern harbour – where the market area is now. The Mausoleum, a gleaming white structure, would have been as impressive as a lighthouse when seen from the sea.

It is believed that this building was the first example of the dead being commemorated in the middle of the living city. It was a new idea to the Greeks, Egyptians and Persians, who had until then built tombs and monuments to the dead in special places outside their cities. Some archeologists believe that Alexander was so impressed with this radical notion when he came this way a few years later that he pre-ordered such a thing for himself at Alexandria.

What was it like, this Mausoleum, that it almost immediately became a wonder? Of the ancient writers, Pliny has the best account, which he included in the part of his *Natural History* that deals with stone and what the great sculptors did with it. The

Mausoleum was partly impressive because of the sculptures it housed, rather than simply as a very big building; it was like a huge sculpture gallery rather than like a pyramid.

Wrote Pliny:

Scopas, Bryaxis, Timotheus and Leochares ... jointly carved the sculptures of the Mausoleum ... The tomb built for Mausolus, king of Caria, who died in the second year of the 107th Olympiad. These artists (and Pytheos, who carved the four-horse chariot on the top-most point) in particular were responsible for making the building one of the Seven Wonders of the World ... considering it to be a monument to their own glory and their art.

Writing earlier, Vitruvius mentioned that the other great sculptor of the period, Praxiteles, also worked there.

As well he might. Praxiteles carved the greatest sculpture of the era – perhaps ever – the Venus of Cnidus. On this measure of beauty the Venus in the museum at Rhodes and others are based. Pliny tells of a man who fell in love or lust with the statue and hid himself in the temple at Cnidus. He '... embraced it intimately; a stain bears witness to his lust.' Life imitating – or perhaps, intimate with – art?

As well as carving the chariot figures Pytheos is regarded as the architect of the whole Mausoleum. He is credited with having written the original book on which Vitruvius based his work.

The Mausoleum was rectangular in shape, set on a marble terrace 242 metres long and 105 metres wide, surrounded by a gleaming wall of white marble. There was a podium built on the terrace, and this was surmounted by a massive colonnade of columns, roofed by a low pyramid of twenty-four steps on top of which Pytheos's sculpture of the four horse chariot stood.

The podium, about twenty metres high, was probably stepped back in three stages to allow for two ledges of larger-than-life-sized sculptures of human figures and sculpted reliefs of battles.

Between the columns of the colonnade were the huge sculptures of Mausolus's dynasty. More sculptures of people and lions were on the pyramidal roof, as well the horses.

Some later writers were sceptical about Mausolus's reasons for erecting the Mausoleum.

Lucian (120–180 AD) in the *Dialogues of the Dead* imagined Mausolus debating Diogenes the Cynic in the underworld. Diogenes asks Mausolus: 'Why are you so proud and why do you expect to be honoured more than the rest of us?'

'Because I was handsome and tall and victorious in war. But most of all, because I have lying over me in Halicarnassus a gigantic monument such as no other dead person has, adorned in the finest way with statues of horses and men carved most realistically from the best quality marble,' answers Mausolus.

Diogenes replies, 'Handsome Mausolus, your strength and beauty are no longer with you here. If we were to have a beauty contest, I can't see why your skull should be thought better than mine. And as for your tomb and that expensive marble, it may give the people of Halicarnassus something to show off and boast about to tourists, but I can't see what benefit you get from it, unless you're claiming that you have a heavier burden to bear than the rest of us, being weighed down by so much stone.'

The solid stone interior structure of the Mausoleum was still largely intact until the 1200s, although many of the sculptures had tumbled down in ancient earthquakes and some must have also been souvenired. In the 1200s, the entire colonnade and roof came down. Yet even after this, the bulk of the main building survived another 200 years.

The Knights of St John had begun building the Castle of St Peter in 1402, and between 1494 and 1522 used the Mausoleum as a quarry, containing as it did conveniently pre-cut squares of excellent green coloured volcanic stone. The marble of the sculptures and the facade were burned on the spot in lime kilns to make the mortar for the new walls.

At the Castle of St Peter I saw some of the stones of the Mausoleum, and also the cement made from burning some of the greatest works of sculpture. I wondered how this transformation of the elements would have appealed to Scopas or Lucian, or Mausolus himself.

By 1522, the knights had used all the easily accessible aboveground stones. They needed more, and started to dig. In 1581 Claude Guichard, a French writer, published an account of the events of 1522 (quoted by archeologists John and Elizabeth Romer in their book *The Seven Wonders of the World*):

> They had great success, for they soon discovered that the deeper they dug, the more the structure was enlarged at the base, providing them not only with stone for burning but also for building.
>
> One afternoon they saw an opening like the entrance into a cave. Taking candles, they went down into it and found there a large square chamber surrounded by marble columns with their bases, capitals, architraves, friezes and cornices carved in relief. The space between the columns was lined with slabs and bands of marbles of different colours, ornamented with mouldings and sculptures which matched the rest of the work, and inserted in the white ground of the wall, where histories and battles were also represented in relief.
>
> Having admired this at first, and entertained their fancy with the singularity of the work, finally they pulled it down, broke it apart and smashed it, in order to use it for the same purpose as the rest.
>
> Beyond this chamber they found afterwards a very low doorway leading into another room like an antechamber, where there was a tomb with its urn and its gabled lid of white marble, very beautiful and of marvellous lustre. This tomb, for lack of time they did not open, the retreat already having sounded ...

Unlikely as that story sounds, the sarcophagus did disappear. Guichard says corsairs or pirates got at it that very night. Methinks Guichard protested too much. It would have been surprising in the extreme if the knights themselves did not loot Mausolus's tomb at the time. Whether there was an elaborate room above the tomb chamber or not is also open to question. If there was, it too disappeared into the lime kilns. Some gold spangles and alabaster fragments possibly from the sarcophagus lid were found by the Danish archeological team under Dr Kristian Jeppeson in the 1960s.

Thus the great Mausoleum had been systematically demolished. The site was filled in with soil from the hill above, houses were built on it, and the quarry site was forgotten for 300 years.

The final battle of the knights actually took place on Rhodes in 1522, after which they all left for Malta; however, some of the sculptures and some of the friezes had been used in the Castle of St Peter. A dozen or so friezes of mythical battles between the Greeks, Amazons, centaurs and others were incorporated as decoration, as well as a couple of big cats from the roof of the Mausoleum.

By the nineteenth century, travellers' reports of what had been built into the castle walls had reached the eager ears of the growing band of diplomat–looters intent on stocking the storerooms of the British Museum. Lord Elgin had carted away the beautiful frieze from the Parthenon in Athens in the early 1800s, and Lord Stratford de Redcliffe, British Ambassador in Istanbul, had gained a *firman* (permission) from the Ottoman sultan to remove the 'Amazon' frieze from the castle in 1846.

In 1856, an assistant keeper of the British Museum, Charles Newton, obtained a *firman* to look for the site of the Mausoleum and ship his findings back to England. With Vitruvius in one hand, maps he'd asked the Admiralty to compile in the other, and an eye for the lie of the land in Bodrum, he soon located the site of the building. With some difficulty, he then bought the houses built above it.

Charles Newton dug an area he called the 'quadrangle', so-called because all that was left of the outline of the great building was a rectangular area, a foundation cut into the rock and filled with fragments. This was where the main tomb was.

Newton wrote later:

> The whole of the quadrangle was filled with the remains of architecture and sculpture. The quantity of these fragments was so great that it would have been impossible to specify their exact position on the plan, nor would such information be of any value in reference to the majority of marbles, which had evidently been rolled and pitched out of the way by the spoilers of the tomb, as they removed successive courses of masonry.

Newton found some more pieces of the Amazon frieze, including a fragment of a gracefully carved Persian horseman, butchered by a knightly sledgehammer.

Newton and his Royal Engineers (there were as yet no scientific archeologists) cut and filled this area for about three months, then moved slightly to the north to a twenty-six metre area of the field in front of the local imam's house.

Here he found, tumbled from the topmost levels of the Mausoleum, fragments of horses, lions, a head of Apollo, two colossal human figures – pieces of sixty-six statues in all.

This was the greatest trove left from the Mausoleum. The pieces survived because they had fallen between the slope of the hill and the wall of the Mausoleum's platform in antiquity and were quickly buried by soil from the hill and undiscovered by the knights' cement industry.

The statues and other architectural fragments were shipped back to the British Museum, where some are on display but others have been in storage for over one hundred years.

The colossal statues from the top level of the Mausoleum found by Newton were about all that remained of the human work of the great sculptors. There was as a statue of a man, probably not Mausolus, as Newton hoped, but an early portrait of a

Greek individual nevertheless, one of the hundred or more strolling and posing between the columns. The lions are also individual portraits.

Newton's technique of excavation was to fill as he dug, which meant there was still a good deal to discover when modern archeologists under Dr Jeppeson dug the area scientifically between 1966 and 1977, leaving the site as it is today.

Jeppeson exposed the foundations of the Mausoleum, including the burial chamber. Its front door was still intact, but it had been tunneled into by ancient tomb robbers, leaving a few gold spangles. The tomb is not in the centre of the platform; it is believed that it was built on a previous tomb, perhaps that of an earlier Artemisia. Jeppeson also found the ritual deposit of animal remains: sheep, goats, cows, chickens, pigeons, a goose and a few dozen eggs.

What I found at the Mausoleum site was green grass, tadpoles and frogs in the pool below the wide staircase that marks Mausolus's tomb, and a 'plug-block' of greenish stone which blocked its entrance. I stood in this, and listened to the frogs. Fluted columns lay around a level above the water, and above that – the present ground level – was a porch covered in red tiles where a few of the finds by Jeppeson were displayed, including some slabs of the Amazon frieze. Also displayed was a plaster cast of the frieze preserved in the British Museum – a kindly gesture from the repository of so much ancient loot.

Inside the porch was another room with some smaller artefacts and a model of the Mausoleum. The Byzantine writer Gregory of Nazianzus in 382 AD imagined himself to be the building. 'I was a wall, a wall set upon bases and rising upright, then flat with flanks which met together at a point, a tomb, a hill upon a hill. But what did that mean? Nothing to the gold lovers who shook me from top to bottom.'

Rose Macaulay wrote a wonderful and eccentric book in 1953

called *Pleasure of Ruins*. 'Ruinelust' is what Macaulay aptly calls the emotional attachment to ruins, which I evidently share.

> Since down the ages men have meditated before ruins, rhapsodised before them, mourned pleasurably over their ruination, it is interesting to speculate on the various strands in this complex enjoyment, on how much of it is admiration for the ruin as it was in its prime ... how much is association, historical or literary, what part is played by morbid pleasure in decay, by righteous pleasure in retribution (for so often it is the proud and the bad who have fallen), by mystical pleasure in the destruction of all things mortal and the eternity of God (a common reaction in the Middle Ages), by egotistic satisfaction in surviving (where art thou? here still am I), by masochistic joy in a common destruction ... and by a dozen other entwined threads of pleasurable and melancholy emotion, of which the main strand is, one imagines, the romantic and conscious swimming down the hurrying river of time, whose mysterious reaches, stretching limitlessly behind, glimmer suddenly into view with these wracks washed onto the silted shores ...

But a ruin is a different mess of pottery than is an archeological site. The Mausoleum is a site, with not even a column to mark the place or to excite the romance. But the stories stir the imagination. It was a wonder.

I walked back along Mausolus's ancient street, across to the *otogar*, and bought a ticket to Kuşadasi for TL 350 000. In the purple darkening sky, the castle loomed above the twinkle of the market area. Behind the point the Turkish gunboat sat solidly at anchor.

The sellers of evil eyes were packing up. Not enough tourists this early in the season to keep awake. Down Atatürk Street, on the way to the *pansyon* I stopped at a garish cafe with a red and green winking plastic fountain where six policemen were wolfing down quantities of beer and fresh flat bread.

Out the back, the baker proved to be a master of making the two halves of the *pide* separate and rise so that it arrives like a delicious pastie full off fragrant air. The *kebap* cooker sat at a throne behind a big trough of charcoal. He used a cylinder of tin over coals to get them glowing and burning, and cooked deliciously marinated *kebaps* of chicken, lamb or the spicy favourite minced lamb, the Adana *kebap*.

This was my kind of place. Efes beer arrived without asking; fresh chopped salad; the bread; and a nod in the direction of the sweating *kebap* man brought a chicken and Adana in a few minutes. This was a song without words; so what if it cost a million Turkish lire. They even had dessert! A kind of sweet honey and vermicelli custard thing called *kùnefe*.

In the bustle and smoke, I had another of those spasms of loneliness that must strike at solo travellers but which hardly anyone ever mentions. It must have something to do with language. I felt that this friendly waiter or that smiling *kebap* cook would love to have a yarn about the shocking form of the football team Galatasaray, the rise and rise of the Islamic Party, Refeh or the scandals of (then) Prime Minister Tansu Çiller. But we were stuck with the sign language for 'another beer' and my mastery of the word for the bill: *hesap*.

Next morning, an invigorating sunny day with a cold breeze, I set off for the Castle of St Peter via the evil eye salesmen putting out their wares, the boy selling the *Turkish Daily News*, the fruit and vegetable shop – one *mooz* (banana) TL 50 000? What the hell, I'll have two – and the quiet bustle of a tourist port at a civilised hour of the morning. Decks were being swabbed, ropes coiled, coffee drunk on the poop deck.

On the pleasant fifteen minute stroll, the castle loomed into view at the end of the point, the sun sparkling on the water.

Construction of the Castle of St Peter was begun during the tenure of Philebert de Naillec, Grand Master of the Knights of

St John between 1396 and 1421. It was evacuated in 1522 after their headquarters at Rhodes was captured by Suleiman the Magnificent.

It is now something of a castle in a botanic garden, with the ramps and walls and towers surrounded by all manner of Mediterranean plants and flowers, and a flourishing colony of peacocks and peahens.

All around the exterior of the paths and walls is an impressive collection (biggest in the world!) of amphorae, the ancient shipping containers, earthenware storage jars with pointy ends and, usually, handles. If I'd had a mind to do it, I could have learned all there is to know about distinguishing the different manufacturers of these practical objects. I did find out that Kos amphorae have a double handle and a crab-shaped seal, that Byzantine amphorae had pointy ends and no handles but had round lids sealed with resin, and that, most importantly the amphorae from Chios, used for the best wine in the ancient world, had button-shaped handles on the base and were sealed with a sphinx.

Today Queen Ada, another sister of Mausolus, receives visitors at the highest point of the castle. She stares across the secret harbour towards the Mausoleum, where her brother once lay. Dressed in a silk *peplos*, a dress trimmed in gold, Ada was at one end of a small room. She looked like a super model, and had a facial reconstruction done by English art-in-medicine experts Drs Richard Neave and John Prag of Manchester.

Ada, if it was Ada, was discovered near Bodrum in 1989, her grave untouched since she died around 330 BC. She was in her forties when she died, had all her teeth, and had given birth more than once.

I walked into Ada's sanctuary and the room automatically lit up. Ada's model was at the end, with her coffin and skeleton on the right and her jewellery on the left. There were three rings, two bracelets, two necklaces and an absolutely exquisite gold crown: a golden wreath of flowers and leaves.

The real Ada was another sister of Mausolus, and met Alexander the Great as he passed through. This was as close as I was going to get to meeting Alexander, or Mausolus. Alexander didn't have all that much time for women, we are told, but perhaps he drank a toast of Chian wine from that *oichonoe*, or wine jug, Ada's favourite, also found buried with her. *That* wine jug! This was ruinelust of a high degree.

It took Alexander considerable trouble to take Halicarnassus from the Persians, and when he did so he wanted to appoint Ada as his satrap, reinstating Mausolus's dynasty. Alexander often appointed or reappointed local rulers under guidance of one of his officers. Ada is supposed to have agreed to this if Alexander became her adopted son. He said he would not 'disdain the name of son'. Ada sent him baked delicacies, sweetmeats and succulent roasts of meat (such as are still to be had in Halicarnassus!), but Alexander declined the food, supposedly saying, in the royal third person, 'For his breakfast, his preparation was a night march; for his lunch a sparing breakfast.'

Outside the castle an empty souvenir shop beckoned. I bought a few small trinkets and was talking to the salesgirl as she put them in a bag. Standing next to us was a smiling woman and a small child. The girl gave me a postcard of an extravagantly dressed baby. He had several evil eyes around his neck and a pink headband twined with gold coins dangling. She pointed to the kid and then the card. 'It is him! The baby in the postcard!'

'It's a beautiful baby,' I say. 'What's his name?'

'Kemal,' says the proud mum.

Kemal! Of course. What else would you call a baby round here – unless you chose Mausolus.

One of Mustafa Kemal's secularising decrees was that all Turks should, from 1934, have a surname. He chose Atatürk for his. Mustafa Kemal Atatürk. Before that everyone was Mehmet son of Bodrum, or perhaps Ahmet son of Izmir. This baby was Mustafa son of Halicarnassus at the very least.

There was a market on top of the *otogar*. I bought another big handful of saffron for TL 100 000, a bag of nuts, a TL 50 000 *mooz*, and hopped on the bus for the short trip to Kuşadasi.

Kuşadasi is another harbour town, smaller and not as pretty as Bodrum, but as it is handy to Ephesus and other nearby ancient cities it is a prime cruise ship port. The bus stopped at an *otogar* on a hill some distance from the town. Here, in a rank of *taksis*, I met Çafer Yanmaz, or 'Silent Çafer' as I came to know him.

At one end of the harbour, where the cruise ships and the ferry from Samos berth, is a small forlorn market area. Silent Çafer drove through here and up a steep street to an Otel that proved to have the tiniest room I'd stayed in so far. It was a cupboard looking out into a white wall, room enough for a bed (A soft bed! Soft pillows! Early night tonight!) for TL 700 000 with breakfast. Okay.

I arranged with Silent Çafer via hand signals to pick me up the following day and take me in his yellow *taksi* to three other cities of my imagination: Priene, Miletus and Didyma. It was going to cost US$50, which seemed to be the universal daily rate for a dragoman with car.

Ali, the young desk clerk at the Otel, was from the Black Sea coast of Turkey. He had come straight here to an uncle of an uncle's hotel in Kuşadasi and hadn't been anywhere else in Turkey; not even Istanbul. He was doing his national service next year, and said he would see more of Turkey that way. Like most young Turks I spoke to, he faced a year or two in the army with a kind of weary resignation coupled with a little excitement.

National service marks a turning point in the lives of 'ordinary' Turkish boys. They mark time until it happens and then think about life again after it. With youth un- and under-employment said to be around 70 per cent in many places, the army is an attractive option – except for the potential death aspect. Ali hoped to be posted back to Trabzon near his family, not to the south-east where it was freezing cold and boys were being killed every day.

Waiting for Silent Çafer next day, I caused the Great *Taksi* Incident. I say caused. Put it down to a problem with communication – with Ali. He asked me why I was waiting ...

'Why you sit, wait?'

'I am waiting for a *taksi*.'

'*Taksi!*'

'Yes, in fifteen minutes *taksi*: Priene, Didyma, Miletus.'

'Ahhh. Never seen these places. How much it is?'

'Oh,' thinking furiously about whether Silent Çafer had undercut the local rate or not, 'Seventy dollars all day. Lunch.'

'Okay. I am cheap. Wait.'

'No,' weakly. 'No no. Coming – Çafer is coming.'

Ali returned. 'I fix. You pay too much. Only is sixty dollars. Coming coming coffee?'

'No, yes coffee, no *taksi*.'

'Is okay. I fix.'

Minutes later a cup of Nes arrived and a few minutes after that a big Turk.

'Okayokayokay.'

'Oh no.'

'Sixty dollars – Priene, Didyma, Miletus ... just stones ...'

'No, wait.'

Of course Silent Çafer turned up. Two yellow *taksis* out the front. Who could I explain to?

'Ali. Look! Already book this *taksi*.'

Ali, astonished: 'But you say ... He yesterday *taksi*.'

'I know. I asked him to come back.'

'Seventy dollars!'

Silent Çafer looked at me: huh?

'Yes! No! Tell this driver ... I already ...'

He said, 'You pay me ten dollars to come!'

Me: 'Hang on, it's not the season just yet!'

Silent Çafer broke into a long stream of consciousness piece in Turkish, presumably about the rights and wrongs and ethics of gazumping. The other driver agreed, nodded, and also made a long speech, the gist of which was presumably that tourists out of season are really, really stupid. He got in his *taksi* and rolled down the hill. Ali looked exasperated. How was he going to bill this episode?

Silent Çafer said, 'Is okay. We go.'

We went, first to Priene, about forty kilometres across the flood plain of the eponymous Meander River, and passed through a small village up the side of a hill to the entrance gate below the looming Mt Mycale.

Silent Çafer parked under a tree. 'You be back two hour.'

The path from the entrance was of marble but roughly laid, so that the intrepid walker's dodgy ankle was put immediately under pressure. Onwards, and upwards. After about a kilometre, a wide platform or terrace opened up, with a spectacular view across to where Miletus must be, the next promontory to the south. When the area below was still covered by sea, as it was BC, it must have been awe inspiring. Above loomed what looked to be a two or three hundred metre high cliff, almost straight up. The acropolis of Priene was up there somewhere.

There was no-one here. The wind whispered in the pines, in and around the right-angled grid of streets. Ahead were the pillars of the Temple of Athena, to the right a marvellous Greek theatre, and to the left a patchwork of the foundations of houses.

Hippodamus of Miletus, ancient town-planner, philosopher extraordinaire and friend of the great Athenian Pericles, either designed or influenced the design of Priene when its Greek inhabitants wisely began shifting from somewhere on the flood plain below. That was after the city was destroyed by the Persians around 360 BC.

They were still building the Temple of Athena when Alexander visited Priene, liberating it from the Persians. He is said to have stayed in a house just up the road while he besieged Miletus in 334 BC. (Was it the house in which I was standing? These foundations?) While he was here Alexander also helped defray the expense of building the temple. Prienians, less proud or poorer than Ephesians who had turned down a similar offer from Alexander, accepted his money. It was recorded by an inscription from the temple now in the British Museum (where else?). After Alexander's liberating visit, another inscription was carved at Priene: 'There is no greater blessing for Greeks than the blessing of freedom.'

The Athena Temple is built on a site as spectacular as any in Turkey. Designed by Pytheos, the temple now has five restored twelve-metre Ionic columns contrasting with the huge rough cliff behind and the smooth fields that were once the sea below.

Priene went into decline a thousand years ago, left to the wind and the rain. The splendidly named early sufferers of ruinelust, the Society of Dilettanti, visited in 1764. German archeologists dug in the 1860s and 1890s and the Istanbul Archeological Institute has been doing conservation work since the 1970s.

The decline was probably because access to the outside world was too difficult. It had a communications problem; the port below the town silted up, and, while it was easy to defend, it was also hard to get to. That is still the case. No tourist hordes here on a windy, watery beautiful spring day.

Miletus, on the low shore across the way, also went into decline with the silting of the River Meander and the Gulf of Latmus. It is often swampy, and occasionally under water. The flood plain grows cotton and sunflowers and what looks to be rice. Silent Çafer grunted at my question, '*Riz*?'. And gum trees: they're all over Turkey too.

Miletus has a history going back to 1500 BC, when ancient Milesians are said to have fought 'like the Trojans' against the raiding Greeks. Milesians were seafarers and colonisers who founded towns as far away as the Crimea and the Black Sea coast.

The site of Miletus has something of a bad reputation as being too wet and squelchy, or else too hot and vast in the rest of the year. Guidebook writers talk about it being dark and brooding and melancholy, and the air solid with mozzies. The Turkish writer Evilya Celebi noted in his *Book of Travels* in 1670: 'The air is so heavy that even the donkeys cannot bray.'

Best known of the ancient Milesians was Thales (636–546 BC) who is credited with predicting eclipses, measuring the height of the pyramids by comparing the length of a man's shadow with his actual height at a certain time of day, and propagating the basic philosophy, 'Know thyself.'

Herodotus wrote of an event in Athens during the time of Pericles in 494 BC: 'When Phrynichus produced his play *The Capture of Miletus*, the audience in the theatre burst into tears. The author was fined a thousand drachmae for reminding them of a catastrophe which touched them so closely, and they forbade anyone ever to put the play on stage again.'

This play was about the revolt of the Ionian cities, including Miletus, against the Persians in 500 to 494 BC. These older Ionians killed all the male Carians and 'married' the Carian women. Herodotus says of this savagery:

The Ionians took no women with them but married Carian girls, whose parents they had killed. The fact that these women were forced into marriage after the murder of their fathers, husbands and sons, was the origin of the law established by oath and passed down to their female descendents forbidding them to sit at table with their husbands or to address them by name.

The story in the play clearly had no effect on one Aspasia, another of the very smart women of the region, who became

Pericles' mistress and taught him much of what he knew. Herodotus knew her, as did the city planner Hippodamus.

Silent Çafer stopped near a bedraggled row of Coke stalls, under a row of welcoming *Eucalpyptus nondescriptus* and in front of the great loom of the theatre.

'*Bilet?*' I said.

'Hundred thousand okay.'

'Cheap ruins, okay.'

The theatre has not been restored to the extent that similar but smaller theatres in Jerash have been. Climbing over the stage buildings, finding weedy carvings of centaurs and leopards and other more real forms of gladiatorial combats, the overgrown and under-restored atmosphere gives a feeling that you are 'discovering' this place. No-one tells you to get off, or not lift that stone, or crawl under things. It's the acme of ruinelust.

Among the barracker factions in Roman times in this theatre were the Blues, one of whom has inscribed his favourite seat in the outer with the words: 'place of the goldsmith of the Blues'. My football team in Australia is Carlton: the Blues. I hadn't thought the lineage was so ancient.

From the top of the hill behind the theatre I looked out over where the sea had once lapped the harbour entrance. I saw a pond with white floating flowers in front of the restored Ionic stoa, or verandah colonnade, which had fronted the shops of the harbour square. Waterlogged, the pond reflected the columns in a postcard view of a ruin.

I climbed down the hill and found the entrance to the harbour, the Lion Harbour. Here huge lions guarded the harbour entrance. One was still reluctantly doing so, up to its neck in water. There was the circular base and part of the carving of the large harbour monument that commemorated the victory of Octavian over Mark Antony in the Battle of Actium in 31 BC. A triton, with human torso and the tail of a fish, and bearing a paddle, sat in a boat.

Gymnasium, stadium, warehouses, houses – most of the later Roman city is under the swampy ground, with some pieces poking up. Miletus: 'The first [city] settled in Ionia, and the mother of many and great cities in Pontus and Egypt, and in various other parts of the world', as the Milesians used to say.

The most picturesque remaining ruin is the most recent: the Ilyas Bey Mosque, built in 1404 and now disused (the people of the village closest to Miletus moved away after the earthquake of 1955 which brought down the minaret). The roof is covered in a green lawn. Outside the wall a donkey chewed methodically, while inside a man cut green fodder.

On the path back to Silent Çafer's *taksi*, I visited the large Baths of Faustina. Faustina was the wife of Roman Emperor Marcus Aurelius, 161–180 AD. Inside was a pond with a fountain lion sitting in the sun, white flowers on green water, and a statue of the river god of the nearby River Meander wondering now where his river had gone. A small Turkish boy stood guard.

'German?'

'No.'

'English?'

'No.'

'America?'

'No.'

'Russia?'

'No, sorry.'

'What please?'

'You guess?'

'Okayokayokay – Frenchman.'

'Nope.'

'Spain man.'

'No.'

'Sorry. No know.'

The kid was very thin. He had teeth missing, and was dressed in a dirty jumper with no shoes. He gave me a smile, and a flower. 'Tell me.'

'Australia.'

'Ohh,' a tinkle of laughter, 'thank you. Number one.'

I am his first Australian, I thought. Man from another planet.

We drove to the Temple of Apollo at Didyma, twenty kilometres south. The road followed the general route of the Sacred Way which had connected Miletus with one of the most famous oracle temples of the time. Apollo himself is supposed to have taught the first oracle, one Branchus of Miletus. After Branchus, the priests who tended the temple became known as Branchidae, and the temple as Apollo Branchidae.

The archaic temple was built around a sacred spring and a sacred laurel tree. The oracle was world famous partly because of her style. She apparently spoke deliriously with her feet in the sacred spring when asked a question, and the answer was rendered into poetry by a priest.

Xerxes destroyed the archaic temple of Apollo, probably after he won the Battle of Lade off Miletus, in 494 BC. The Branchidae gave up the treasure of the temple to him in exchange for their lives, and he let them settle in Sogdiana in Persia.

The temple then went into a decline and the sacred spring dried up – until Alexander arrived in the area a hundred years later. The sacred spring gushed once again, and the oracle, handily still around, wisely foretold an Alexandrian victory over the rest of the world. Alexander ordered the building of a huge new temple, the one now on the site, 120 columns in all, which 500 years later was still not finished.

Alexander also later found the descendants of the Branchidae, and had them executed for their forbears' treachery.

Because of its size and extended plinth, the temple was never entirely buried and forgotten. Richard Chandler, one of the Dilettanti, came in 1764 to find: 'The columns yet entire are exquisitely fine, the marble mass so vast and noble, that it is impossible to conceive greater beauty and majesty in ruin.'

Back in Kuşadasi, I stumbled down the steep hill from the Otel to the newspaper kiosk and bought yesterday's English newspaper.

The Frankish leader was visiting near Tyre and Sidon. The Israelites were exchanging blows with an Islamist group. It was quiet in Damascus. In Anatolia, Kurdish tribesmen were being killed in the snow. A caravan had arrived in Antioch from Aleppo and the Euphrates. Greeks and Turks had planted flags on disputed rocklets. Nothing had changed.

CHAPTER TWELVE

THE TORTOISES
OF EPHESUS

THE ORIGINAL AUSTRALIAN AND New Zealand Pension (and 'Genuine Non-ripoff Carpet Shop') was a white two-storey building with a rooftop terrace and dining room. Vines trailed over the walls, and flags of many nations hung about, including mine. Sounds of cleaning and singing came from the rooms.

'Yeah mate, leave your pack over there, we'll fix you up later.'

Mine host was an Australian Turk. Been out, got married, unmarried, back again. Got a backpacker girlfriend from 'Brsbn'. 'Gunna go back one of these days.'

From the pension there was a view of the one restored column of the wonder of the world that had once been here, the Temple of Artemis.

The room was clean, had a pine bed, no water, was big enough to swing a cat, window onto the courtyard, sunshine, Turkish flag fluttering.

'Wanna beer? Nah? Okay see ya later.'

Selçuk is the closest town to the restored ruin of Ephesus – about two kilometres down the road. It is right next to the site of the Temple of Artemis, which itself is next to the old Isa Bey Mosque, which is below the ruins of St John's Church, which is below an Ottoman fortress. Just about the whole history of this part of Turkey can be found here, from the bronze age beginnings to the returned Aussie Turks making a living in the backpacker tourist trade.

Ephesus was for thousands of years just about the most wonderful place in the world. Only in the last 1500 years or so, in the Christian and Muslim eras, was it less than splendid, and now, in the 'Tourist Age', restoration work done on the Roman ruins of the city has made it a compulsory stop on the tourist trail and the cruise ship itinerary. They bus up from Kuşadasi and back in two-thirds of a day.

Ephesus was a port before the estuary of the River Cayster silted up. Great trading and temple towns were built on rivers and

overleaf: Stadium Street, Ephesus, Turkey

hilltops such as this up and down the coast. They survived for as long as the rivers flowed and the harbours were dredged, and the gods were propitiated: Ephesus and Miletus on the sea, Didyma and Priene in the hills.

Leaving backpack and book bag behind, I sauntered to the site of the Temple of Artemis just five minutes from the pension. The site is a pit more than 200 metres long, and eight or nine metres below the level of the road. It is fenced off and is right next to the *jadarma* post, a police training institution. 'No photo', said the sign. The lads were square bashing out the back as I walked down from the entrance gate.

Visits to the large Temple of Artemis in Jerash, and to the Temple of Apollo at Didyma gave some idea of the scale that this temple was built on. It must have been very big indeed.

I had stopped here once before at the height of summer. It was baked hard then, nothing to see except old Coke cans and the column. The often-photographed stork's nest on the top of the column wasn't there. There was no fence, and the pit was as dry as history. But the excavations are in fact below the water table for most of the year, and the trenches dug by the Austrian archeologists who have been working here through the 1990s fill up, as does the whole area of the temple and the altar. It is a lush green depression in spring, with ponds.

On closer inspection, large marble slabs which were part of the platform the temple stood on, and perhaps part of the road that leads from the temple to Ephesus, were visible through the water. A family of caretakers lives within the enclosure in a house screened by eucalypts and willows. They have cows, a few sheep, peacocks and peahens, roosters. Daisies and poppies pop up. Little yellow and black birds dive into the green pools.

Here was fecund life in all her glory, the spot where the original earth mother goddess Cybele had been worshipped 5000 years ago. Cybele–Artemis came to represent all the earth mother goddesses from the region and beyond. Mary, mother of Jesus, is supposed to have lived in a house not far away, where she came to stay after the crucifixion. Perhaps the continuum of woman-worship at Ephesus runs from Cybele through Artemis to Mary and beyond. It seems hardly coincidental that two of the contemporary women worshipped, by the media at least, are named Madonna and Diana, the Roman name for Artemis.

Artemis herself may be seen in two extraordinarily beautiful but weird statues, having twenty-nine or more breast-like symbols of fertility and fruitfulness, in the museum in Selçuk just around the corner. The statues were found in the 1950s, artfully buried a thousand years before against the depredations of the temple-destroying Christians. They are first century AD copies of the cult statue herself. One Artemis has a temple on her head, rows of animal figures, necklaces of pearls and grapes, and a belt of bees – the bee being the town symbol of Ephesus. The other, made from a green marble, also features bees and breasts (or are they bull's balls?), lions, goats, griffins, deer, sphinxes, and flowers.

There was something else, moving in the water and on the marble slabs, poking out. Moving stones? No, they were tortoises. There were hundreds of little tortoises swimming in the ponds, sitting in the sun on the marble slabs, snoozing on the grassy banks. I made a movement and the nearest dozen clacked and clambered back into the safety of the water.

I chortled out loud. The archeologist who spent twenty years looking for and excavating this wonder of the world was named John Turtle Wood.

Pliny the Elder said there were 127 columns twenty metres high in the first marble temple. It was the biggest temple in the world, one that had a profound effect on the spirit of the region and its economy for close to two thousand years. According to Pliny, it was built by a Cretan architect, Chersiphron, who had visited Egypt – and presumably been as impressed as everyone else has been by the forest of columns at Karnak.

The forest of columns idea in temple design has an echo in the bush coloured marble in the public foyer at Parliament House in Canberra, a secular temple where the rough Australian demos is played out. Parliament House is sunk in a green hill, a preternatural archeological site, crawled over by tourists, while beneath the earth orators, sophists and rhetoricians ply their trade.

Croesus destroyed earlier wooden temples when he conquered Ephesus, but set about building the first huge new marble one straight away, in around 560 BC. John Turtle Wood found a column drum dedicated to Artemis by King Croesus when he excavated – and sent it to the British Museum.

The temple built by Croesus was destroyed by the madman Herostratus on 21 July 356 BC, the day of Alexander the Great's birth. The second marble temple was begun shortly afterwards and was still being constructed as 22 years later Alexander passed through. He offered to pay for its rebuilding. The Ephesians, however, were well capable of rebuilding their own temple. A sensible adviser, perhaps the chief priest, the Megabyxus, told Alexander that it would not be wise for one god to be seen to pay homage to another. But Alexander did appoint his architect, Cheirocrates, to supervise the building, and perhaps paid for the sculptor Scopas to carve some of the front row of columns, which were fabulously and unusually ornate.

The platform this temple stood on was three times the size of the Parthenon in Athens. It was built ten large marble steps higher than that of Croesus, allowing the building, and Artemis herself (from a window in the side of the temple), to be seen from the harbour, then nearby. In front was the altar building, a huge affair where, among other things, the meat for Ephesus was slaughtered daily. Today it is another pond.

This second Artemesium was destroyed by the marauding Ostrogoths in 262 AD, but was built again with many of the destroyed fragments sealed beneath a pathway. An earthquake damaged it in the 300s, and in 401 St John Chrysostom ordered it sacked and plundered and the lime kilns set to work.

Standing in the pit excavated by John Turtle Wood makes it easy to understand how difficult it was for him to find this place. I was five metres or more under the present level of the land. Back in 1863 there was nothing sticking up, and no detailed Homeric guidebook such as the *Iliad* provided for those seeking the location of Troy.

Wood was employed in Smyrna as an architect–engineer building the railway. He took leave in 1863 and devoted himself to finding the temple. He obtained the necessary *firman* from the Ottoman government and from the British Museum, where he would send the antiquities he hoped to find. He lived outside Smyrna and for the first years of his work commuted the fifty miles from there every day, four hours each way.

He broke a collarbone on one occasion and had a trial hole collapse on him on another. By the end of 1863, all that he had discovered from seventy-five deep holes and numerous trenches was that the plain of Ephesus had silted up to a height of three metres or more.

In 1864 he started to excavate the odeum – a small 1400-seat town-meeting theatre also used as the council chamber, the bouleuterion – for the British Museum, and also had a small number or men excavating the large mound covering the proscenium of the Great Theatre.

In his report Wood wrote of the difficulties of taking paper pressings of inscriptions because of the wind; of sickness; a visit by HRH Prince Arthur; problems with workers; and murder. A dreadful smell at the theatre turned out to be the body of a murder victim, most probably killed by one of his men.

In 1866 he started in earnest on the Great Theatre. There he found inscriptions regarding the procession of gold and silver images of Artemis from the temple to the theatre and back to the temple. These images had been made by a rich first century

THE TORTOISES OF EPHESUS 247

Roman, Caius Vibius Salutarius, and were to be paraded on 25 May, the birthday of Artemis. The month of May was known as Artemesion.

The images were to be carried from the temple to the theatre through the Magnesian Gate, where the young men (the ephebe) of the city would take them. Afterwards they were to come back to the temple via another gate so the whole city could see their splendour. Salutarius left a fortune for the chief priest at the temple, the Megabyxus, to invest at 9 per cent to pay for these annual tributes. Megabyxus literally means 'drone bee'. He was attended by priestesses called the Melissae or honey bees (hence the seductive name Melissa).

St John wrote of one procession, describing priests blowing rams' horns and incense so thick in the theatre that he could barely see the images of Artemis. The cult image, a much larger version of the statues in the museum, was carried on a litter or on a chariot.

Caius Vibius Salutarius wrote on the wall of the theatre of a procession in which the whole city took part: magistrates, administrators, priests and priestesses of the temple, musicians, dancers, young people; some carrying instruments for the sacrifices, others leading animals, some on horseback and others carrying personal images of Artemis.

Wood thought that if he could find the city gates described by Salutarius, he could follow the wheel ruts in the marble to where the temple might be. Later that year he found the Magnesian Gate, which had three openings, one for pedestrians and two for chariots and wagons.

Clearing away a mass of earth in front of the gate, he followed the path until it 'bifurcated'. One rutted road led to Selçuk and was made of massive marble blocks; the other, less worn, road led to Magnesia on the River Meander – hence the name of the gate – and was hardly worn down at all.

Wood took the path most travelled, and dug along the course

of this road for two more seasons. He was digging three metres down, finding Roman ruins along the side of the road but no temple. Wood sunk holes on the boundaries of the barley fields and at a grove of olives at another boundary some half a mile distant. Following a modern boundary, he dug another hole and struck a corner and then a stone inscribed in the reign of Augustus. at 6BC, saying that the wall was to be maintained by the temple.

Wood wrote in his report:

> The great question of the whereabouts of the temple was now decided. Six years had elapsed since I had first begun the search ... The discovery of the peribolus (boundary) wall and the inscriptions built into it occurred early in May 1869, and it was at that time that I had several narrow escapes from being taken prisoner by the same band of brigands ...

On 1 December 1869 he found a column base, and on 9 December one of the mutilated capitals.

> What building could this be but the great Temple of Artemis? On the last day of the year of 1869, the marble pavement of the temple, so long lost, so long sought for, and so long almost despaired of was at last actually found at a depth nearly twenty feet below the present surface of the ground.

The *mudir*, or mayor, of the district came down to see these 'wonders', and Wood showed him ancient column drums and capitals.

> I told him they were the remnants of an ancient mosque or church in the time of the ancient Greeks, when they did not worship the one true God but had many gods, male and female, and that this church was dedicated to the worship of a female, whose statue forty or fifty

feet high, was set up inside it. 'Ah,' said the *mudir*, as if a new light had broken in upon him, 'they were Protestants.'

Wood discovered that, just as at Halicarnassus, lime kilns had been set up in ancient times to burn the limestone and marble for its 'cement' … that great Middle Eastern industry again. Only one of the fabled column drums with its beautiful carvings by Scopas that the ancients had mentioned remained – a badly damaged drum that took months to be hauled to the sea. It was sent to the British Museum. The British Museum stopped subsidising Wood's dig in 1874, though he kept working for a few more years. His last season was in 1884, and he died in England in 1890 at the age of seventy.

Archeologist John Romer, musing on the discoveries of more recent diggers at the temple, such as the Austrian Dr Anton Bammer, has argued that there is a 'continuity of sacredness' about this spot.

An ancient beach, a freshwater spring, Mycenaean pottery and a small altar discovered since Wood's dig suggest that this was very sacred 3500 years ago. They've found gold and ivory ornaments and offerings dating back to the first known temple, around 850 BC.

The archeologist's discovery of the rough stone bases for wooden columns in the manner of the classic Greek design are, Romer says, the oldest known example of the typical Greek temple, the ancestor to the Parthenon. There is nothing much of the temples to be seen now. I sat on the grassy bank above the ponds and pools and cows and peacocks and tortoises.

A man, the gatekeeper, walked over and sat next to me. I thought he wanted entrance money. He didn't. He placed his hand on my arm and pulled out a tourist brochure, the cover of which showed the site with men at work. It was a photograph of the site being dug.

This man pointed at one figure. 'Me,' he said. And another, 'My father.'

I pointed at a cow. 'Your cow.'

'Yes, yes,' he said, delighted.

'We live here,' pointing at the house, 'and work here when archeologist come.'

'Is peaceful. Lots of tortoises,' I said to him.

'Yes.'

'Not much of Artemis.'

He unrolled a corner of his *galabyia*-like garment and pulled out a coin. It looked old, but might have been a reproduction such as you can buy at the Archeological Museum in Istanbul. He passed it to me. It had a worn picture of the columns of the temple, and a smudge where Artemis might have been, sur-mounted by the shape of a pediment. It looked worn enough to be real – Roman, probably. Not worth a lot anywhere, except here.

'You take. Artemis.'

'No thanks, I can't. No money.'

'No, not want money. You take.'

He unrolled another corner of his garment and pulled another coin out. This was very black and my eyes were not in good enough shape to see what it was. He tapped my arm.

'No, no. I can't. Sorry.' If real, illegal, if not, not worth a watch.

He tapped my arm again.

'Watch. For watch two coins. Old, very old. I find here. Artemis coin.'

If true, very tempting, but I had been gulled already, in Egypt, in Jordan, in Syria. 'No I can't. I need my watch.'

'You give me watch!'

I thought briefly of John Turtle Wood and the brigands. 'No.' I gestured in the direction of the police training establishment. '*Jadarma*.'

'Okayokayokay. Someone else buy.'

I took the road from the temple up to the top gate, the Magnesian Gate of Ephesus rediscovered by John Turtle Wood, quite high on the hill of Mt Pion, and then began the breathtaking walk down the Street of the Curetes to the Marble Way.

Only 10 per cent of the site of Ephesus has been excavated, but what has been gives you a good a feel for what it must have been like to live in a prosperous Roman city.

Originally Ephesus seems to have been based around the other hill, Ayasuluk Hill, where the Church of St John and the modern Selçuk are built. But in the 300s BC, the story goes, after Alexander's visit, Lysimachus blocked up the drains and caused a flood in town, making the citizens rebuild it on the present site.

Ephesus was built over the next 200 years. It became capital of the Roman province of Asia in 129 BC, and styled itself, in boosterish inscriptions, as 'First and Foremost Metropolis in Asia'. Bigger than Smyrna! Longer-lasting than Troy! It reached a population of 250 000 in the 200s.

It flourished, as the extraordinary extent of the buildings and public utilities such as the water and sewerage systems disclose. It was one of only three Roman cities to have street lighting (Rome and Antioch were also lit), with fifty lamps down the street to the harbour.

This big city had all fashions of philosophy represented, Christianity included, and continued to prosper until the 500s; two great councils of the early Church were held there, in 431 and 449. With the silting of the harbour, however, and the movement of the Roman empire to Constantinople, Ephesus went into a decline.

Most people seem to have shifted back to the more defensible hill of Ayasuluk in the 500s, which is where the Byzantines had built the first fortress. Then came an 800-year interlude before the Turks extended the fortress and built the mosque of Isa Bey. By the time John Turtle Wood arrived 550 years later, Ephesus was a forgotten desolate and abandoned place.

Even after the small boom in tourism occasioned by Wood's excavations, it was still remote and difficult to get to. In 1936 H. G. Morton could famously write that at Ephesus there was 'no sign of life but a goatherd leaning on a broken sarcophagus or a lonely peasant outlined against a mournful sunset'.

But the ongoing excavation and partial restoration of Ephesus in the last forty years has restored it to a new place of honour as the biggest and best Roman city in the eastern Mediterranean, or anywhere else.

The path down Curetes Street from the Magnesian Gate is composed of the large and now slightly uneven marble slabs uncovered by Wood, and lined with the gymnasia, temples, ceremonial gateways, fountains, the odeum, a grain exchange, and marketplace–agora.

The prytaneion, or town hall, was on the right next to the small theatre or odeum. This was where the Ephesian town council (prytanes) had its 'offices' and meeting room, where dignitaries received visitors, and where the flame of Hestia (or Vesta) was kept burning. Hestia was the goddess of the hearth, honoured in every Ephesian home. The prytaneion was destroyed in the 400s in the riots of St John Chrysostom, but not before the two beautiful statues of Artemis were buried, to be uncovered in the 1950s and placed in the Selçuk museum.

Just below the Gate of Hercules, I heard a thrush singing, stopped and sat on a stone opposite Trajan's Fountain. All these reconstructed buildings, or parts of them, are cut into the fennel-flowered side of the hill. I wondered what was still to be found in the streets and lanes that must be covered there. The beautiful Library of Celsus was almost glowing in the sunlight down the hill. There was no-one else in sight for a few minutes. I felt like I was waiting for a passing chariot – back to the future perhaps, with John Turtle Wood aboard.

A beautiful square opens out from the corner of the Street of the Curetes and Marble Street. On one side is the Gate of

Mazaeus and Mithridates, built around 4 BC. This pair were freed slaves of the Emperor Augustus, and the gate is consecrated to him. Augustus visited Ephesus in 16 BC to pay homage to Artemis.

The little square also has the most beautiful building in Ephesus, the Library of Celsus. It was not built until 110 AD by Gaius Julius Aquila as a monument to Gaius Celsus Polemaenus, his late father who had been Governor of Asia. Restoration began in the 1950s.

The library once held 12 000 books in niches inside the two rows of double Corinthian columns, watched over by four reproduction female statues representing wisdom (Sophia), valour (Arete), thought (Ennoia) and knowledge (Episteme). It is an arresting facade, and sitting on the steps you can almost hear the voices of Ephesians going about their business.

Outside, along Marble Street, is a footprint carved on the path, pointing the way to the brothel, and also pointing toes in the direction of the theatre. In the theatre is a late Roman graffito saying, 'Carn the Greens! And the Christian emperors!' The Greens were one of the sporting mobs of the time, along with the Blues, Reds and Whites …

It was in this theatre that Paul preached to the Ephesians on one of his trips around the eastern Mediterranean in the years 54 and 56. On his third trip to Ephesus, Paul spent some years here, re-baptising Christians and arguing with the Jews in the synagogue, and holding public meetings in the lecture hall of Tyrannus. Ephesus was a diverse commercial city, a thriving seaport, and a centre of silver and jewellery manufacture for the adornment of the locals as well as souvenirs for visitors to the Temple of Artemis. In fact the local economy was based on a kind of cult religious tourism.

When Paul inveighed against the idolaters of Ephesus, telling the Christians to put on all of God's armour, it did not seem to

Demetrius, a silversmith of Ephesus, to be a business opportunity. Demetrius's stock-in-trade was making silver models of the temple, and according to the Bible (Acts 19) 'it brought a great deal of profit to his workers'. Demetrius called together a meeting of silversmiths and goldsmiths and jewellers and others to discuss the threat of Paul's preaching to their business.

Demetrius told them that there was a danger that their business would get a bad name; that the temple of the great goddess Artemis would come to mean nothing, and that her greatness would be destroyed.

Demetrius was obviously a passionate and inspiring speaker; the crowd was stirred up, saying, 'Great is Artemis of Ephesus!' In the riot that ensued, the crowd rushed out, grabbed a couple of Paul's acolytes and dragged them off to the theatre. Paul wanted to go there himself, but was persuaded by local authorities and friends that harm might come to him if he did. Instead, another associate of Paul's, Alexander, tried to speak in defence of Paul and Christianity. But the audience would hear none of it and shouted 'Great is Artemis of Ephesus' for two hours.

By this time the local authorities were somewhat worried, and the town clerk found himself addressing the meeting. He said, 'Fellow Ephesians! Everyone knows that the city of Ephesus is the keeper of the temple of the great Artemis and of the sacred stone that fell down from heaven. Nobody can deny these things. So calm down and don't do anything reckless. You have brought these men here even though they have not robbed temples or said evil things about our goddess. If Demetrius and his workers have any charges to make against anyone, we have our authorities and the regular days for court up at the odeum. But if there is something more it will have to be settled by a legal meeting of citizens, for after today there is the danger that we will be accused of a riot. So everyone please go home.'

At least that's the Bible story.

The stone he referred to is the great beam that puzzled

Alexander's architects and engineers in the construction of the temple in the 300s BC. Artemis herself is supposed to have helped them lower the lintel.

Sitting on a carved seat in the gymnasium opposite the theatre, where the actors used to rehearse and train, I heard, beneath the sound of a tourist group cheering and clapping in the theatre, a scrabbling clicking sound in the bright green grass growing around the marble slabs. This sound went on for several minutes. A rabbit? A snake? The intrepid naturalist clambered along a marble length, pulled aside a thistle, and there were two tortoises making love in the sunshine. At least wanting to. The smaller male seemed to have been merely tapping the rear bumper bar of the female when I disturbed them.

Outside the museum in Selçuk I met Sedat, who runs a small knick-knack and jewellery shop …

'Business? You ask business? Buy from me and I will have some business. Troubles. These Kurds and these fanatics they are the ruin of my business. Christians okay, there is plenty to see around here, but they are so easily discouraged.'

I imagined Demetrius walking by saying, 'Well we've warned everyone about Paul and these Christians. Paul says he doesn't want anyone's gold or silver or clothing – doesn't believe in it. Well, that's the point! Jewellery and adornment is our business! Idols and graven images – that's us! Gold, silver, precious stones – what would this place be without them?'

Sedat offered tea, and I asked him what else he had, not being very interested in another bad carving of the many-breasted Artemis or the other silver trinkets or postcards. He showed me a case inside his shop. Most things were displayed outside, gathering dust. I spotted a couple of ring-seals: semi-precious stones carved intaglio so that when pressed into wax or clay they leave a raised cameo. Set in a gold-coloured frame, they look oldish. The export of genuine antiques is forbidden in Turkey, so the rule of thumb is: if it looks very old, it isn't. While antiquity smugglers are at work in Turkey, as elsewhere in the world, the practice ought not be encouraged. Everything looks better in context – Ephesian objects, if they can't survive in situ, are best in the local museum, such as the excellent one in Selçuk. Ripped out of context, whether in London, Melbourne or, to some extent, Istanbul, objects are deprived of meaning. It's like watching Balinese dance in a Victorian theatre.

Sedat profusely admired my accidental and unintentional connoisseurship, which was simply based on the observation that those green and red stones, though somewhat crudely carved, were not carved yesterday – last year perhaps, or last century, but 2000 years ago, I didn't think so.

Bargaining was brief and brisk. 'Jewellery, my friend … we have made a living selling it since the days of great Artemis. Take them back to Australia, but tell no-one that Sedat sold below cost. But I would lose money rather than have day with no sale.'

Next morning I walked towards St John's Church, on the flank of the hill of Ayasuluk above the museum. The Church, or Basilica, of St John has been partially restored over the past seventy-five years, and work is still going on. The great church was dedicated in 535 but was built on the site of earlier church buildings. St John himself is buried beneath these antipodean feet, and his story lives here. Stories live everywhere around Ephesus: the rocks and ruins sing them like crickets. But on this day the aura was disturbed by a scrum of Turkish schoolchildren who swarmed onto the marble plinth and sang an aggressive, secular-sounding song. They marched around the site, stopping and singing.

Below the church, the mosque. No Christian tourists were here, no kids, nor was there an entry fee. The Isa Bey Mosque was built in 1375 by Damascene architect Ali ibn Dimiski on the instruction of Isa Bey, son of the Emir of Aydin. The stump of

only one minaret remains, but there is a peacefully quiet courtyard, and an equally quiet prayer hall. The hall is supported by
Roman columns brought from Ephesus. I took off my shoes,
although the attendant said with his hands and eyebrows that I
needn't have bothered with such matters. I left them at the door
anyway and padded around the elegantly stark interior.

The attendant had some of the beautiful cards you get all over
Turkey – reproductions of faïence, embroidery and tiles. I bought
some tile cards, put on my shoes and headed back to the pansyon.
Outside, a man was making brass shoeshine boxes, and another,
antique carvings.

At the *pansyon*, the sun setting behind Mt Pion, the travellers
gathered on the roof, fresh from the day's perambulations.
Accents from all over the world assembled: Canada, the United
States, 'Briiian mate, we ain't Great, are we?', and Straya.

Most had been to Ephesus, some were back from Kuşadasi,
one had been asleep most of the day. A couple of people had
arrived from Izmir, and Pergamum to the north. One group of ten
had their own bus and had set up their own kitchen on the roof.
They had left London some weeks before with the idea that they
would drive to Cape Town. Why not?

Somewhat world-weary adventures began to unfold: rip-off
pensions in Kuşadasi, good deals in Izmir, crazy bus drivers,
carpet stories. As someone prone to taking taxis, I listened without letting on about my traveller's heresies.

Everyone had a Turkish carpet story except me, as I was heading in the carpet direction. I told my story of investigating carpets
in Saqqara in Egypt: the silk, the ladies weaving, the cost, the
amusement of the owner when I said I wanted to know the 'real'
cost; I might as well have asked, 'How long is a silk thread?'

These were young travellers who genuinely lived on $10 a
day, who had been away for months and had no plans. I developed a great respect for their hardy constitutions, their refusal to

be beaten down by the non-system, and their optimism about what the next day would bring.

They were not in a hurry like me. On the other hand a few of them seemed to see less. Dressed in a wild assortment of layers of T-shirts, old jeans, elaborate walking boots, caps and hats, and warm jackets, they exuded the friendly odour of the road.

The Efes beer did the rounds, I got out my nuts, and found I had a great deal of trouble understanding the Strayan accent.

'Whereya from? Straya? Wheir? Sinny Melbn Brsbn?'

It seemed to me that the language had become a spoken kind of Arabic; or maybe Aramaic, where all the vowels disappear and everything is in a curly script, with a rising inflection on the end.

'Brnswck? Yeah evryones bin to Brnswck.'

'Errr! Errr! Thght y'mnt Brnswck Hds Qnsld! Bstard!'

'Nehhh. Nver bn t'Mlnbn!'

Listening, I developed the notion of the Three Traveller's Questions: Whereya from or whatareya? Wheryagoin? Howlong-yabinaway?

Whatareya? helps define your putative religion and relation-ship to the world. Saying you are an Australian avoids, for the most part, messy questions about whether you are Christian, Muslim, Hindu, Jew. I think that's why the Japanese are welcome everywhere too; apart from being noisily inquisitive and curious, they are also likely to be some unfathomable secular Buddhist Shinto background.

Wheryagoin? or Wheryaheaded? When people know who you are by what you are, they want to know 'what next'. This is the opportunity for the interlocutor to say, 'Yeah Ibinthere.' There's this and that worth doing, and this that and the other thing that are not.

The ultimate question in the traveller's stakes is, 'Howlong-yabinaway?' Tourists have been away just a week or so, and are always passing through. Genuine travellers must have been on the road for a month or more.

At the *pansyon* that night, I qualified under the general traveller heading, but disqualified myself by having a bus to catch and definite things to do in the next couple of weeks. Having started in Egypt gave me a certain amount of kudos, because everyone else was based in or coming from Europe.

As it got dark we moved into the dining room, a warm carpet-covered room with a couple of tables and the prospect of copious amounts of food: lentils, vegetables, rice and the red wine of choice, known as 'Dikman'.

At the table I stumbled to there was an English couple with accents that sounded like they were sending themselves up, a big moose of a Canadian girl all in black, a couple of earnest Americans from Utah and the Strayan girl from Brsbn.

While we drank more Dikman, I recalled out loud the Priapus figure in the museum holding a tray up with his … which did not go down all that well with the Utah-ans. I told some of the stories of Ephesus, Artemis and Alexander, St Paul and Demetrius, and said that I was headed for Gallipoli.

'I been there,' said the man who had been everywhere. 'Nothin' there, except dead men.'

The Strayan said she hated war and wondered how anyone could get involved. 'Sometimes you don't have a choice,' I told her. 'Sometimes that's the way it is – it comes to you.' I tried to explain the difference between Vietnam and Gallipoli, but the wine had made me fuzzy in the thinking.

Next day I caught a bus to Çanakkale by way of Izmir – Troy and Gallipoli on my mind.

CHAPTER THIRTEEN

GALLIPOLI
STORMED

ETTING ON TURKISH BUSES is the easy part; getting off at the right spot, as I had already discovered, is more difficult. No-one tells you whether the bus will stop at the *otogar*, by the side of the road or, in Çanakkale, at the ferry terminal on the Asian side. Last time I had been on this bus, it had stopped at the ferry terminal, and everyone who wanted to stay in Çanakkale got out while the bus waited for the ferry to come across the Dardanelles from Ece-abat.

This time the ferry was close to shore and the bus barely paused before I realised that it was not going to stop. I shouted at the conductor. 'Hey, Çanakkale!'

'You want get off?'

'Yes, Çanakkale! My bag is underneath.'

'Can no stop. Ferry she wait.'

'Stop the bus, I want to get off!'

'You get off on other side please.'

'This side! Çanakkale!'

'Okayokayokay.'

Horns sounded. The conductor got out his tool to open the underside door of the bus so I could get my backpack out, the bus inching forward.

'Why you not get off?'

'Why you not stop?'

'Why you not tell me?'

'Ahh, ptah!'

And it was not even summer yet.

Çanakkale is a town that lives for the ferry. It connects the hinterland of Turkey to Istanbul, seven hours distant on the other side of the Dardanelles.

The mythical Leander used to swim across the Dardanelles – known to the legend-writers as the Hellespont – at Abydos, just north of Çanakkale, to see his girlfriend Hero who was confined in a high tower at Sestus. One night the wind blew out Hero's

overleaf: Turkish memorial, Anzac Cove

guiding light, and Leander drowned. Hero saw his body at the base of the tower, jumped and was reunited with him in death.

Lord Byron repeated the feat (the swimming part) more successfully in 1810 – in the reverse direction. Byron remarked that the distance, while not more than a mile, had a hazardous current. 'So much so, that I doubt whether Leander's conjugal powers must not have been exhausted in his passage to Paradise.'

I'd arranged to stay in the Anzac Rest House which was somewhere across the Dardanelles near Anzac Cove. Exactly where it was, how to get there, and where to buy supplies was something I would deal with when I crossed the Dardanelles. The Rest House was said to be more like an old Australian beach hut than anything else, and I was excited about spending time by myself at Gallipoli. It would be the climax of my little odyssey.

I checked into the Anfartalar Hotel for the night, partly because of the name, but also because it was right on the quay, just past the wonderful smells of the fresh *pide* and *kofte* and *kebap*. The Anfartalar Hills are the high points above Anzac.

From the Anfartalar balcony – wrinkled carpet in the corridor, creaky lift, soccer on the TV – the view across the Dardanelles was misted over with rain. This spring in Turkey was wet and cold. The Anzac April of 1915 fortunately only had a couple of days of this weather. The snow came later.

I walked down along the quay, looking for fish to eat and newspapers in English. The news was sold out but there were plenty of fish.

'Sorry, no English news today.'

'*Turkish Daily News* [the English language paper]?'

'Turkish news yesterday.'

The Kalel Sultaniye Fort is fifteen minutes walk along the quay. First built in the time of Mehmet II in 1454, it was in use in 1915 and it still is today. If you wander too close to the top of the walls a sentry will have you scurrying off.

There's a naval and military museum in the square beside the fort, where old World War I guns can be viewed, as well as a reconstruction of the famous Turkish minelayer the *Nusrat*, which helped destroy the British and French fleet sailing down the Dardanelles in March 1915 by laying and relaying the mine-field. This victory on *18 Mart* is the Turkish 'Anzac Day' – the difference being that they celebrate a win. The naval attempt to 'force the Dardanelles' was the prelude to the landing in April. Had it been successful and the Turkish resistance simply folded – as the British apparently believed it would – the landing would have been unnecessary. But the naval attempt was an exercise in military arrogance that did not count on the Turks actually defending their country. Across the water the huge soldier carved in white permanently reminds visitors of the date.

This piece of naval folly was accompanied by Australian sub-mariners in the AE2 who in fact did some damage before being damaged themselves and captured, spending the duration as pris-oners of war under very arduous conditions.

Napoleon, a somewhat romantic strategist asked in 1808 'Who is to have Constantinople? That is always the crux of the problem.' After *18 Mart* it seemed that much more than romantic naval statements would be required for France and Britain to have that city.

I found a restaurant full of steam and smoke, tables full of young Çanakkalians rubbing each other's legs, smoking like chimneys, downing *arak* at a great rate of knots, watching the soccer on the TV and holding conversations with three or four tableloads of other people all at the same time. I was ushered to a corner table which was ceremoniously cleaned of scraps and cats. They had some fresh-looking snapper-like fish in the glass case, which I pointed to.

'One? Two?'

'One is enough.'

'Salad?'

'Okay.'
'Beer?'
'Yes, please.'
'My friend, you are welcome in Turkey.'

The *taksi* rank is opposite the clocktower square in Çanakkale. A dozen drivers forlornly watch the rain. It is thirty-two kilometres, or about fifty minutes, to Troy over the pine-covered hills on the main Izmir road.

The sullen driver drove fast in the wet, wanting his million Turkish lira. After twenty kilometres there was a turn off to Truva, or Troy, passing through flat agricultural land, damp cows huddled. The souvenir shop at the entrance gateway was uninhabited. In a taxi you pay an entrance fee for yourself, and a small parking fee for the driver to sit and wait.

Troy, the location of the ten-year Trojan War where the Archaean Greeks tried to invade the mainland, and Anzac Cove, where the Australians tried to do the same thing 3500 years later, are within fifty sea-miles of each other, on either side of the entrance to the Dardanelles.

The stories of the Greeks and the Trojans are told in Homer's *Iliad*; the stories of the Australians are told in Charles Bean's *Official History of Australia in the War of 1914–1918*. Both Homer and Bean believed that the way to tell the story of their respective battles was through the stories of the individuals concerned: Achilles, say, or Captain Lalor. Homer knew the spirits of each of his heroes, but Bean seems to have talked to every Australian at Gallipoli, or his mate. Bean was there, Homer was writing 500 years later.

The connections between Troy and Gallipoli were in the minds of some Australian soldiers in 1915. Our dead lie in the same corner of memory with the ancient dead. One Australian soldier, a Melbourne University graduate Private V. Finch, wrote in his diary that when he sailed for Lemnos from Egypt 'he was thinking hard about the old Greek and Latin poets and what they had to say'. And not just the graduates. Versifying and yarning were high on the list of self-made entertainments for Australians of that time.

The Anzac Book, edited by Charles Bean, is a collection of poems, stories, yarns, paintings, sketches, photographs and jokes from Anzac in 1915. It was published in 1916, and contains some wonderfully funny, dry and droll material, as well as a lot that is serious and sad. Among the poems are hymns to nicotine, a clean bath, food and the history of the place. The Anzacs, many of them at least, were well aware of where they were, and what the significance of it was.

'L.L.' wrote 'The Graves of Gallipoli' at Anzac, 1915:

Some flower that blooms beside the Southern foam
May blossom where our dead Australians lie,
And comfort them with whispers of their home;
And they will dream, beneath the alien sky,
Of the Pacific Sea.

'Thrice happy they who fell beneath the walls,
under their father's eyes,' the Trojan said,
'Not we who die in exile where who falls
Must lie in foreign earth.' Alas! Our dead
Lie buried far away.

J. Wareham of the 1st Australian Field Ambulance contributed 'The Trojan War, 1915':

We care not what old Homer tells
Of Trojan war and Helen's fame.
Upon the ancient Dardanelles
New peoples write – in blood – their name.

Homeric wars are fought again
By men who like old Greeks can die;

Australian back block heroes slain,
With Hector and Achilles lie.

No legend lured these men to roam;
They journeyed forth to save from harm
Some Mother–Helen sad at home,
Some obscure Helen on a farm.

And when one falls upon the hill –
Then by dark Styx's gloomy strand,
In honour to plain Private Bill
Great Agamemnon lifts his hand!

Homer's *Iliad* tells the story of the last part of the Trojan War, an embroidery on one of the raids on the mainland of Anatolian Turkey, called Troas or the Troad by the Archaean Greeks. They were from the great Bronze Age civilisation centred on Mycenae in the centuries 1500–1200 BC. Agamemnon was their great king. What might be his mask – it is named for him – glows magnificently in the National Museum in Athens. Troy – a layer of the mound I was standing on – was destroyed around this time.

Homer seems to have written his story down 500 years after this, in the 700s BC. Izmir, or Smyrna, just down the road, was Homer's home town. He must have known the lie of the land from personal experience, and he apparently combined direct observation of a place very like one of the citadels built here, Troy, with attributes of the inhabitants at the time of the Trojan War. These attributes can be confirmed through archeology.

The Greeks used 'hollow boats' and the description of their armour matches Mycenaean paintings and carvings. The walls of one of the cities of Troy are beautifully constructed. The Trojans, interestingly, have the epithet 'horse-breeding' applied to them by Homer. Horse breeding continued in the Troad until late Ottoman times.

It seems probable to me that a raid on Troy by Bronze Age Greeks from across the Aegean did occur, and that Homer wrote down the story from an oral tradition, adding to it and making it the remarkable work that is the *Iliad*. Five hundred years is not such a long time for a story to persist: the tales of *Arabian Nights* are more distant from us than the events of the Trojan War were to Homer. And it is such a great story, it strains belief to think that it would not have persisted with the storytellers of those days.

What happened in the Trojan War is simply told. Paris, son of King Priam, with the approval of the goddess Aphrodite, took Helen, wife of King Menelaus of Sparta, back to his home city of Troy. Agamemnon, King of Mycenae, a Greek ally of Sparta, headed an expedition to avenge this kidnapping. Agamemnon recruited an army of Greek heroes and their troops, including Achilles and his Myrmidons, his best friend Patroklos, Ajax and Odysseus. Their expedition (and Helen's face) launched a thousand ships to lay siege to Troy for ten years. Troy was defended by Paris and Hector.

In the tenth year of the siege, Achilles left after a dispute with Agamemnon. The Trojans then looked like winning, burning some of the Greek boats. Patroklos persuaded Achilles to lend him the Myrmidons and his armour to attack the Trojans again.

While the attack was successful in driving the Trojans back inside the walls, Patroklos was killed by the Trojan Hector while wearing Achilles' armour. Achilles, angry, then returned to kill Hector. After this there was a truce, with funeral games (giving Homer the opportunity to invent sports writing) honouring Hector. Achilles was later killed by Paris with a shot to the heel.

Towards the end of the siege a single-combat encounter took place between Menelaus and Paris, which the husband won. Helen, who is said to have spent ten years weaving her sorrows, was afterwards united with Menelaus, but not before Aphrodite spirited Paris away in a cloud for a last few nights with her.

Helen and Menelaus had incurred the displeasure of the gods, and rightly so – and were battered around the eastern Mediterranean, landing as has been noted, on the island of Pharos in Egypt.

But Troy fell when the Greeks gained access to the city by hiding in the Trojan Horse, then sacked and burned it. Homer does not tell this part of the story – it is a later addition.

The rather expressionist 'replica' of the Trojan Horse, a twenty-five metre high wooden construction, that stands outside the site is a photo opportunity for contemporary visitors. The site while rich in story is poor in relics.

Troy received visitors for a thousand years after the supposed date of the Trojan War, 1250 BC. Later historical heroes came to the place where they thought the earlier legendary heroes had died.

Alexander sacrificed at the 'grave' of Achilles in 334 BC on his way to conquering the known world. The site of a Hellenistic grave mound has been found near here, dedicated to Achilles. Alexander, who carried Homer's works around with him, regretted not having a 'singer' of that quality, but he took a shield that was supposed to have been used in the Trojan War, and left his own armour.

Julius Caesar visited in 48 BC, and Augustus regarded Troy, or Ilion as it was also known, as the 'mother city'. Aeneas, a Trojan, according to Homeric prophecy and stories preserved in Virgil's *Aeneid*, survived and escaped, founding Rome. Romans thought they were the descendants of Trojans.

When I stood inside the entrance looking for the glory that was Troy, I saw only humble rubble and a few low walls. Troy might now be the most disappointing wonder in the entire region, a sad mound distant from the sea, ploughed by trenches, with confused layers of stone exposed, a walking track to perambulate, and numbered signposts of the views.

Heinrich Schliemann, the German eccentric who made a fortune in St Petersburg trading in indigo, was a lifelong addict of Homer. He became an archeologist to try to prove Homer right. He used Homer and some ideas of the American Consul at Çanakkale, Frank Calvert, to locate this spot, and excavated between 1871 and 1890. While destroying some things and enthusiastically getting other things completely wrong, Schliemann pioneered the first scientific methods in archeology, such as the notion that sites like Troy might have been built up layer upon layer, and that the deeper the layer, the older the find. Although his original trenches destroyed some of what he meant to discover, in the end he did demonstrate that if Homer's Troy was anywhere, it was here.

Schliemann found what he claimed was Priam's treasure – gold and jewellery objects that he displayed around his wife's neck, and which were smuggled to the museum in Berlin 1880. They were thought lost in the destruction of the city at the end of World War II. Then, not very surprisingly, this treasure turned up in the Pushkin Museum in St Petersburg, Russia.

The Turks want their treasure back, as the Greeks want the bits of the Parthenon from the British Museum. They each seem to have an equal chance. In any event, the material is from the Troy II level – a thousand years before the presumed date of Priam and the Trojan War.

The site of Troy is confusing to the visitor because of the impossibility of exposing successive layers of material ranging over 3000 years without disturbing what is on top.

What *is* on top, numbered Troy IX, is the Roman town called Novum Ilium with which Augustus was concerned. It began in 85 BC, when the preceding Greek city was destroyed by one Fimbria and flourished under the patronage of the Roman imperial family until the establishment of the Roman Empire further up the Dardanelles at Byzantium, or Constantinople as it became in 328 AD. This seems to be when the silting of the bay of the River

Scamander also helped shift the balance of commerce to the other end of the Dardanelles. The visible remains of Troy IX are a pretty odeum or concert hall, and the bouleuterion, or council house.

Other buildings, such as the Temple of Athena, were begun in the Greek era, when the town was known as Ilion: Troy VIII. This is the Troy that Homer knew in the 700s BC, and which Alexander visited. It existed from about 1000 BC to 85 BC. There's a dip where the 6000-seat theatre was in the north-east of the site and a few stones from the Temple of Athena.

Over the years much Trojan material has gone to Berlin and London, but in recent years most of it has stayed in Turkey, and is now on display in one of the new rooms of the Archeological Museum in Istanbul. It would be wonderful if some of the potsherds, arrowheads, plate, jewellery fragments, scraps of gold and pieces of stone were here at Troy, but they are probably more accessible in Istanbul. The museums there are just about worth a trip to Turkey in themselves.

Troy VII is an interregnum period between the Greeks and the Trojans of the Trojan War, which seems to fit with the discoveries and general design of Troy VI, dated between 1700 and 1250 BC, when there is a layer of earthquake debris or some other form of destruction consonant with the burning and destruction of the city. Ash from a fire is also evident a hundred years later. For want of a better date, the Trojan War occurred in 1250 BC.

Visitors can see the east wall of this city, Troy VI. Some 300 metres of the 550 metres of ancient wall survive. In addition there is the east tower, a massive stone building jutting out eight metres, with three-metre thick walls. Was this the tower from which King Priam watched Paris fight Menelaus?

The walls of Troy 1 (3000–2500 BC) and house foundations of Troy II (2500–2300 BC), as well as a fine stone ramp, can also be seen. Troys III, IV and V were mostly destroyed by

Schliemann, though they have been characterised as poorer and meaner additions anyway.

Priam may have watched from the north-east bastion, another massive construction, once surrounding a more ancient well, with a height of nine metres. From up here I looked out across the plain of the Dardanelles towards the river Scamander.

Perhaps the Trojan War never happened; some scholars certainly believe that it did not. But regardless of its veracity, it has had a tremendous influence on life and literature in this region and elsewhere.

When Mehmet II inspected the place in 1463, according to Critobolous of Imbros, and was shown the tombs of the heroes Achilles, Hector and Ajax, he said, 'It is to me that Allah has given to avenge this city and its people ... Indeed it was the Greeks who devastated this city, and it is their descendants who, after so many years, have paid me the debt which their boundless pride had contracted ... towards us, the peoples of Asia.'

I walked around the walls again, wet without an umbrella, and woke up another Mehmet, in the *taksi*.

The winds are high, and Helles' tide
Rolls darkly heaving to the main
And Night's descending shadows hide
That field with blood bedew'd in vain
(Byron, *Don Juan*)

My ferry ride across the Dardanelles, or Hellespont, to the Anzacs' 'fatal shore' was under dark, threatening clouds. But I felt exhilarated by the prospect rather than any sense of foreboding. A sense of dread is not a useful faculty in Turkey.

On the ferry, a local trader with a suitcase pestered some Americans to buy socks. 'Please Missus, you have nice big feet. Please, one, two, I give you, just five dollar.' She complained, she walked the deck, she came back, she gave in.

Across the Dardanelles from Çanakkale is the town of Ece-abat, which is more a ferry and bus stop than a town. A straggle of shops line the shore near the ferry wharf. Buses struggle off onto the shore, and roar and belch smoke on the road to Istanbul.

The first task was to find a taxi driver who might be able to find the Anzac Rest House for a suitable price. Anzac Cove is some twenty-three kilometres from Eceabat, and the cottage is north along the coast from there, towards Suvla Bay. 'Just ask for the English cottage,' someone in Australia had cheerfully said. 'You'll be right.' The sky threatened something, maybe snow.

The first taxi driver I asked about going to 'Anzac, English cottages, you know?' looked somewhat frightened, clutched my arm and took me to the next driver, a man with a droopy mous-tache, a weary cap and a wary eye. 'Anzac, Anzac!' said the first driver.

'Anzac *turizm*, yes, please,' said the second. 'Two million.'

'Sorry my friend. I don't want a tour. Just a ride to Anzac Cove. Rest House. The English cottages. War Graves Commis-sion huts … you understand?'

'Just a ride, two way, I show everything.'

'No,' I said firmly, 'one way. I am staying at the cottage.'

'You stay night? Is rain soon.'

'Yes, I stay. I am Australian.'

'Okay Australian. Not English [suspicious] ?'

'Australian.'

'Ossie. Okay. Friends.'

'How much?'

'One million.'

'Sorry. No.'

'Okay. How much you pay?'

'Five hundred thousand.'

'Ptah!'

'Okay. Next taxi.'

'Okay 600 000.' That was about US$9, a small fortune for a taxi driver in Eceabat on a cold and wet April morning.

But first, supplies for a few days. Fresh *ekmek* steamed in glass-fronted cases outside a small shop. Eggs, coffee, some weird plastic-wrapped sausages, *bali* (honey), tomatoes, cheese, olives – boxed and bagged in a few moments and we were off through the green wet countryside of the Gallipoli Peninsula.

Soon the rain fell in buckets. As we drove slowly along the road above the beach at Anzac Cove it was clear that the driver did not quite know where he was going. The tall thrust of 'the Sphinx' (the name for the prominent formation of the cliffs) above us was shrouded in rain. Looking up the cliffs of mud and low gorse it looked an impossible task to scale them. A bushfire had been through the area a couple of years before, and the small pine trees I remembered from my first visit seemed to have gone.

Further up the road was the Canterbury Cemetery, where twenty-seven New Zealanders of that regiment are buried, and 200 metres beyond that, a knot of large pine trees.

'Here is it I hope.'

We pulled in to the driveway, the rain now pelting down. There were two or three huts in the trees. One was a workshop. A man was carving a headstone.

'Is it. Go now. Please.'

Thunder cracked directly overhead. A bolt of lightning sizzled to a point in the hills above us. It was very dark.

I got out and stumbled a few paces to the man in the workshop. He pointed towards the other cottages. I was soaked already. I went back to the *taksi*, gave the driver, now in a state of fright, his wad of notes, pulled my pack and bags out and splashed across to a hut.

I opened the door. It smelled of an Australian beach house unused since last summer. There were no beds, nothing. Must be the other hut, closer to the beach. I went out for a reconnoitre, looking for a key. The rain was even heavier. The sky was almost pitch black, the thunder cracked and rolled.

Gallipoli in April … this was like a Tasmanian rainforest in mid-winter. The taxi gave a mournful blast as it passed by on the road back to Eceabat.

At the other hut, a door. It opened – no keys needed around here. Must be it. Bringing wet pack, bag of books, box of tucker, I went inside.

It was a small cottage with pressure lamps, a stove, wood, maps and pictures on the wall of the main room. Bean's books. I had landed, at last. Looking out the window, the beach slopped just across the road, grey and foam flecked. A hedge of rosemary. Pine trees sighing and dripping. The thunder, sounds of battle in the sky above, silence everywhere else.

I had a catch in the throat, just thinking of landing at dawn down the beach from here on an April morning seventy-one years ago. Must have been getting a cold.

Wood, matches, a fire in the combustion stove, stripped off, dry clothes, planned the campaign.

When the Anzacs landed it was before dawn, with a clear bright moon. The night of 24–25 April was dark and stormy, one of the rare wet spells of the whole campaign. The gorse and underbrush that tangled the hills above the beach would have been wet all day. The Anzacs were soaked from the landing on the beach. The survivors would have spent the first night wet as well, in their hollows in the soft clinging clay, bullets from the Turks fizzing above.

My plan for early the next morning was to walk up from the beach at Ari Burnu, the little point at the north end of Anzac Cove where the first Anzacs came ashore – wrong place of course. I wanted to walk where they had walked and to get as far as they had got, up over Plugge's Plateau. I would look down on Shrapnel Gully, cross the Nek, up to Chunuk Bair and back down the front line of trenches past Quinn's and Steele's posts to Lone Pine.

The names were the roll call of a boyhood that understood what all this meant by a process of osmosis, before the doubts of adolescence erupted.

Thousands of Australians have made the pilgrimage to Gallipoli, especially in the last ten years or so; some to add the sense of place to a grandfather or great-grandfather's story, some just to honour the single most emotion-charged event in the creation of the Australian nation, and some to tick off another shrine among the churches, battlefields and tombs of old Europe. And some, I am sure, could not articulate why they come. They just feel they must. I had made my initial pilgrimage in 1993, and even without relations here, I was back, pulled by the stories and by the secular sanctity of one of the most peaceful places in the world.

Gallipoli is remarkable for many reasons, not least of which is that it must be one of the few battlefields where the wild geography has preserved its shape and form from the battles in 1915 until now. At other places you must divine events from stories, but at Gallipoli the hills and gullies still exist, and in many cases the trenches and rifle pits too.

And then there are the thirty-one cemeteries. Charles Bean made the report, reprinted in his book *Gallipoli Mission*, when he returned here in 1919 that the dead should remain buried where they fell, or as close to it as possible:

> I urged that the Australian Government should as soon as possible express its wish as to whether graves should be retained in their present positions, and men's remains buried where they lay, or whether graves should be concentrated in a few large existing cemeteries. I had already recommended the former system and I now urged that this could well be carried out at Anzac provided that the whole of the area was vested in the Imperial War Graves Commission.

Bean's 1919 report 'envisaged the whole Anzac area as one

big graveyard, which would probably be visited by thousands of Australians and others yearly, and in which the dead, merely by being buried where they fell or where their comrades had carried them, would commemorate their achievement better than any inscription.'

So, instead of huge and overwhelming ranks and files of white crosses there are small, elegant and private cemeteries and memorials, in occasionally inaccessible spots, the stone glowing white in the afternoon sun, amid the glowing green. One, at Plugge's above the beach at Ari Burnu, has just twelve men buried in it.

The stone from which the cemeteries were constructed, Bean noted approvingly, came from across the Dardanelles and was 'of the same class as that which the Homeric walls of Troy were built'.

Bean's great, simple idea is one of the main reasons why, as John North wrote, 'No battleground so easily lends itself to retrospective sentimentality' for those pilgrims who tread the ground.

For most Australians, Gallipoli represents a potent mixture of emotions: nationalism, sadness, nostalgia, anger, death, love and beauty. Hatred seems not to form much of the mix. Charles Bean – and Mustafa Kemal, the first President of the Turkish republic – were responsible for shaping our sensibilities in regard to Gallipoli, whether we know it or not.

Mustafa Kemal, one of the most remarkable political leaders of the twentieth century, famously directed the defence of the tottering Ottoman Empire at Gallipoli as a means to the creation of modern Turkey eight years later.

His statement made in 1934, inscribed in white stone on the beach at Anzac Cove, is the other reason why Gallipoli is a unique place. This is what he said:

Those heroes that have shed their blood and lost their lives ... you are now lying in the soil of a friendly country. Therefore rest in peace. There is no difference between the Johnnies and the Mehmets to us where they lie side by side here in this country of ours... You, the mothers, who sent their sons from far away countries, wipe away your tears; your sons are now lying in our bosom and are in peace. And having lost their lives on this land they have become our sons as well.

No-one has ever stood in front of this memorial, read the letters proud on the standing stone, and not cried. I did on my first visit. I would again. I don't know what it is. The sentiment is a bit hackneyed, but it nevertheless conveys the reconciliation that we needed after such a futile invasion – reconciliation perhaps aided by the tyranny of distance. We Australians have not had to come this far again as soldiers, and the Turkey of Mustafa Kemal and his successors has been admirably non-expansionist.

Bean wrote a poem called 'Abdul' for *The Anzac Book*, which has the feeling of reconciliation that is the most remarkable feature of Australian–Turkish relations – and remember, he wrote this in 1915. The final two verses are:

Yes , we've seen him dying there in front –
Our own boys died there, too –
With his poor dark eyes a-rolling,
Staring at the hopeless blue;
With his poor maimed arms a-stretching
To the God we both can name ...
And it fairly tore our hearts out;
But it's in the beastly game.

So though your name be black as ink
For murder and rapine,
Carried out in happy concert
With your Christians from the Rhine,

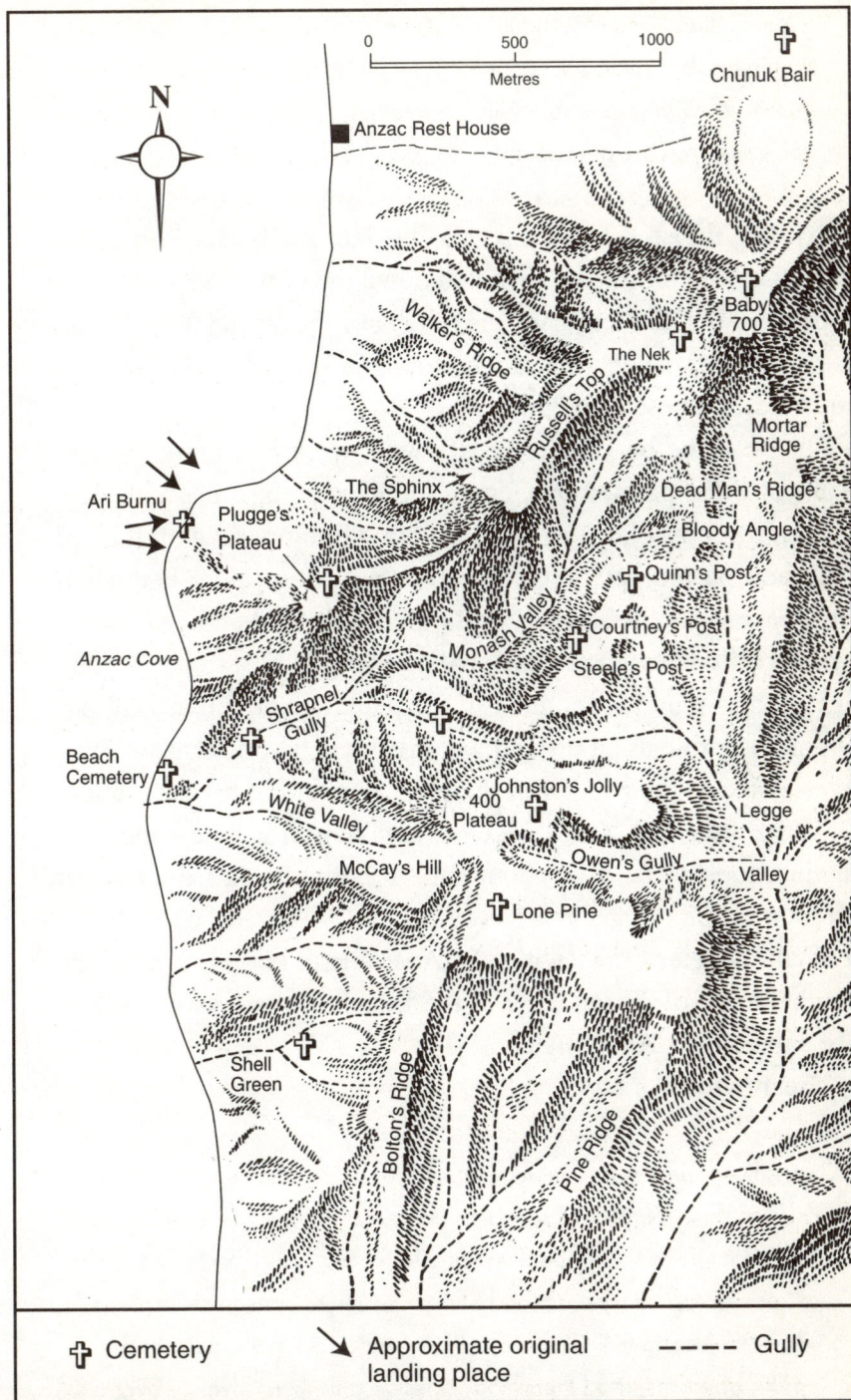

Chunuk Bair

0   500   1000
Metres

■ Anzac Rest House

N

Baby
700

Walker's Ridge

The Nek

Russell's Top

Mortar
Ridge

Ari Burnu

The Sphinx

Dead Man's Ridge

Plugge's
Plateau

Bloody Angle

Quinn's Post

Anzac Cove

Monash Valley

Courtney's Post

Steele's Post

Shrapnel
Gully

Beach
Cemetery

White Valley

400
Plateau

Johnston's Jolly

Legge

McCay's Hill

Owen's Gully

Valley

Lone Pine

Shell
Green

Bolton's Ridge

Pine Ridge

✝ Cemetery   Approximate original
                    landing place   – – – – Gully

Anzac Cove and surrounding hills

We will judge you Mr Abdul,

By the test by which *we* can –

That with all your breath, in life, in death,

You've played the gentleman.

Next day, the storm had passed. Outside, the breeze shipped in from the Mediterranean. I walked down the beach to Anzac Cove – passing the Canterbury Cemetery and the World War II concrete pillbox which had fallen from the eroded cliffs and now squatted on the sea's edge.

In from the beach, the wildflowers were blooming, descendants of those painted by George Lambert on his visit with Bean in 1919; poppy-like flowers, but with white mixed with the red, pink and purple petals. George Lambert, born in St Petersburg (maybe his parents came across Heinrich Schliemann?) was a wonderfully talented professional painter and occasional *Bulletin* artist who found his moment in the paintings he did at Gallipoli and in Palestine as an official war artist. He is somewhat unfairly overlooked in the rollcall of the great painters of his generation.

Ari Burnu and Mustafa Kemal's memorial is where the main landing took place. It is about half an hour's walk from the hut, on a small spit of land at the northern end of Anzac Cove. There's a small cemetery here with 151 Australians buried in it. At the southern end of Anzac Cove is the Beach Cemetery where there are another 295 Australians.

Bean wrote:

As officers and men tumbled out of the grating boats and waded ashore, they found themselves faced by a country utterly different from that which had been described to them ... They had been told to rush across the beach and shelter under a bank such as lines nearly all beaches. They were to drop their packs there, quickly form up, fix bayonets, load their magazines ... and then advance over a belt of open land to a comparatively low ridge, which they would climb ... reorganise, and then push off towards specified points on a long ridge about a mile inland.

But that was nothing like the country in which they landed. They found themselves on the foot of an exceedingly steep, almost precipitous hill 300 feet high which, except for a minor lower knoll around which the boat grounded, rose straight from the bank that bordered the shingle. How this happened was made clear ... by the voice of the naval commander in charge of the tows, just before the first shots: 'Explain to the colonel that the dam' fools have taken us a mile too far north.'

The 'minor knoll' is right on the beach, and is where the Ari Burnu Cemetery is laid. Today the road cuts across above this knoll, before the steep ascent to Plugge's. There is a bank above the beach, below which the waves slop on the stony, shingly beach. Succulents creep down from the high-water mark. Some small iris-like flowers peep from the sand and stones of the bank. When the tide is in, the beach is just a few metres wide; when it is out, perhaps seven or eight metres.

The bank is shoulder height when you're standing on the beach, and would have afforded some protection from shots fired from higher up. You can see the Sphinx, the prominent formation of the cliffs high above, and the impression of ridges beyond the beach, but you cannot see much immediately in front of you other than the bank, and the steep hill rising above it.

Bean again:

It was too steep for normal hill climbing – they had to help themselves up by their rifle butts and haul themselves by the stems and roots of the low holly and arbutus scrub that thickly covered the slope. Men could only be seen if they moved. In that respect the Turk had the advantage, and a fair number of the climbing men were wounded and left hanging among the scrub.

From the top of the bank I saw a ridge above me, perhaps the objective: 'First Ridge'. High above that, a white monument glistened in the weak sunshine – Chunuk Bair, or one of the memorials along the road to it.

Over the bank, across the road, over a drainage ditch, and I began to climb the slope in the same way, minus rifle but encumbered with cameras. The soft sticky clay had already made me ten centimetres taller as I struggled up the hill, pulling on branches and finding some of them coming loose – dead from the fire. Low gorsey plants, holly and flowers bent on the cold wind.

After a stiff fifteen-minute climb I reached the top of Plugge's (pronounced Pluggeys and named for a New Zealand commander). I found seventeen graves marked in the small, sacred place. It was quiet, just the wind rushing in my ears. A bird squeaked somewhere near. Below at Ari Burnu a bus pulled up. Half-a-dozen people walked to the cemetery. Up here the only shooting going on was of pictures.

I walked to the inland end of Plugge's – maybe fifty metres. From below, it looks as if this plateau connects directly with the next ridge – where the Sphinx emerges from Walker's Ridge and Russell's Top and the Nek – and on to the hill known as 'Baby 700'. Higher than Baby 700, Chunuk Bair looms. Lone Pine is to the right from here, on another ridge line.

But between Plugge's Plateau and Russell's Top is a precipitous drop, perhaps fifty metres, to a low narrow spine. On the other side there is another drop down to the gullies, Shrapnel and Monash. If this seems confusing, it is. The countryside is wrinkled in and on itself like mother's bread.

Across from Plugge's, on the seaward sides of the ridges, and along Shrapnel Gully can be seen horizontal bands, like sheep tracks on the side of a hill. These are the remains of 1915 trenches and tracks which eventually terraced the whole area, at times providing shelter from snipers, at others mined by the Turks; sometimes they were nests for Australian soldiers, other times overrun.

On that day in April 1915, various parties of soldiers were plunging down the steep sides of the gullies, more were landing on the beach, and the fight was carried on in small, isolated places. Bean found some of their remains on his 1919 expedition lying where they fought and died. He wrote:

> How in this strange country, amid the sweet smelling thyme on the uplands on that beautiful bright spring day, the fight which after the first rush had seemed almost over, gradually became intense again and swayed hour after hour on the Second Ridge until the factor that wins or loses battles – the strain upon nerves – became almost unbearable so that to many brave men the smell of thyme long afterwards brought a shudder.

During that first morning, the Australians, except for some thrusting parties, held up at the line of the Second Ridge – which was about as far as they ever advanced. This is the ridge that runs down from Chunuk Bair to Lone Pine. Another Third, or Gun, Ridge runs down from Chunuk Bair, diverging away from Second Ridge. Gun Ridge was the original day one objective.

Others, some landing to the north of Ari Burnu on North Beach, scrambled up the gravelly cliffs next to the protuberance of the Sphinx and gained Russell's Top, clearing it of Turks.

These men then advanced northwards along this flat-topped ridge until it began to narrow – this was what was known as 'the Nek'. After the senior officers were killed here, others advanced, joined by yet more, including Captain J. P. Lalor (grandson of Peter Lalor of the Eureka Stockade), who had come up the other side from Shrapnel Gully. Lalor dug in beneath the stem of the Nek and died there during the day as the Turks pushed the Australians back from their attempts to take Baby 700 beyond it.

One reinforcement, Lieutenant B. Y. Chapman, wrote in his diary, in 1915, 'The original men must have been a combination of mule, goat and lion to have succeeded as they did.'

This is what I tried to do, scrambling like a clumsy goat from a gun pit on the top of Plugge's down the steep side, aided by the horizontal skeletons of tracks, then up the side of Russell's Top to the Nek and Walker's Ridge. At the top there were many gun pits and trenches, still two or three metres deep. Inside one, the sides washed away by the recent rain, was a length of leg bone – Turkish or Australian, who could tell.

All around were other things exposed by the rain: pieces of pottery, even a buttonhole surround, and unidentifiable pieces of metal. Most I left where they were, except for a couple of buttonhole reinforcements. Along Walker's the small pines flourished in an impassable tangle; you could see over them but could not walk through them. Pictures from the war show this area – most of it quickly chopped, blasted and destroyed – with no trees. It's hard to imagine charging through this sort of foliage.

By the end of the first day, the position at Anzac was very serious. The Australians had not gained their objectives. The Turks had fought back well at the northern end of the line on Walker's Ridge. A toehold had been held in the area of Lone Pine. Sixteen thousand men had been landed but more than 2000 casualties had been taken. Lalor was dead. (He is buried in the Baby 700 Cemetery.)

As Bean noted, 'Instead of driving one and a half miles inland with a front of four miles, the troops were clinging to a bare foothold on the Second Ridge little more than half a mile inland, on a front of a mile, and even in the centre with only one ridge between them and their landing place.'

Withdraw? Or, as commanding general Hamilton signalled to General Birdwood on the spot, 'There is nothing for it but to dig yourselves right in and stick it out … PS You have got through the difficult business, now you have only to dig, dig, dig, until you are safe.'

And they did, from April to August, with no sign of a breakthrough. It was decided to give the operation one last chance –

with reinforcements – in August. One of the saddest days in Australia's brief military history was about to occur.

The charge of the Light Horse brigades at the Nek on 7 August 1915 was one of the most awful, and seemingly criminal, episodes of confusion and futility at Gallipoli or anywhere else in that war so wasteful of life. Australia might have lost more men in a single battle in France later on, but the image of the Nek, most beautifully pictured in the great George Lambert painting called *The Charge of the 3rd Light Horse Brigade* (in the Australian War Memorial), is the one that remains and still hurts.

Lambert surveyed this spot with Charles Bean in 1919, when the detritus of the charge was still around. The ground was orangey brown, rough and broken up by bomb and digging and battle. The Turks had themselves charged here in April, when they were scythed down like rows of wheat. Many of their bodies remained where they fell – sometimes providing a skerrick of cover for the Australians.

In the painting, the looming height of the hills Baby 700 and Chunuk Bair can be glimpsed ahead. Between lay the Turkish machine-gun batteries and ranks of riflemen.

The Nek is narrow, perhaps 150 metres across, falling away steeply on both sides. Clambering up here, the low pine trees obscure the view. Today, the Australian cemetery faces a Turkish monument, screened by trees. The road up to Chunuk Bair passes both. It is green, as are all the cemeteries.

The Turks placed a memorial here after the Anzacs left in December 1915, marking the spot where they stood and defended their country. It is called Sergeant Mehmet's Memorial. According to the Turks, Mehmet fought and died here, saying, 'I die happily for my country, and you, my comrades, will avenge me.' Mehmet, immortalised by Mustafa Kemal as the Turkish everyman, was avenged not through defeating the British imperial invasion but by his commander later defeating the Western victors at both conference table and in the mountains of Anatolia.

With the establishment of the Turkish republic in 1923 also came the preservation of this place, sacred to both Mehmet and the gallant 600 Australian Johnnies.

On this spot, as at others on the front line, occurred one of those lulls in the killing – an armistice. After the Turkish attack of 19 May, where thousands of men of both sides were killed, it was agreed that a day's respite was required to bury the dead. Australian and Turkish burial parties worked from seven-thirty in the morning to four-thirty that afternoon, burying them where they lay.

Bean, revisiting in 1919, recalled a couple of Turkish comments during the armistice. One Turkish captain said, 'At this spectacle even the most gentle must feel savage, and the most savage must weep.' Another Turk, pointing to the graves, said, 'That's politics.' And pointing to the dead, 'That's diplomacy.' At the end of the day, an Australian said to a Turk near him, 'Goodbye old chap. Good luck.' The answer, Bean says, came in Turkish, 'Smiling may you go and smiling come again.' This expression, in Turkish *gule gule*, is always used by the person remaining. This place was not going to be taken.

The Nek Cemetery is a flat grassed area surrounded by a stone wall, with a cross. It is in the fifty metres of ground that the Australians had to pass over, and is where most of them died. On the Australian side of the spot the slowly collapsing trenches are filling themselves in. Today the ground is soft from the rain, wildflowers opening in the sun.

There are five identified graves at the Nek, and five headstones commemorating graves whose exact location is not known. There are also 316 unmarked burials, in rows under the grass, mostly of the 8th and 10th Light Horse regiments.

Of all the Gallipoli cemeteries, this should be the most affecting, but it is in fact the least. Perhaps the scale of the events it commemorates is too big.

Lambert's painting shows men – boys – some in shorts and

pith helmets, a couple in long trousers and hats, running, falling, bending forward. They carry rifles, bayonets fixed. The Turks rise up in a forward trench, just about where their memorial now stands, picking off the men without fear of being shot themselves. Peter Burness, in the definitive account of the charge, *The Nek*, points out that the Light Horse charged with unloaded rifles, wearing shorts.

Other attacks were supposed to support the charge at the Nek, but none distracted the Turks. One was by Harry Chauvel's Light-horsemen (at Gallipoli without their horses) attacking from Quinn's Post. Chauvel called the murder off after one wave of troops had been cut down by enfilading machine-guns.

At the Nek there was no-one alive or senior enough to call it off. Three waves of men, each of 150, stood up in the trenches and faced the certainty of being hit and the probability of being killed. We know now, and the commanding officers should have known then, that this was simply a massacre. To call it anything else is to demean the bravery of the men who died and are lying under this green grass.

Survivors recalled the sound of the Turkish storm of fire. Burness writes, 'Each enemy soldier sighting down his rifle must have squeezed the trigger as soon as the Australians burst into view. The rifle and machine-gun fire erupted as a roar sweeping through the Australians' ranks.'

Charles Bean was nearby in 1915 '... when [the] tremendous fusillade broke out. It rose from a fierce crackle into a roar in which one could distinguish neither rifle nor machine-gun. But just one continuous roaring tempest. One could not help an involuntary shiver: God help anyone who was out in that tornado.'

After the first line was cut down, 'Everyone fell like lumps of meat,' New Zealand-born Captain George Hore wrote.

We saw our fate in front of us, but we were pledged to go and, to their eternal credit, the word being given, not a man in the second line stayed in his trench. I jumped out and looked down the line, and they were all rising over the parapet. We bent low, and ran as hard as we could. Ahead we could see the trench aflame with rifle fire. All round were smoke and dust kicked up by the bullets. I felt a sting on my shoulder. I passed our first line, all dead or dying it seemed, and went on a bit further, and flung myself down about forty yards from the Turkish trenches. I was a bit ahead of my men ... I looked around and saw them all down, mostly hit. I did not know what to do. I was protected a little [by] a very little fold in the ground and by a dead Turk — dead about six weeks!

And yet, another line of 150 men went. And then another. Into the Valley of Death rode the gallant 600 at Balaclava. Ours went 150 at a time, without their horses. Trooper Harold Rush of the 10th Light Horse is buried nearby on Walker's Ridge. His stone says, 'His Last Words. Goodbye Cobber and God Bless You'. He was killed in the second wave.

I walked over Baby 700 and its cemetery of 493 burials, and up the hard road to Chunuk Bair, wind whispering softly, a thrush, in the pines. At the top there is a monument, the only one in Gallipoli not designed by English architect Sir John Burnet, a tall tapering pylon of New Zealand architect S. Hurst Seager. It stands next to a double-lifesized bronze of Mustafa Kemal, looking across to the Dardanelles. And around the perimeter are a number of restored Turkish trenches, lined with pine logs, from which you can look down the hill and recognise the bravery of the New Zealanders who briefly held this position in August, and the impossibility of holding it against superior numbers without the promised support that never came.

From here you can just see the Straits, far off, and the wisdom of Mustafa Kemal in knowing that he had to defend this hill no matter what the cost. It commanded everything in the vicinity.

The New Zealanders buried or commemorated here number

1484. They held this place for the night of the 8 August. It was as brave as the day before's charge at the Nek had been. Bad timing. The New Zealanders, and later British and Gurkha troops, were killed or driven off the next day and night.

This is where Mustafa Kemal said to his Mehmets, 'I am not ordering you to fight, I am ordering you to die.' Just below the top of Chunuk Bair a circle of large monuments, like huge white stone billboards, tells the story of Mustafa Kemal and his men's deeds in August 1915. Mustafa Kemal took a bullet in the breast pocket here, and was saved from death by a watch presented to him by the German general Liman von Sanders. If it hadn't been for that watch …

No-one else was here on this cold April day. It had taken me perhaps four hours of brisk climbing and walking to make the four or so kilometres up from the beach, to Chunuk Bair where the Australians had hoped to get on the first day, but never did. Without pack, without being shot at, and knowing where I was going, roughly speaking, it had taken that long – and I was tired.

From here, the folded maze of the topography is clear, in the sense that you can pick the tops of the ridges as they wrinkle down and rise higher to the north and east. But from the ground, walking up, there is no such clarity. In describing such well-known places as Plugge's, the Nek, Shrapnel Gully, even having walked them, it is difficult to convey the impossibility of the terrain. A worse place to stage the first modern amphibious landing and invasion could hardly have been picked.

I began to walk down the hill, along the line of the Second Ridge, towards Lone Pine. It is so steep in the beginning that even on the macadam you have to be careful. It levels out after a kilometre or so, the distance from Chunuk to the furthest defended trenches: Quinn's, Courtney's and Steele's posts. They are on the right, the seaward side, as you go down the hill.

On the landward side of the road, where most of the Turkish trenches were, is a series of newish Turkish memorials. A small bronze old man and a little girl bring flowers to a grave site, a huge Turkish infantryman thrusts his bayonet at the Dardanelles, a 750 kilogram cannon named Mesudiye Topu lies on the ground. This is a three-tiered open-framed white tower – four legs with a sort of cupola on the top. A red Turkish flag flutters in the chill breeze. Off in the green down the hill are other Turkish cemeteries.

Our cemeteries are named for Australian officers: Lieutenant Colonel Richard Courtney, Major Thomas Steel and Captain Hugh Quinn. These spots were taken on the first day and held until the evacuation. Quinn's Post Cemetery has 473 burials and Steel's and Courtney's 225. From Quinn's you can look back up the road along the line of no-man's-land to Chunuk Bair high above, the new memorials marking the spots. To your left, behind the ridge and across a ravine, is the Nek. Keep going down the road, and on the left is Johnston's Jolly, so named because Colonel George Johnston had some artillery pieces there to 'jolly-up' the Turks up the hill. There are 181 men buried there.

Across the road from Johnston's Jolly in the pines is a maze of filled-in trenches, part of the defensive position around Lone Pine. You can follow them for hundreds of metres, stumbling across bits of barbed wire now and again, as well as tree roots.

Lone Pine and Johnston's Jolly were part of what was first called the 400 Plateau, a flat piece of pine-covered dirt on the 400 yard contour. It was taken briefly on the first day, but not regained until 6 August, as part of the bloody August offensive.

There are 1167 burials at Lone Pine, and another 4932 names recorded on the Lone Pine memorial as killed in the vicinity. This windswept place with a lone pine now flourishing, is the one tree hill of Gallipoli, the loneliest killing field. There was nothing cosy about the long list of names or the futility of their sacrifice. Seven Victoria Crosses were awarded to Australians at Lone Pine. Perhaps by this time compassion fatigue was beginning to set in, as well as physical fatigue.

I set out on a course which I judged would lead me to somewhere south of the Hell Spit Beach Cemetery, from where I could see Shell Green, where the famous picture of the cricket match had been taken. Major George Macarthur-Onslow was batting, executing a Victor Trumper-like drive. The game was played in December 1915 as part of the appearance of normality designed to deceive the Turks and cover the withdrawal of all troops.

I plunged across uneven ground and down into a gully which was not where I thought it should have been. I think it must have been White's Valley, rutted by trenches and tracks covered in dead wood and rubbish from the fires. Once at the bottom there was nothing for it but to climb up the other side, and then down again. From the top I spotted the 4th Battalion Parade Ground Cemetery, glowing white as the sun slowly descended off to the west. Down to the bottom. I reached a trackless place with 116 burials.

A steep climb up and along the ridge led me to the intersection of Rest Gully, Monash Valley and Shrapnel Gully. There is a white sand watercourse (dry on this day) at the bottom, with small smooth rocks, and dead branches. Some bush bashing for half an hour through these obstructions, and I emerged at the Shrapnel Gully Cemetery as the sun dropped over the ridge. The site, where 683 men are buried, is preserved from the water by a retaining wall.

I walked across the modern road to the Beach Cemetery and looked north along Anzac Cove and out into the Aegean.

The story of the evacuation of Anzac is well known. It was the most successful part of the whole operation, with the fewest casualties – the guns on the water drip that automatically went off; a mine or two set off under a Turkish trench; the deception.

When Bean, Lambert and the Historical Party came back in 1919, they found the graves at Anzac had been largely undisturbed. The wooden crosses had been burned, and probably the bodies still in the open, looted, but there was a lot for Bean and the burial parties to find. Some of the material he had sent back is in the Australian War memorial, such as the back pack of a soldier who died at the Nek, riddled with bullet holes.

The Commonwealth War Graves Commission pamphlet about the cemeteries around Gallipoli has a chart in it which shows that Australia only had 26.52 per cent of the dead in the Gallipoli area, and that the United Kingdom had 68.02 per cent (New Zealand 4.85 per cent, India 0.24 per cent, Canada 0.22 per cent, other 0.15 per cent). And that doesn't count the French. Or the Turks. How come Australians have stolen all the glory? How come the Turks and the Australians are the best of mates? The British had more dead in the overall campaign, including Helles.

Perhaps it is because it just means more to us. We came, in a sense under sufferance, as the Turkish nationalists like Mustafa Kemal did. The Ottomans and the Germans were in charge of him, the British in charge of us. Perhaps that's another clue to its importance to Australians.

Bean looked, and wrote, while Lambert sketched. The paradox of our national archetype is that it sprung from independence, disobedience and giving cheek – such as was provided in Cairo before the Light-horsemen came here – but reached an apotheosis in being given a mad order, and obeying it.

Someone once said that the past, history might feel quaint or old fashioned to us, but it wasn't quaint for the people who lived in it. These boys – it breaks your heart to see that some died here at the age of sixteen – volunteered for something, but surely not for what happened to them. A modern Australian sensibility cannot go back and fill those big boots. Sitting on that memorial I knew I couldn't.

Anzac was abandoned on 19 and 20 December 1915. The Australians killed numbered 8141. One survivor left a message in a dugout, known as a 'wosser' or 'wazzir' after that place in Cairo. The message was perhaps ironic.

To Johnny Turk: we hand over to you the entire contents of our humble abode. Anything which may benefit you individually you are quite welcome to. You are a fair fighter and deserve all you get. We appreciate the way you have respected the Red Cross.

Nearly every generation of Australians has had to make its own decisions for life or for sacrifice. I did over Vietnam, my father did, my grandfathers did. Each of us had our own wars to fight, or not, and maybe it is just the distance of time that burnishes the first Anzacs so brightly, and why they still ride so magnificently tall for anyone who comes here or cares to remember. They put the question to us: what would you have done? Would you have risen in the third wave out of the trench at the Nek and run into a roaring wall of bullets? If not, why not?

Your answer might be that war is wrong, that this or that war was wrong. You might be like me, who made a decision not to participate in the war in Vietnam; feeling quite strongly that *not* accepting the order to do so was the Australian way, yet feeling equally strongly that I was part of the Australian military and national tradition.

In 1996 there was a lot of discussion about Samuel Huntington's thesis about international relations 'The Clash of Civilisations', a thesis supposedly proved by Australia's failed desire to become 'part' of Asia when we are really part of the western Protestant 'civilisation'. Forget about the wrong-headed notion that we want to become Asian; Australia's quest to sort out our relationship with all manner of other civilisations can be traced back to Gallipoli, when we might have established an individual identity.

Basic to the confusion some commentators have with Australia's relationship with the world is that they find it difficult to accept that we have a distinct and unique culture, 'civilisation' if you like, that is of our own making – not British, American, or Asian–Australian. And the first time we realised, or should have, that we had national interests and ideas that were distinctively our own was, if you leave aside the first Test match in Melbourne in 1877, at Gallipoli.

At Gallipoli, Australians, through blood-sacrifice, paid a high price for being qualified to say we were a separate, fully independent and sovereign nation (and 'civilisation'). The double tragedy is that our young men paid that supreme price for something, 81 years later, we still have not yet fully achieved: the full political and emblematic representation of an independent culture, a republic. Worse is that some Australians do not want to achieve it. I know that if you could travel back in time and ask the Anzacs what they fought and were prepared to die for, they would not mention a republic, and would mention the King of England. They would talk about their mates and empire, and probably not talk about the Commonwealth established just fourteen years before. But I maintain that by what they did, and how they did it, those extraordinary men made a new nation. There was a kind of clash of civilisations in World War I, but it wasn't really between the tribes of Europe, it was between the old order and the new nations, including for a few months, the new Australia and the new Turkey. Just as it had been in the Trojan War.

I walked back up Anzac Cove, along the sighing sand, onto the road at Ari Burnu where I had started. A taxi was going the other way. I waved at it, and it stopped. One of the handy words I had learned was *yarun* – tomorrow. I spoke it.

'*Taksi yarun?* Anzac Rest House?'

'Okayokayokay.'

'*Saat üç? Yarun?*'

'Okayokayokay.'

Gule gule, I concluded as he burned off down the road into the dark. A Turkish taxi driver miss a fare? Unlikely. He would show up. I hoped so, I had a bus to catch.

CHAPTER FOURTEEN

A BUS TO
BYZANTIUM

THE BUS TO ISTANBUL is a long way from the romance of Yeats'
'Sailing to Byzantium'. And as far as I know there is no way anymore to sail from Çanakkale or Eceabat to Istanbul.

Yeats had never come closer to Istanbul than Italy. He must
have deduced the sublime image of the glowing dome of Hagia
Sophia, the minarets and spires, the skyline that evokes such
mystery from the old prints of his imagination. In 1927 he wrote:

> Once out of nature I shall never take
> My bodily form from any natural thing,
> But such a form as Grecian goldsmiths make
> Of hammered gold and gold enamelling
> To keep a drowsy Emperor awake;
> Or set upon a golden bough to sing
> To lords and ladies of Byzantium
> Of what is past, or passing, or to come.

In 1930 he had another dream of Byzantium.

> Night resonance recedes, a night walker's song
> After a great cathedral gong;
> A starlit or a moonlit dome disdains
> All that man is,
> All mere complexities,
> The fury and the mire of human veins

Although seduced by the romance of Yeats' Byzantium, I
hated leaving Gallipoli, and perhaps I should not have. I could
have got more supplies, stayed another couple of days and gone
home. I felt my trip was at an end. I thought of Samuel Beckett's
Waiting for Godot: 'I can't go on. I must go on.' That is the epi-
taph of the traveller.

I fought the smokers on the bus, dismounted at the biggest
otogar in the world (it was like an international airport for buses),

overleaf: Istanbul skyline

and took a taxi to the Hotel Historia, a cheaper old converted wooden house below the Blue Mosque. I had stayed here before. It was comfortable, handy to the Hagia Sophia, the train station, Topkapi, the covered bazaar – all the old haunts.

Istanbul, first known as Byzantium, then Constantinople, and also to nineteenth century diplomats and travellers as the Sublime Porte, was damp, cold and magical.

That night it was all I could do to walk in the hastening gloom to the railway station to buy a ticket to Athens, buy the English newspapers, walk up the tram line to the university and the covered bazaar and back. I ate slop at the Vitamin Restaurant with a Japanese backpacker who had been everywhere in Europe, Africa and Asia except Australia. I had one up on him there.

Next morning, I went to the Hagia Sophia to restore my spiritual batteries.

Charles Bean came here in 1919, before Mustafa Kemal had won the war of independence and before the occupying Allies had departed. It was also before Kemal's 1932 decree, which turned the mosque, formerly the great church of St Sophia, into a museum. Before all that, Charles Bean stood …

… gazing up at the wonderful dome and pendants where the mosaics of the old Christian church – huge figures of seraphim, with their wings hiding their faces, feet and bodies – were most clearly discernible under the Turkish whitewash.

Everywhere you could see the relics of the Christian symbols … In the vestibule were camped Turkish troops, with their camp fires burning – a regular garrison – a precaution taken, I believe, in the expectation that the Greeks might rush the great building and hold a Christian service there … Three British officers came silently to a point near us, and they too stood for a while gazing up. One was Allenby; you couldn't mistake his clipped moustache and big chin –

not an unworthy successor of other conquerors who must have stood
there ... I wonder if any stood there as modestly as he ...

The crusading Egyptian Expeditionary Force, with Chauvel's
Light Horse, finally had an end to their story – their commander,
standing in the ceremonial centre of the defeated Ottoman
Empire, and all it had been heir to, and all that succeeded it.

This is the third church to stand on the site. The first church
was planned by Constantine when he made Constantinople the
capital of the Roman Empire in 330 AD, and opened in 360. It
was destroyed in the riots of 404. The second church was
destroyed in the Nika riots of 532. Just a few months after the
revolt, work began on the mightiest building the Christian world
had seen, planned by Isidore of Miletus. It was a wonder of its
age, and the last wonder for me on this odyssey. St Sophia was
reconsecrated in 563 AD after earthquake damage.

On the day I visited there was a huge tower of scaffolding
extending to the top of the inside of the dome, where renovations
and cleaning were going on. The mosaics, now uncovered thanks
to Mustafa Kemal, glowed quietly. Strange that the Turks simply
covered the images up – the eighth century Christian iconoclasts
did much more damage to Christian imagery in Constantinople.
The mosaics aren't as gorgeous at Hagia Sophia as the ones at the
Kariye Church, but they are less 'restored' and shiny, more wise
and experienced.

I left, and spent the rest of the day finding warm places to stay
out of the sleeting rain. Drinking tea at the covered bazaar I met
an Iraqi man who had been working for Care Australia with the
Kurds in northern Iraq. He wanted me to get him a visa to Australia, because he was in fear of his life. Saddam Hussein was
after anyone and everyone. He had a nationalist *fatwa* on his
head. What could I do? I bought him a tulip glass of tea.

Sirkeci Station at night is the train station at the end of the world.

It was bitterly cold. The waiting room attracted drafts like bliz-zards. The cafe was called the Orient Express but, naturally enough, was closed.

The train for Athens for which I had paid four million Turkish lire was supposed to leave at ten p.m. When I arrived there was not only no sign of a train, but no sign of life at all. The ticket office was still open, but as I had a ticket and merely wanted information they suddenly lost all capacity to speak English. The information booth was closed. Inspection of the platform found a kind of steamed up station official's room, but no amount of banging on the window would get whoever or whatever was in there to come out into the cold.

While cooperation between Turkey and Greece over ferries is grudgingly maintained because there is so much tourist traffic and money to be shared, and air services operate efficiently, the railway on the European side is run-down and neglected.

Part of the reason (chicken and egg, cause and effect) seemed to be that there was little interest in a twenty-four-hour plus timetabled trip to Athens. Only a dozen people shared the wait-ing room with me – mostly backpackers taking advantage of the $50 trip, which included of necessity a night's 'accommodation'.

Near midnight I met Ulrich, of the fraternity of blue back-packs. Ulrich was about nineteen and was doing his national ser-vice in an orphanage. He was a student archeologist who had been to Troy and back in a day, heading backwards to 'Cher-many'. Ulrich said the train must go now at eleven-forty. There was no train. He said there was a strike. I chanced a trip outside the station and bought supplies for the journey. Ulrich looked after backpack and book bag.

A pleasant pretty girl sold me biscuits in little packages, a large bottle of water, chocolate, nuts to the value of TL 400 000 or US$5. She said yes we have no Turkish delight. Not on this night. On the way back to the station I spent my last TL 100 000 note on ten oranges from a coffee seller.

A train pulled in to platform two, the wrong platform. A couple of locals eyed it warily and spoke rapid Turkish. They were young and had an exhausted six-year-old daughter asleep. They had suitcases with wheels. He went away, he came back – he couldn't get an answer either. The child cried, the woman cried – the man slapped the wall.

Half an hour later, a clot of backpackers made a rush for this train, which was still sitting on the wrong platform.

'Whaddya think Ulrich?'

'Wrong platform, wrong train.'

'Someone will tell us, surely.'

'Ja, maybe.'

'Otherwise half of Istanbul would be sleeping here in the station.'

'Oh ja, ja. I think so.'

'They would have to learn to shut the door.'

I only had warm weather gear. It was getting colder. It was too cold to snow.

Half an hour later another train pulled in, halfway up platform one. The couple and the child made a run for this train and climbed aboard a carriage. They were willing to go anywhere to get out of the waiting room. A lot of shunting seemed to be going on as a small engine picked a few carriages from here and from there.

This time I took a look. A policeman – at least he was a man in a uniform with a gun. 'Is this the Athens train?'

'No questions. You will be told.'

It was now about one a.m. It was so cold that standing on the platform for three minutes induced a series of shivering fits. I raced back to the single bit of steam heat in the waiting room. There was no-one left but Ulrich and our packs.

The train across at the other platform pulled out.

Just then the man with the gun ran past the waiting room shouting, 'Athene *sefit* [one]. Platform one okay.'

We got into a carriage. Red-faced officials like a troop of police marched down the corridor as we were looking into the compartment. 'No. No.' We were pushed and shoved.

I lost my temper a little and pushed one back – a very dangerous thing to do on a train. But he stopped pushing me, in amazement.

'Why?' I asked.

'Not train.'

'Where is the Athens train?'

'Athene ptah!'

'Where is train?'

'Off. Out!'

There was a phalanx of officials in his direction and, discretion being the better part in a foreign country, I picked up my dignity and walked out of the carriage and up the platform. I was shunted into another carriage, with full compartments. I was then pushed into one with a spare seat among seven dozing English people. Ulrich had disappeared.

'Hello.'

'Where have you come from?'

'More to the point, where is this carriage going?'

Somehow the carriages had filled from somewhere else, and in the mysterious comings and goings of the trains, a Greece-bound group had found itself in a carriage. Don't ask me how. At least we'll get across the border in this, I thought.

Pythion, Greece, nine a.m. Ulrich was in the cafeteria. The coffee was good, the Greek man friendly. There was yesterday's cakes and ouzo not raki tipped into coffee mugs for thirty people. The train had lost a carriage or two. Some people, I hoped they had woken up, were headed for Bulgarie on the ten-fifteen train. Our carriage looked, in the daylight, as if it had been retired from Melbourne and shipped across. Perhaps that is why it had taken so long.

To Thessaloniki, close to Pella, Alexander the Great's birthplace and birthplace of Mustafa Kemal. It was late in the evening. All change! A small part of me wanted to get off, but most of me was so downtrodden by this insane journey that when I saw a sign for a train to Athens in twenty minutes I got on.

Ten hours later, Athens.

Stumbling out of Athens Station at three in the morning, accosted by ouzo scented street crones, I found a railway hotel not far from the station.

The desk man, a dapper European gent in a tight black coat and rose red tie, asked where I had come from.

'Istanbul, Damascus, Amman, Cairo, Melbourne.'

'Ahh, Cairo. You have heard the news?'

'No, I have been on the train …'

'The massacre. Eighteen Greeks. Old ladies. In Egypt …'

'Where in Egypt?'

'The Pyramids Road. At the hotel.'

What hotel? Surely it couldn't have been the Mena House …? (It wasn't.)

That was the moment when a great wash of emotion, like being dumped by an Ocean Road shore break, hit me. It was a combination of exhaustion, travelling on nerves and a fractured schedule, and the backwash of the hijacking.

I stared at the desk clerk. He must have thought I was another Australian macadamia. I picked up the key, went upstairs, and took a very long shower.

Perhaps I had seen too many tombs and cemeteries between Alexandria and Athens, too much historical death. I couldn't cope with any more.

I left that railway hotel and shifted to a pension in the Plaka, the tourist centre of Athens. Staying in the Plaka was like living in a market: great early in the morning, painfully crowded and noisy at other times. I liked it a lot.

I spent two days in the National Archeological Museum, one of the great quartet of museums in this part of the world, along with Istanbul, Damascus and Cairo. I examined the so-called Mask of Agamemnon dug up by Schliemann at Mycenae. Yes, this should have been his. It was as extraordinary as Tutankhamun's mask. It glowed.

I spent an afternoon on the Acropolis, at the Parthenon. It was beautiful, but I didn't think I could put it on my list of Ancient Wonders still in existence. There was really not much of a story attached to it, except that it had survived. But it does need its marbles back. Why can't the British Museum have the plaster casts? And put the originals in the nice little museum on the Acropolis with the pollution-damaged caryatids.

I was invited for Sunday lunch with my friend and Citroën manager George's Aunty Irene, in a place out of Athens called Varkiza, on the coast.

After many friendly interrogations, I found out that a bus to Varkiza first meant a bus to Glifhada. I walked past overgrown diggings, across a couple of roads to Andrea Singrou, and did find the right bus. I had to stand all the way. So this is where everyone was, on a bright spring day – going to the beach.

At Varkiza the homing beacon in my head made me get off. It seemed the right sort of place. Water nearby. Irene and Con waiting at the bus stop.

'You are Australian boy,' she said, looking up, a tiny dark-haired woman in her sixties. Con smiled, shook hands. His English was rusty through lack of interest.

Irene was born in Alexandria. She had gone to Australia in the late 1950s, becoming a teacher in Richmond, Melbourne, and returned with her daughters to Greece, part of the Hellenic nesting instinct, in the 1970s. They couldn't go to Egypt. There is family back in Richmond and elsewhere in Australia – brother, nephews and nieces. Here in Athens the two daughters have married, they have children, they sound Australian.

They are part of the extended Australia, as much as Australia is part of the extended Greece (or Turkey, or Egypt). Athens feels a lot like Melbourne, or perhaps Melbourne is a lot like Athens and we don't know it.

One husband is a wood merchant and is going to build an Australian type of wooden house one day. A wooden house! Probably the first ever in this city of cement and marble.

Australia seemed to have become, once more for Greeks, a kind of far off-land, a paradise of pensions and beaches. The disappointment now is in having left it. Australia is Paradise Lost. The Greeks have been a great colonisers, perhaps the pre-eminent colonisers in history, from the Pontic coast of the Black Sea in the Bronze Age, to the Ionian islands and the Turkish coast, Alexandria, to Melbourne. This Mediterranean colonising had none of the Imperial overtones of later Europeans. These Greeks traded and mingled and merged, and many of them have returned to modern Greece, voluntarily and otherwise. Athens feels a lot like Melbourne of the 1960s – with monuments.

Perhaps that is why my journey's end in Athens is like a journey's end in Australia. The plain but tasty food on the windy balcony, a couple of beers, Sunday afternoon drive in the Range Rover down the coast, a visit to a haunted hot spring, where people disappear perhaps – very Australian. Back at the apartment Con and the children had been having a siesta: very Greek. That's how you can tell a Greek Greek from an Australian Greek. The Greek Greeks nap, the Australian Greeks go for a drive.

Next day I went early to the airport, thinking that after hijackings and massacres, security might be a bit tighter. But no, there was no X-raying of baggage, no searching of hand luggage, and no interest in whatever antiquities someone might have in their pocket – not by EgyptAir, by Greek customs, not by anyone. Oh, there were two handsome policemen marching around with guns on their hips, chatting to pretty girls. Athens is notoriously the least secure airport in the world, but this, given recent events, verged on the ridiculous.

Finally, aboard the EgyptAirbus bound for Sydney via Cairo. An announcement from the captain, first in Arabic. I couldn't make out a word. I'd lost the plot in Arabic, even the seat numbers. Then he spoke in English.

Just thought he'd mention that the plane *was* going to Cairo. Whew.

But first it was going to Rome.

Oh boy. Hijacked again.

BIBLIOGRAPHY

The literature of the eastern Mediterranean is, of course, immense. Literature in all its varieties, including travel writing and storytelling, probably began in this neck of the woods. I have listed here and briefly annotated the books I used and found useful before, during and after my trip.

Guidebooks

A flourishing field. I used the Everyman Guides to Egypt, Athens and the Peloponnese, and Istanbul as motivational books before I went. Somewhat hard to find in Australia, they were originally published in French by Gallimard and recently (1993–95) in English by David Campbell Publishers. They are beautifully designed, colourful and packed with historical, archeological and literary information as well as information on bird life and architecture. While not very useful in terms of finding a hotel or a bus, they are both the best introductions and souvenirs that I know of the areas they cover.

Also in this before-and-after category are the Insight Guides (APA Publications); specifically, Insight Guides to Turkey (1993), Egypt (1991), Cairo (1992) and Greece (1994). These contain interesting writing and excellent photographs but are tourist oriented.

The grandfather (and best) of all guidebooks was E. M. Forster's *Alexandria: A History and a Guide* (Michael Haag, London, 1982). Unfortunately this is now out of print; however, Michael Haag has recently produced the best picture book of the city, *Alexandria* (American University in Cairo Press, 1993). Of all the local guidebooks to be found on sale at sites from Egypt to Turkey, this one is well worth bringing home.

As on-the-road guidebooks, the Lonely Planet Guides vary in quality and usefulness. Despite their standard format, much depends on the predispositions and interests of the original researchers and writers of the guides. They are more personal than many other guide series because they are designed for individual travellers rather than groups of tourists.

I found the Lonely Planet guides to Egypt, Turkey and Greece invaluable on the road, if occasionally, and understandably, out-of-date. The maps are not to my taste; that is, I find them difficult to use 'on the ground' and occasionally misleading. On the other hand, the bus information is an accurate starting point. The accommodation guides also provide useful places to begin (there are always other places nearby). The prices quoted for everything have almost all failed to 'keep pace with inflation', as they say. The specific titles I used were: *Lonely Planet Travel Survival Kit: Egypt and the Sudan* by Scott Wayne and Damien Simonis (3rd edn, 1994), *Turkey* by Tom Brosnahan (4th edn, November 1993) and *Greece* by Rosemary Hall (1st edn, February 1994).

Major international rivals of the Lonely Planet guides for the backpacker market are the Rough Guides. Of British origin, these are comprehensive, well written, have better maps and a less hippie-esque parcel of attitudes. Why didn't I use them? Dumb nationalism I guess. The Rough Guides are well worth reading when planning a trip.

If you have to carry around one fat guidebook for any country, on balance I would recommend Lonely Planet, but if the edition available is more than a year or two out-of-date, choose a later Rough Guide.

If you are an American college student, Let's Go might suit. If you are a plush tourist, take a Frommer's, and if you are driving in Greece or Turkey the modern alphabetical Baedekers are well worth having in the glove box.

In Syria I used Michael Haag's *Cadogan Guide to Syria and Lebanon*, not as colourfully produced as his book on Alexandria but indispensable before travelling as well as while in Syria. Published in 1995, this book is much more enlivening, practical and up-to-date than the Lonely Planet *Travel Survival Kit to Jordan and Syria* available when I travelled. Anthony King's *Syria Revealed* (Boxer Publishing, London, 1995) is also pretty good, though less exciting than Haag's book.

The modern classic in the Syrian field is Ross Burns' *Monuments of Syria* (I. B. Taurus, London, 1992). Burns is an Australian diplomat who worked for some years in Syria, and his book is a labour of love. Alas, it is almost impossible to find in Australia, but is (or was) widely available at sites and bookshops in Syria. This is the 'Blue Guide' for Syria.

Back home, or for the two-book traveller

For the historically minded, the bibles of monuments are the Blue Guides. If you want to know what you are looking at in some ancient Egyptian tomb or some uninterpreted site in Turkey or Greece, these books are for you. From a travel practicality point of view they are too fat to be useful, but they are unrivalled in scholarship and the detail of description. These guidebooks are the cribs for the other guidebook writers: *Blue Guide Egypt* by Veronica Seton-Williams and Peter Stocks (3rd edn, 1993), *Turkey* by Bernard McDonagh (2nd edn, 1995) and *Greece* by Robin Barber (6th edn, 1995), all published by A & C Black, London.

And the other books. . .

I have given both the edition I used and first publication where it seemed relevant. Bear in mind that this is the list of an accidental reader.

Ascherson, Neal, *The Black Sea*, Vintage, London, 1996. Peripheral geography but central argument about the ancient frontier between civilisation and barbarism. Wonderful.

Barrett, John, *We Were There*, Penguin Books, Melbourne, 1988. Australian experiences in World War II.

Bean, C. E. W. (ed.), *The Anzac Book*, Harrap, 1916. Edited at Gallipoli, an extraordinary anthology.

Bean, C. E. W., *Anzac to Amiens*, Penguin Books, Melbourne, 1993 (1946). One volume abridgement of the great work, *The Official History*.

Bean, C. E. W., *Gallipoli Mission*, ABC Books, Sydney, 1990 (1948). Account of Bean's trip back to Gallipoli in 1919.

Bean, C. E. W., *Official History of Australia in the War of 1914–18*, vols 1 & 2 *The Story of Anzac*, 8th edn, Angus & Robertson, Sydney, 1938.

Bean, C. E. W., *Gallipoli Frontline*, selected & annotated Kevin Fewster, Allen & Unwin, Sydney, 1990. Bean's diary 1914–1915.

Bernières, Louis de, *Captain Corelli's Mandolin*, Minerva, London, 1995. A novel, but one which contains a lot of the truth about World War II on the Greek island of Cephalonia.

Boardman, John (ed.), *The Oxford History of Classical Art*, Oxford University Press, Oxford, 1993. The standard reference to all the art of classical Greece and Rome in and out of situ.

Brugger, Suzanne, *Australians and Egypt 1914–1919*, Melbourne University Press, 1980. Interesting but academic history backgrounding the First AIF in Egypt.

Burness, Peter, *The Nek*, Kangaroo Press, Sydney, 1996. The best history of the terrible charge.

Cavafy, C. P. , *Collected Poems*, trans. Edmund Keeley & Philip Sherrard, Chatto & Windus, 1990. Nearly all the poems 'work' in English. Essential to civilisation.

Casson, Lionel, *Travel in the Ancient World*, Johns Hopkins University Press, 1994. The only history of this subject, entertainingly written.

Chisholm, Alex H., *The Making of a Sentimental Bloke: A Sketch of the Remarkable Career of CJ Dennis*, Georgian House, Melbourne, 1946. Contains the full text of Dennis's 'Battle of the Wazzir'.

Clayton, Peter & Price, Martin (eds), *The Seven Wonders of the Ancient World*, Routledge, London, 1988. Solid accounts of the archeology and history of the wonders.

Clogg, Richard, *A Concise History of Greece*, Cambridge University Press, 1992. A good path through the thickets of modern Greek history.

Dennis, Peter et al., *The Oxford Companion to Australian Military History*, Oxford University Press, Melbourne, 1995. Most of what needs to be known, in one volume.

Denton, Kit, *Gallipoli – One Long Grave*, Time–Life Books, Sydney, 1986. Documentary style, reliable text, excellent pictures.

Downing, W. H., *Digger Dialects*, eds J. M. Arthur & W. S. Ramson, Oxford University Press, Melbourne, 1990 (1919). A dictionary of the First AIF's Australian English.

Durrell, Lawrence, The Alexandria Quartet (one-volume edn), Faber, London, 1968. A great rambling ruin or archeological site of a novel set in Alexandria before World War II.

Fakhry, Ahmed, *Siwa Oasis*, American University in Cairo Press, 1990. The Egyptian archeologist's account of the stories of Siwa and its people.

Forster, E. M., *Pharos and Pharillon*, Knopf, New York, 1923. Forster's beautiful essays originally published in the *Egyptian Gazette* during World War I.

Fox, Robin Lane, *Alexander the Great*, Penguin Books, Harmondsworth, 1986. The best and most enthusiastically written biography of the great man.

Gammage, Bill, *The Broken Years: Australian Soldiers in the Great War*, Penguin Books, Melbourne, 1975. A classic in its own right.

Ghosh, Amritav, *In an Antique Land*, Granta Books, London, 1994. This book travels from modern Egypt to the trade with the fabled Malabar Coast of India via papers found in the synagogue in Cairo. Wonderful.

Gullett, H. S., *Official History of Australia in the War of 1914–18*, vol. 7 *Sinai and Palestine*, 12th edn, Angus & Robertson, 1944. Essential account of the Light Horse and the Palestine campaign.

Haddawy, Husain (trans.), *The Arabian Nights*, W. W. Norton, 1995. Excellent translation from the Muhsin Mahdi text.

Herodotus, *The Histories*, Penguin Books, London, 1972. The original story.

Homer, the *Odyssey*, trans. E. V. Rieu, Penguin Books, London, 1947. The classic translation in modern English. There are others.

Homer, the *Iliad*, trans. E. V. Rieu, Penguin Books, London, 1950. Likewise, the classic version in English.

Irwin, Robert, *The Arabian Nights: A Companion*, Penguin Books, London, 1995. Fascinating background to the stories.

James, Robert Rhodes, *Gallipoli*, Angus and Robertson, Sydney, 1965. Still the best general history.

Jones, E. H., *The Road to En-Dor*, The Bodley Head, London, 1930. The story of how some English (and Australian) officers escaped from a Turkish prisoner of war camp in World War I using a ouija board.

Keeley, Edmund, *Cavafy's Alexandria*, Princeton University Press, 1996. Pioneer background to Cavafy's place in Alexandria.

Khayyam, Omar, *The Ruba'iyat*, trans Peter Avery & John Heath Stubbs, Penguin Books, Harmondsworth, 1981. Limpid translations; edifying notes.

Kinross, Patrick, *Atatürk*, Phoenix, London, 1995. Definitive biography of Mustafa Kemal.

Lawrence, Cyril, *The Gallipoli Diary of Sergeant Lawrence*, ed. Sir Ronald East, Melbourne University Press, 1981. Fascinating and terrible.

Lawrence, T. E., *The Seven Pillars of Wisdom*, Penguin Books, Harmondsworth, 1962. Mad but great parallel journey to that of the Light Horse.

Lewis, Bernard, *The Middle East*, Weidenfeld & Nicolson, London, 1995. Deserves to be called magisterial, especially about the post-Christian, pre-Islamic Middle East.

Lewis, Bernard, *The Arabs in History*, 6th edn, Oxford University Press, 1993. The classic account.

Lindsay, Jack, *Cleopatra*, Constable, London, 1971. Stimulating biography by a neglected Australian writer.

Long, Gavin, *Australia in the War of 1939–1945*, Series 1: Army, vol. 1 *To Benghazi* & vol. 2 *Greece, Crete & Syria*, Collins/Australian War Memorial, 1986 (1952). Not Bean, but very good all the same.

Maalouf, Amin, *Samarkand*, trans. Russell Harris, Abacus, London, 1994. Lebanese-born Maalouf's novels are romantic in the best storytelling tradition.

Maalouf, Amin, *Leo the African*, trans. Peter Sluglett, Abacus, London, 1994.

Maalouf, Amin, *The Crusades through Arab Eyes*, trans. Jon Rothschild, Schocken Books, New York, 1985. The fascinating point of view of the invaded.

Macaulay, Rose, *Pleasure of Ruins*, Thames & Hudson, London, 1984. Beautifully written account of why we love looking at them.

Mahfouz, Naguib, *Palace Walk*, trans William Maynard Hutchins & Olive E. Kenny, Anchor Books, New York, 1991.

Mahfouz, Naguib, *Palace of Desire*, trans William Maynard Hutchins, Lorne M. Kenny & Olive E. Kenny, Anchor Books, New York, 1991.

Mahfouz, Naguib, *Sugar Street*, trans William Maynard Hutchins & Angela Botros Samaan, Anchor Books, New York, 1991. There is no better entry point to understanding modern Egypt than these novels of a family growing up in Cairo before and after World War I. Mahfouz is the Dickens of Egypt.

Mahfouz, Naguib, *Miramar*, trans. Fatma Moussa Mahmoud 1978, eds Maged el Kommos & John Rodenbeck, Anchor

Books, New York, 1993. Alexandria in the post-Nasser 1950s.

Maughan, Barton, *Australia in the War of 1939–1945*, Series 1: Army, vol. 3 *Tobruk and El Alamein*, Australian War Memorial, 1966. Not Long, but straight.

Mitchell, Elyne, *Light Horse*, Macmillan, 1978. The best book by Harry Chauvel's daughter, with good reproductions of the Lambert and Powers paintings.

Moorehead, Alan, *Gallipoli*, Hamish Hamilton, 1956. Another classic account.

Moorehead, Caroline, *The Lost Treasures of Troy*, Phoenix, London, 1994. Really a good biography of Heinrich Schliemann.

Murnane, William J., *The Penguin Guide to Ancient Egypt*, Penguin Books, London, 1983. A useful guide to what may be seen at the actual sites.

Nixon, Allan M. (ed.), *Somewhere in France: Letters Home – the War Years of Sgt Roy Whitelaw 1st AIF*, Five Mile Press, 1989. And also in Egypt.

Norwich, John Julius, *Byzantium: The Early Centuries*, Viking, London, 1988.

Norwich, John Julius, *Byzantium: The Apogee*, Viking, London, 1991.

Norwich, John Julius, *Byzantium: The Decline and Fall*, Viking, 1995. These wonderful books rescued a thousand years of history.

Pick, Christopher (ed.), *Egypt: A Traveller's Anthology*, John Murray, London, 1991. Nicely selected and arranged tidbits.

Pinchin, Jane Lagoudis, *Alexandria Still: Forster, Durrell and Cavafy*, Princeton University Press, 1977. The original and still interesting work on the three writers and the city.

Pliny the Elder, *Natural History: A Selection*, trans. John Healy, Penguin Books, London, 1991. A remarkable early encyclopedia.

Plutarch, *The Age of Alexander and Makers of Rome*, Plutarch's

Lives, trans. and rearranged Ian Scott-Kilvert, Penguin Books, Harmondsworth, 1973. Wonderfully clear and readable.

Reeves, Nicholas, *The Complete Tutankhamun*, Thames & Hudson, London, 1990. All you need to know, and more, about the Pharaoh.

Roditi, Edoard, *The Delights of Turkey*, New Directions, New York, 1977. Post-modernist refashioning of Turkish tales.

Romer, John & Elizabeth, *The Seven Wonders of the World*, Michael O'Mara Books, London, 1995. From the TV series, delicious archeology, evidence and argument about the relationship between the ancient wonders and modern sense of wonder. Essential.

Saleh, Mohamed and Hourig Sourouzian, Official Catalogue, the Egyptian Museum, Cairo, Verlag Phillip von Zabern, Mainz, 1987. The only catalogue necessary to cart around on the journey.

Seal, Jeremy, *A Fez of the Heart*, Picador, London, 1996. Looking for the history of modern Turkey by way of a hat. Great.

Shelley, Percy Bysshe, *Poetical Works*, Oxford University Press, 1967. For Ozymandias.

Smith, Geoffrey, *Arthur Streeton 1867–1943*, National Gallery of Victoria, 1995. Splendid reproductions in the catalogue of the eye-opening national touring retrospective 1995–96.

Steel, Nigel and Peter Hart, *Defeat at Gallipoli*, Macmillan, London, 1994. Interesting for its slightly revisionist British military history point of view.

Streeton, Arthur, 'Letter from Egypt', the *Bulletin*, 21 October 1897.

Wood, Michael, *In Search of the Trojan War*, BBC Books, London, 1987. Also originally a TV series, the book is wonderful on Homer, Schliemann and the archeology of both.

Wray, Christopher, *Arthur Streeton: Painter of Light*, Jacaranda, Brisbane, 1993. A good short biography.

Yeats, W. B., *The Poems*, Everyman, London, 1990. All of them.

The author and publishers thank the following for permission to reprint copyright material as detailed below.

Every effort has been made to trace and acknowledge copyright. The publishers apologise for any accidental infringement and welcome information that would rectify any error or omission in subsequent editions.

American University in Cairo Press for a section of William Maynard Hutchins & Olive Kenny's translation of *Palace Walk* by Naguib Mahfouz (Anchor Books, 1991)

The Australian War Memorial for extracts from the work of C. E. W. Bean in the following books:
Official History of Australia in the War of 1914–18, vols 1 & 2 *The Story of Anzac* (Angus & Robertson, 1938)
Gallipoli Mission (ABC Books, 1990)
Gallipoli Frontline, selected and annotated by Kevin Fewster (Allen & Unwin, 1990)
The Anzac Book (Harrap, 1916)

The Australian War Memorial for extracts from H. S. Gullett's *Official History of Australia in the War of 1914–18*, vol. 7 *Sinai and Palestine* (Angus & Robertson, 1944)

Kangaroo Press for passages from *The Nek* by Peter Burness (1966)

Allan M. Nixon for a passage from *Somewhere in France, Letters Home: The War Years of Sgt Roy Whitelaw* (Five Mile Press, 1989)

Random House (UK) Ltd for lines from C. P. Cavafy's 'The God Abandons Antony' in *Collected Poems*, translated by Edmund Keeley & Phillip Sherrard, edited by George Savidis (Chatto & Windus, 1990)

Thames & Hudson Ltd for a passage from *Pleasure of Ruins* by Rose Macaulay (1984), © Estate of Rose Macaulay

Valerie Yule for passages from *The Gallipoli Diary of Sgt Lawrence*, edited by Sir Ronald East (Melbourne University Press, 1981)

HarperCollins*Publishers* for the map of Anzac Cove by Arthur Banks, previously published in *Gallipoli* by Robert Rhodes James (Angus & Robertston, 1965)